NOT TO BE
FROM THE

D1631554

THE ARDEN SHAKESPEARE

GENERAL EDITORS: HAROLD F. BROOKS
AND HAROLD JENKINS

THE COMEDY OF ERRORS

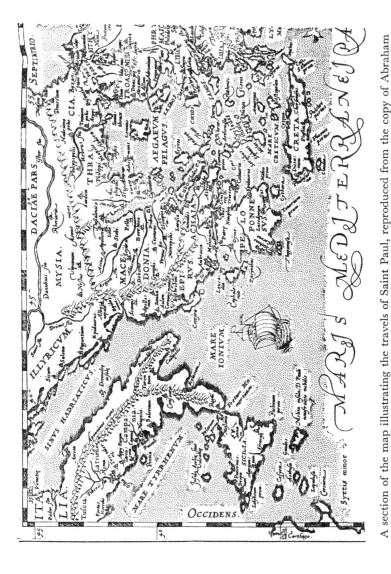

A section of the map illustrating the travels of Saint Paul, reproduced from the copy of Abraham Ortelius, *Theatrum Orbis Terrarum* (1584) in Yale University Library. See Introduction, pp. xxx–xxxi.

THE ARDEN EDITION OF THE
WORKS OF WILLIAM SHAKESPEARE

THE COMEDY OF
ERRORS

Edited by
R. A. FOAKES

METHUEN & CO LTD
11 New Fetter Lane, London E.C.4

The general editors of the Arden Shakespeare have been W. J. Craig (1899–1906)
succeeded by R. H. Case (1909–44) and Una Ellis-Fermor (1946–58).
Present general editors: Harold F. Brooks and Harold Jenkins.
The Comedy of Errors was first published in the Arden Shakespeare in 1907,
edited by Henry Cuningham.
Second edition 1925
Third edition 1933
Fourth edition 1940
This edition, completely revised and reset, first published 1962
Reprinted 1963
Reprinted 1969
SBN: 416 47460 8
5·3
Printed in Great Britain by
The Broadwater Press Limited
Welwyn Garden City, Hertfordshire
Editorial matter © 1962 Methuen & Co Ltd

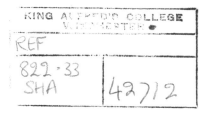
DISTRIBUTED IN THE U.S.A. BY BARNES & NOBLE INC.

CONTENTS

PREFACE

THIS edition is not based on Henry Cuningham's earlier 'Arden' edition, but I have used some of his notes, with appropriate acknowledgement. I owe a great deal to other scholars, particularly to the editorial work of J. Dover Wilson, and to the massive labours of T. W. Baldwin on Shakespeare's early plays. The introduction and commentary register my disagreement with Professor Baldwin's answers to many questions, and perhaps do not sufficiently indicate how often, in an important and original discussion, he has taught his successors what questions to ask.

I am grateful for their help to Professor Clifford Leech, Mr J. C. Maxwell, Mr Bernard Harris, Dr F. D. Hoeniger, and Dr G. K. Hunter. My greatest debt is to the General Editors, and especially to Dr H. F. Brooks, who has generously enriched each section of the book out of his deep understanding of the early Shakespeare, and his wide knowledge of earlier literature.

R. A. FOAKES.

University College, Toronto
May 1961

ABBREVIATIONS AND USAGES

1. *Editions of* The Comedy of Errors:

Herford — C. H. Herford, Eversley Edition of Shakespeare (1900).

Cuningham — Henry Cuningham, Arden Shakespeare (1907, reprinted with slight corrections, 1926).

N.C.S. — A. Quiller-Couch and J. Dover Wilson, New Cambridge Shakespeare (1922).

Baldwin — T. W. Baldwin, Heath's American Arden Shakespeare (no date given; 1929).

2. *Other Abbreviations*:

Abbott — E. A. Abbott, *A Shakespearian Grammar* (1869, etc.). References are to sections, not to pages.

Baldwin, *Shakspere's Small Latine* — T. W. Baldwin, *William Shakspere's Small Latine & Lesse Greeke*, 2 vols. (1944).

Bullough, *Sources* — *Narrative and Dramatic Sources of Shakespeare*, ed. Geoffrey Bullough, Vol. 1 (1957).

Chambers, *E.S.* — E. K. Chambers, *The Elizabethan Stage*, 4 vols. (1923).

Chambers, *W.S.* — E. K. Chambers, *William Shakespeare, A Study of Facts and Problems*, 2 vols. (1930).

Greg, *First Folio* — W. W. Greg, *The Shakespeare First Folio. Its Bibliographical and Textual History* (1955).

J.E.G.P. — *Journal of English and Germanic Philology.*

Jonson — *Works*, ed. C. H. Herford, Percy and Evelyn Simpson, 11 vols. (1925–52).

Kellner — L. Kellner, *Restoring Shakespeare* (1925).

Kökeritz — Helge Kökeritz, *Shakespeare's Pronunciation* (1953).

Lyly — *The Complete Works of John Lyly*, ed. R. W. Bond, 3 vols. (1902).

McKerrow — *The Works of Thomas Nashe*, 5 vols. (1904-10, reprinted 1958).

Marlowe — *Works*, Methuen Edition, General Editor R. H. Case (1930-3).

M.L.R. — *Modern Language Review.*

Noble — R. Noble, *Shakespeare's Biblical Knowledge* (1935).

O.E.D. — *A New English Dictionary*, ed. J. A. Murray, H. Bradley, W. A. Craigie, and C. T. Onions (13 vols., 1888–1933).

Onions	C. T. Onions, *A Shakespeare Glossary* (1911; revised edn, 1946).
R.E.S.	*Review of English Studies.*
Sisson, *New Readings*	C. J. Sisson, *New Readings in Shakespeare*, 2 vols. (1956).
Sugden, *Dictionary*	E. H. Sugden, *A Topographical Dictionary to the Works of Shakespeare and his Fellow-Dramatists* (1925).
Tilley	M. P. Tilley, *A Dictionary of Proverbs in England in the Sixteenth and Seventeenth Centuries* (1950). References are to the numbers by which proverbs are listed, not to pages.
Warner	*The Menaechmi of Plautus*, translated William Warner (1595, reprinted in Bullough, *Sources*).

In the collation, collected editions of Shakespeare subsequent to the four seventeenth-century Folios (F, F2, F3, F4), are referred to by the name of the editor, or editors, with the exception of the 'Variorum' editions of 1773–1821. A full, dated list of major editions is provided in recent volumes of the 'New Variorum' Shakespeare, but does not usually include the recent one-volume editions listed in the collation and elsewhere as Kittredge (G. L. Kittredge, 1936), and Alexander (Peter Alexander, The Tudor Shakespeare, 1951). A useful account of major editions is also provided in Chambers, *W.S.*, I. 275–7. Other works cited in the collation include Cartwright (R. Cartwright, *New Readings in Shakespeare*, 1866); Douce (Francis Douce, *Illustrations of Shakespeare*, 1839); Edwards (T. Edwards, *The Canons of Criticism*, 1748, etc.); Grey (Zachary Grey, *Critical, Historical and Explanatory Notes on Shakespeare*, 2 vols., 1754); and W. S. Walker (*A Critical Examination of the Text of Shakespeare*, ed. W. N. Lettsom, 3 vols., 1860).

The usual abbreviations are employed for stage-direction (S.D.), speech-heading (S.H.) and quarto (Q).

Quotations from Shakespeare's Works are taken from the edition of Peter Alexander (1951), and line-references are to this edition. Abbreviations of the titles of Shakespeare's plays and poems are those of C. T. Onions, *A Shakespeare Glossary*, p. x.

In quotations from early books, *u, v,* and *i* are modernized, where appropriate, to *v, u,* and *j*. Titles are generally modernized and abbreviated.

INTRODUCTION

I. TECHNICAL INTRODUCTION

I. THE TEXT

The Comedy of Errors was printed as the fifth play in the opening section, the comedies, of the First Folio edition of Shakespeare's plays in 1623. It is listed among the plays entered in the Stationers' Register on 8 November 1623, for Edward Blount and Isaac Jaggard,[1] and had not, so far as they knew, or we know now, appeared in print earlier. No significant irregularities have been discovered in the printing of the comedies up to *Twelfth Night*, the thirteenth play in the first Folio,[2] and *The Comedy of Errors* was apparently printed in normal succession after *The Tempest*, *The Two Gentlemen of Verona*, *The Merry Wives of Windsor*, and *Measure for Measure*. These four plays have in common certain features which suggest that they were printed from transcripts, made probably by the scribe Ralph Crane, and perhaps prepared especially for the first collected edition of the plays.[3] The text of *The Comedy of Errors* is of a very different kind. Its most noticeable peculiarity is the persistent 'confusion and inconsistency of the character names and prefixes'.[4] So Egeon, for example, appears as Mer(chant) in the headings of I. i, although another merchant is on stage in I. ii; yet another merchant is brought on in IV. i, without being distinguished in entries or speech-headings, and since he returns in V. i, where Egeon also comes back, a new heading had to be found for Egeon to avoid direct confusion. In the entry and speech-headings of this scene he is called the Merchant of Syracuse, Mer(chant) Fat(her), or simply Fa(ther). The most prominent and confusing variations are in the titles given to the Antipholuses and the Dromios.[5] Antipholus of Syracuse is first named as Antipholus Erotes in I. ii

1. See W. W. Greg, *The Shakespeare First Folio* (1955), p. 59.
2. See Greg, *First Folio*, p. 438; J. W. Shroeder, *The Great Folio of 1623: Shakespeare's Plays in the Printing-House* (1956), p. 73.
3. Greg, *First Folio*, p. 100, Note D, and see also pp. 217, 335, 356, 418.
4. Greg, *First Folio*, p. 201.
5. See below, p. xxvi, for further discussion of these titles.

(Erotes, or Errotis, as it is spelt in the entry of II. ii, is probably a corruption of *Erraticus*); his twin of Ephesus enters in II. i as Antipholus Sereptus (i.e. Surreptus). The Dromios are differentiated from the beginning, but only on those occasions when it is essential, as Dromio of Syracuse or Dromio of Ephesus. So a nice confusion occurs in the abbreviations of speech-headings, for *E. Ant.*, or Antipholus Erotes, is Antipholus of Syracuse (II. ii), while *E. Dro.* is Dromio of Ephesus (I. ii). It is only in Act III that the Antipholuses begin to be distinguished like their servants in directions and speech-headings, and then not regularly but when necessary, as of Ephesus or Syracuse. These and other confusions were examined by R. B. McKerrow, who argued that in *The Comedy of Errors* they suggest the hand of the author; from a study of this text and of others which reveal confusions of a similar kind, he reached the general conclusion that 'a play in which the names are irregular was printed from the author's original MS.'[1] He pointed out that a prompter could not be expected to remember differences in character names, and would need to regularize them; an author, on the other hand, might distinguish his characters only when necessary to avoid confusing himself, and might differentiate them simply by their functions—as, in *The Comedy of Errors*, the Duke's name Solinus, and the old merchant's name, Egeon, appear only in the text of the First Folio, not in headings. He decided further that the printed text of this play 'must represent fairly closely what the MS. *looked like* to the compositor.'[2]

McKerrow's argument strongly reinforced what scholars before him had believed, and later scholars have been still readier to claim, that 'the manuscript behind F was clearly the author's, and since it is difficult to believe that the confusion in the character names and prefixes would have been tolerated in a prompt-book, it would seem that the manuscript was most likely foul papers'.[3] Perhaps the manuscript was edited in a rudimentary way for printing, though certainly not to the extent of the plays printed before it; some additions or alterations were probably made. The act divisions given in the Folio seem to have been introduced, as Greg thought,[4] at the time of printing, for the stage direction at v. i. 9, 'Enter Antipholus and Dromio again' (the two characters have just left the stage at the end of Act IV) shows that the action here was meant to be continuous. Some other peculiarities of the printed

1. 'A Suggestion regarding Shakespeare's Manuscripts', *Review of English Studies*, XI (1935), 459–65; the quotation is from p. 464.
2. *Ibid.*, p. 465.
3. Greg, *First Folio*, pp. 201–2; cf. Chambers, *W.S.*, I. 306.
4. Greg, *First Folio*, p. 201.

text led E. K. Chambers and W. W. Greg to postulate the intervention of a book-keeper or prompter.[1]

On the whole the stage-directions seem to be the author's;
several provide information superfluous to a prompter's needs,
such as 'Enter Adriana, wife to Antipholus Sereptus . . .' (II. i), or
even tell us more than the text requires us to know, as at IV. iv. 37,
where the direction, 'Enter . . . a Schoolmaster, call'd Pinch' dis-
closes what is nowhere else mentioned, Doctor Pinch's profession.
Other directions, such as the permissive 'Enter three or four, and
offer to bind him' (IV. iv. 104), and the call for Dromio of Syracuse
to enter 'from the Bay' (IV. i. 85),[2] also point to the author. The odd
form of the direction at V. i. 407, 'Exeunt omnes. Manet the two
Dromios and two Brothers', is also Shakespearian, and similar
directions occur in a number of Folio texts which are thought to
have been printed from the author's manuscript.[3] There remain
a few directions which have seemed to demand further explanation.
The most notable of these occurs at IV. iv. 144, and for a proper
understanding its exact placing in the Folio needs to be appreciat-
ed; it is printed there as follows:

(At the foot of column 1 on H6ᵛ)
 Let's call more helpe to haue them bound againe.
             Runne all out.
(At the top of column 2 on H6ᵛ)
 Off. Away, they'l kill vs.
       Exeunt omnes, as fast as may be, frighted.

It is reasonable to suppose that a stage-direction was somehow
duplicated at this point, but the ready and easy way of accounting
for what happened, by invoking a prompter,[4] is not very convincing. At first sight it looks plausible enough to argue, as W. W.
Greg did, that 'Exeunt omnes' was added by a prompter or book-
keeper on the left of the manuscript page, so 'duplicating the
author's original direction on the right', and that the compositor

1. Chambers, *W.S.*, I. 306; Greg, *First Folio*, p. 201.
2. For further comment on this S.D., see below, p. xxxvi.
3. See, for instance, *3H6*, III. ii. 123, 'Exeunt. Manet Richard.', and *Cor.*, V. ii.
90, 'Exeunt. Manet the Guard and Menenius.'
4. I refer to the putative annotator as the 'prompter' or 'book-keeper' in this
discussion because these are the terms used by Greg. A prompter might be expected to go over a text systematically, and to reveal his intervention in a number of
places, and Greg does not seem to have considered a possibility that a few anno-
tations could have been added preparatory to making a prompt-book, or for
some other reason, by a person connected with the theatre. I prefer the idea of
such an annotator to that of the 'prompter' in accounting for the few odd
directions in *The Comedy of Errors*, though I do not find evidence enough to make
it necessary to think of either.

fitted them together in the printed text. He went on to say 'it is possible that the similar "Exeunt omnes" at v. i. 407 was also an addition by the book-keeper. A duplication at v. i. 189, "Enter Antipholus and E. Dromio of Ephesus", may also be due to him, and Chambers thinks he may have added the words "call'd Pinch" at IV. iv. 37, though why he does not explain.'[1]

However, Greg does not seem to have realized that the direction at v. i. 407 takes a common Shakespearian form, and is not at all analogous to the duplication at IV. iv. 144; it is in fact paralleled by the direction at IV. iv. 129, 'Exeunt. Manet Offic. Adri. Luci. Courtizan'. As for the duplication at v. i. 189, this may well be a compositor's careless expansion of what was in the manuscript—perhaps 'Enter E. Antipholus and E. Dromio'. In other directions of this kind both characters are usually identified as of Syracuse or Ephesus, as at IV. iv. 141, 'Enter Antipholus Siracusia with his Rapier drawne, and Dromio Sirac.', or v. i. 329, 'Enter the Abbesse with Antipholus Siracusa, and Dromio Sir.', and it may be conjectured that here the identification of Antipholus has been transferred to the end of the direction. The phrase 'a School-master, call'd Pinch', as noted above, is probably authorial, and Greg could not see why Chambers wanted to invoke a prompter to explain it; but the reason is, I think, clear enough, and it is the same reason that caused Greg to detect the intervention of a prompter at v. i. 189 and v. i. 407. Both scholars wished to account for the split direction and duplication at IV. iv. 144; this could be plausibly explained by supposing that a prompter made an addition to the manuscript at this point; and this explanation would appear more convincing if the prompter's hand could be found elsewhere.

It was natural that, having discovered signs of the prompter, they should find him useful in elucidating other difficulties.[2] However, there is no need to invoke him elsewhere than at IV. iv. 147, and this passage deserves further scrutiny, to see whether an alternative explanation may not be just as satisfactory. The fact that the passage in F is split between the foot of one column and the top of another needs to be taken into account; it may be that the author

1. *First Folio*, p. 201.
2. Greg at one time suggested, according to Chambers, *W.S.*, I. 306, that the book-keeper was also responsible for 'the first speech-prefixes after entrances', which 'the author seems habitually to have left blank'. I see no reason to accept this; the two occasions on which the prefix is omitted, at IV. iii. 1 and at v. i. 168, are not enough to warrant a general deduction about the author's habits, and both may, in any case, result from mere oversight on the part of author or compositor. The initial prefix of I. i is given in a line to itself in F, as is customary.

wrote one direction in the right margin of his manuscript, but divided it because of its length into two lines, 'Runne all out / as fast as may be, frighted', then, in the accident of printing, and of the division between columns, the direction was split into two and attached to different lines. If so, then 'Exeunt omnes' could be the compositor's addition to make sense of 'as fast as may be, frighted'.

Other inconsistencies, such as the substitution of *Iuliana* for *Luciana* in the entry and initial speech-heading of III. ii, and the replacement of the name *Luce* for the kitchen-wench (III. i. 47) by *Nell* (III. ii. 107), have been explained, the first as a printer's mistake, the second as due to Shakespeare's liking for a pun.[1] For the rest, *The Comedy of Errors* is a good text, with few seriously corrupted passages, and few difficulties that cannot be easily explained as due to the printer's carelessness or mistake. The elaborate theory built up by John Dover Wilson in the New Cambridge edition of the play, that the copy which went to the printing-house was the work of two scribes, one who took down the text from dictation, and another who went over it expanding and correcting,[2] rests on the flimsiest evidence, or on evidence which is more satisfactorily interpreted in a different and simpler way, as Chambers demonstrated.[3]

1. So Chambers, *W.S.*, I. 306, 309; Greg, *First Folio*, p. 201. The substitution of Juliana for Luciana might perhaps be attributable to Shakespeare, if he was writing *The Two Gentlemen of Verona* at the same time as this play, or just before it, and for the moment remembered Julia. The confusion of Luce and Nell may have arisen because Shakespeare conflated, as he was writing the play, two characters from *Menaechmi*; see below, p. xxv.

2. *The Comedy of Errors*, edited by Sir Arthur Quiller-Couch and John Dover Wilson (1922), pp. 65–75.

3. *W.S.*, I. 306–7. Dover Wilson based much of his argument on spellings, believing that 'Obviously a dictated text will be entirely in the spelling of the scribe... As to the remarkable normality of the orthography, this simply implies that the spelling of the scribe closely approximated to that of the printing-houses of his time' (p. 68); he thought he could detect the hand of a second scribe in the spellings of some directions and speech-headings. He did not realize that the play was set up in type by more than one compositor, each with his own preferential spellings (A, for example, prefers *Adr* and *Luc* in speech-headings, while B nearly always has *Adri* and *Luci*); so he traces the spelling 'Courti(e)zan' in stage-directions to one scribe, the spelling 'Cur' in speech-headings to another: 'This difference of spelling seems to us a strong indication that two hands had been at work on the "copy"...' (p. 70). The one exceptional stage-direction, at IV. iii. 43, which has the spelling 'Curtizan', he attributes to the first scribe, who put in some directions. In fact, this is the one place where Compositor A had to set this word in a direction, and he spelt it in the same way as the speech-headings; this compositor was more conservative and faithful to copy than his companion, B (see Alice Walker, *Textual Problems of the First Folio*, 1953, pp. 9–12), and the text here may simply show that A followed his copy, and B used his own spelling where they printed the word in full, while both followed copy in the abbreviation of the

B

It is unnecessary to introduce a prompter or scribes to account for the peculiarities of this text; they may all be explained in terms of an author inattentive to petty details, a printer who added act-divisions, and compositors who solved an occasional puzzle as best they could.

The present text is based on that of the Folio, modernized in order to provide consistent speech-headings and stage-directions, together with spelling and punctuation such as a present-day reader would normally expect. Modernization is always a compromise; the syntax, style, and vocabulary of Shakespeare are not those now in use, and this edition aims at clarifying, not disguising, the differences. Some old forms of words are retained, such as 'porpentine' for porcupine (III. i. 116, etc.) and 'band' for bond (IV. iii. 30, where there is a quibble on other meanings of 'band'). The punctuation differs from that of the Folio principally in reducing to periods, semi-colons, or dashes, many of the colons which are there used lavishly; in general, the aim has been to retain, as far as modern pointing would allow, the phrasing indicated in the original, and changes are not recorded except where the sense is affected.

In the textual apparatus are noted substantive departures from or additions to the Folio text, but not misprints or turned letters. Some curious spellings or forms are also recorded, especially where a measure of editorial interpretation is involved. The many variations in speech-headings are listed; these could sometimes be confusing, and on occasion a sloping bar is used to separate the parts of an entry which might otherwise not be readily understood, as, for example, 'E. Dro. / F.' (IV. iv. 10). Editorial additions to stage-directions are enclosed in square brackets, but in the collation these brackets are not recorded. A plus sign (+) signifies 'many editors'.

II. THE DATE

The play is certainly one of Shakespeare's early compositions, but there is no conclusive evidence to show when it was written; its first recorded performance was given at Gray's Inn on 28 December 1594.[1] Although some features of the play, its shortness,[2]

---

speech-heading. It might be inferred that there was only one spelling, 'Curtizan', in the manuscript!

1. See Appendix II, p. 115, for an account of this performance, staged as part of the Gray's Inn Christmas Revels.

2. It has less than 1,800 lines, and is the shortest play in the Shakespearian canon. The old theories canvassed by Dover Wilson in his edition (1922), p. 76, by Allison Gaw, 'The Evolution of *The Comedy of Errors*', *PMLA*, XLI (1926), 620-

its classical background, its staging,[1] and its nature as the least
romantic of Shakespeare's comedies, might support the view that
it was written for a special occasion and an educated audience,
most scholars have rejected the idea that it was commissioned as
late as the year 1594. Some have believed it to be Shakespeare's
first play, and have sought to push back the date of composition to
1589, or even earlier.[2] A most elaborate theory was developed by
T. W. Baldwin to date the play's composition in 'about December,
1589'.[3] He detected a local allusion in the lines:

> the Duke himself in person
> Comes this way to the melancholy vale,
> The place of death and sorry execution
> Behind the ditches of the abbey here.   (v. i. 119–22)

Here he thought Shakespeare was referring to Holywell Priory, in
a 'vale' near the Curtain and the Theatre; one of these theatres
was indeed built immediately outside the precinct of the dissolved
Holywell Priory in Shoreditch, and the other within the precinct,
where it was divided by a ditch from Finsbury fields.[4] Then, noting
that Shakespeare's company, Lord Strange's Men, were using the
Curtain in the winter of 1589–90, and the Theatre in the following
winter, Baldwin argued that the first performance of the play could
be assigned to one of these seasons, and referred to occasional allu-

---

66, and by J. M. Robertson, *The Shakespeare Canon* (1923), p. 126ff., that the play
might be a corrupt and abbreviated text, or a revision from an old play (either
The Historie of Error, acted 1577, or *A Historie of fferrar*, acted 1583), showing the
hand of Kyd, Marlowe, or Greene, have been demolished by T. W. Baldwin in
his edition (The American Arden Edition, 1928, pp. 101–13), and by E. K.
Chambers, *W.S.*, I. 307–8. They were all troubled by the use of 'doggerel' verse,
such as the tumbling rhymes of the Dromios in III. i, and do not seem to have
realized how common such verses are in plays of this period, including Shakespeare's other early comedies; see, for example, *Love's Labour's Lost*, II. i. 190ff.,
The Two Gentlemen of Verona, II. ii. 120ff., and *The Taming of the Shrew*, I. ii. 10ff.,
and the discussion of such verse by R. W. Bond, *Early Plays from the Italian* (1911),
pp. lxxxi–xc.

1. For further comment on the staging, see p. xxxiv.
2. Peter Alexander stands boldly alone in wanting to date the play between
1584 and 1589, and certainly before August, 1589 (see his *Shakespeare's Life
and Art* (1939), pp. 67–9). He bases this claim on a rigorous, and, I think, un-
warranted interpretation of the allusion to the French civil war; see below,
pp. xx–xxi.
3. In *William Shakspere Adapts a Hanging* (1931); the quotation is from
p. 9.
4. Chambers, *E.S.*, II. 384–6; 400–2. In Thomas Cooper's *Thesaurus Linguae
Romanae*, which Baldwin thinks Shakespeare used (see below, p. xxx), the temple
at Ephesus is described as being 'set in a Fenne or Marshe grounde', which may
have been enough to suggest the lines here.

sions to coldness in the play as supporting this view. He narrowed
the date down to the earlier of these seasons by finding a further
association with the play in the execution of William Hartley, a
seminary priest, in October 1588 in Finsbury Fields, an execution
which he believed that Shakespeare witnessed, and had in mind in
his presentation of Egeon. Finally, he adduced allusions to the
Armada of 1588, to Marlowe's *Tamburlaine* (?1588; the name
Menaphon), to Lyly's *Mother Bombie* (1587–90; the name Dromio),
and to the civil war in France (August 1589–93) as corroborating
evidence.[1]

This makes an ingenious and entertaining story, but it involves
too many hypotheses; it is difficult to see why Shakespeare should
have needed to watch a particular execution in order to conceive
the story of Egeon, who in any case is not executed, and Baldwin's
account is not needed to explain anything in the play. There is no
evidence for linking the play to the winter season of 1589; the
references to 'cold' are proverbial or from common phrases (III. i.
37, 71, and IV. iv. 34), and if the phrase 'the ditches of the abbey
here' may be applied to Holywell, which is doubtful, it would have
been appropriate in any year when Lord Strange's Men (or the
Lord Chamberlain's Men, as Shakespeare's company became after
1594) were playing at the Theatre or Curtain, theatres used by
them until 1598 or later. As for the topical or literary allusions, all
these seem to provide is a *terminus a quo*; the references to the
Armada, to the French war, and to the plays of Marlowe and Lyly
could have been made at any time after 1588.

The editors of the New Cambridge edition follow Cuningham in
selecting 1591–2 as their date for the play.[2] They would place it
within the limits of the French civil war, which ended with Henry
of Navarre becoming Henry IV of France in July 1593, and choose
1591–2 because in 1591 an expedition was sent by Elizabeth under
Sir John Norris and the Earl of Essex to help Henry and the Protestant cause, and the jest in Act III might have been most appropriate soon afterwards. The lines are:

1. His arguments are set out most clearly in the introduction to his edition of
the play (1929), and most fully in *William Shakspere Adapts a Hanging*.
2. Quiller-Couch and Dover Wilson, pp. x–xi; Cuningham, pp. xvi–xviii.
When they wrote, before 1930, the chronology of Shakespeare's plays was
generally accepted as beginning about 1590 or 1591, cf. Chambers, *W.S.*, I. 270,
so that they were putting the play, as they thought, very early in Shakespeare's
career. This chronology is still widely accepted, being based on the first known
references to Shakespeare as an author, which belong to 1592, but a number of
scholars, including T. W. Baldwin and Peter Alexander, now think that Shakespeare was writing plays by the late 1580s.

Syr. Ant. Where France?
Syr. Dro. In her forehead, armed and reverted, making war
    against her heir. (III. ii. 120–2)

Chambers and Greg also accept the period 1589–July 1593 as
fixing the date limits of the play's composition, because of this
reference to the French war,[1] but Chambers is inclined to favour
a time near the end of it. He cites the parallel noted by Dover
Wilson[2] between the lines,

> Heart and good will you might,
> But surely, master, not a rag of money, (IV. iv. 83–4)

and the passage in Thomas Nashe's *Four Letters Confuted* (1592;
certainly earlier than 25 March 1593), 'heart and good-will, but
never a ragge of money'[3]; he points also to the use of 'lean-faced'
and 'hollow-eyed', epithets applied to Doctor Pinch (v. i. 238, 241),
in the description of a villain, Jack Fitten, in the play *Arden of Feversham*,[4] which was entered in the Stationers' Register on 3 April
1592, and published in the same year. There are other slight indications in the play that reinforce the evidence for a date of composition in 1592. One is the apparent echo of Marlowe's play,
Edward II (?1591–2), in the phrase, 'What, will you murder me?'
(IV. iv. 107), which is spoken also by King Edward, and in the
business of the burning of Pinch's beard, and quenching it in
'puddled mire' (v. i. 170–3). In Marlowe's play the King's face is
washed in puddle-water, his beard is shaved off, and he speaks of
standing in 'mire and puddle'.[5] Another is the possibility that the
phrase, 'armadoes of carracks' (III. ii. 135), may refer, not to the
Great Armada, of 1588, but to the Great Carrack, the *Madre de
Dios*, a Portuguese galleon captured and brought to England in

---

1. Chambers, *W.S.*, I. 310–11; Greg, *First Folio*, p. 200. Peter Alexander
argues that Henry of Navarre was rightful King of France, and recognized as such
in England, from the death of Henry III in 1589, and that 'He was heir, therefore,
between 1584 and 1589' (*Shakespeare's Life and Art*, p. 68); but this is to simplify
the confusion of the time in a modern perspective. How differently affairs in
France were seen by Englishmen in those years may be guessed from the tracts of
the period, which refer to Henry always as King of Navarre, not heir to the
French throne; so, for instance, *A Caveat for France* (1588) explains the current
quarrel in France as arising explicitly through the act of Henry III in 1585 of
declaring the Cardinal of Bourbon heir, and excluding the protestant Henry.
H. B. Charlton's account of the French war in 'The Date of *Love's Labour's Lost*'
M.L.R., XIII (1918), 258–66, also disregards the contemporary publications on it.
    2. *Op. cit.*, pp. 107–8.   3. *Works*, edited R. B. McKerrow (1910), I. 301.
    4. He does not appear in the play, but Bradshaw describes him (II. i. 51–2) as
'A leane faced writhen knave, Hauke nosde and verye hollow eied'.
    5. H. F. Brooks drew my attention to these parallels; see v. i. 170–3 and n.

September 1592.[1] None of the evidence for 1592 is very strong; the parallel with Nashe could have been used by either author first, and in any case was possibly a common expression of the early 1590s, picked up independently by each of them[2]; the connection with *Arden of Feversham* is tenuous, the date of *Edward II* is uncertain, and there may be no precise topical allusion in the phrase 'armadoes of carracks'. Nevertheless, the accumulation of pointers to this year should perhaps be allowed some weight, and there has been a tendency to fix on 1592 as the date of composition.[3] If there is an allusion to the *Madre de Dios*, and if Shakespeare is echoing Nashe, then the date of *The Comedy of Errors* would be late in the year; Chambers is inclined to take this view, and even to identify the play with the 'gelyous comodey' produced on 5 January 1593 by Lord Strange's Men,[4] for he feels also that its stylistic development suggests a date after the composition of *Venus and Adonis*.[5]

The firmest element in the evidence for dating the play has been the civil war in France, with its limits of 1589–93. However, a glance at some of the publications of the time relating to France shows how worthless as evidence the history-book dates of the war are. In a letter of 1589, published by Henry of Navarre, and translated at once into English, he discusses events since December 1588, saying, 'this foure yeares space I have beene the argument of the tragoedies of France . . . the subject of civile armes.'[6] Similarly, the

1. See III. ii. 135 and n. T. W. Baldwin thinks that the comparison in this scene of Nell to a globe, and the reference to 'rheum', with its quibble on rhumb-lines (III. ii. 112, 126), may have been stimulated by the appearance of Emery Molyneux's globe in 1592; however, Mercator's globe (of 1541), which was already in use, had rhumb-lines. See E. L. Stephenson, *Terrestrial and Celestial Globes*, 2 vols. (1921), I. 128, 132.

2. There are some references to the stage in *Four Letters Confuted*, and one line is quoted with the note by Nashe, 'I borrowed this sentence out of a Play' (McKerrow, I. 271); this has led some scholars to think that he might have borrowed other sentences too. On the other hand, it is possible that some allusion to Nashe and his quarrel with Gabriel Harvey is involved here, as also at IV. iv. 41ff. (see note to these lines). Shakespeare glances at this quarrel in *Love's Labour's Lost*, a play which the editor of the Arden volume, R. W. David, dates in 1593; see his Introduction (1951), pp. xxix–xlvi.

3. See, for instance, Allison Gaw, 'The Evolution of *The Comedy of Errors*', *PMLA*, XLI (1926), 620–66; E. I. Fripp, *Shakespeare, Man and Artist* (1938), I. 314ff.; R. A. Law, 'Shakespeare's Earliest Plays', *S.P.*, XXVIII (Royster Memorial Studies, 1931), 99–106 (631–8).

4. *Henslowe's Diary*, edited W. W. Greg (1904), p. 15; edited R. A. Foakes and R. T. Rickert (1961), p. 19. The play is entered as 'ne', which probably indicates that it was new or newly-revived.   5. *W.S.*, I. 311.

6. *A Letter written by the King of Navarr* (1589; dated at the end, 4 March 1589), A3r. Compare *A Caveat for France* (1588), A2r, 'These three yeares and more hath *France* ben tormented with this war . . .'. In this text the beginning of the war is set in March 1585.

upper limit, 1593, seems not to have been regarded at the time as marking more than a truce, and it has recently been shown that as late as 1597 writers in England were referring to the civil war as still in full swing.[1] It would seem, then, that the allusion in III. ii could have made its point at any time in the decade after 1585.

A case has also been made out for regarding the earliest known performance as the first, and the date of composition as 1594.[2] In presenting his argument for this date, Sidney Thomas appeals to the similarities between the lyrical power shown in some passages in *The Comedy of Errors* and Shakespeare's narrative poems, *Venus and Adonis* and *The Rape of Lucrece*, published in 1593[3]; to the legal terminology in the play, which, he believes, would have been appropriate to an audience trained in law[4]; and to the appropriateness of a play based on and challenging comparison with classical sources (Plautus's *Menaechmi* and *Amphitruo*) for the formally, that is, classically, educated gentlemen of one of the Inns of Court.[5] He also thinks that Shakespeare borrowed the name Dromio from Lyly's play *Mother Bombie*, which was printed in 1594, presumably after the entry in the Stationers' Register of 18 June in this year,[6] and detects a connection between the description of Pinch (v. i. 238–42) and the appearance of the apothecary in *Romeo and Juliet*, v. i, a play usually ascribed to 1595.[7]

1. Sidney Thomas, 'The Date of *The Comedy of Errors*', *Shakespeare Quarterly*, VII (1956), 377–84.
2. *Ibid.*; this is the general argument of the article.
3. See the exchanges between Adriana and Luciana in II. i, between them and Antipholus of Syracuse in II. ii, and between him and Luciana in III. ii. Some verbal parallels between the poems and the play are noted in the Variorum edition of the *Sonnets*, edited Hyder E. Rollins (1938), and in T. W. Baldwin, *On the Literary Genetics of Shakspere's Poems & Sonnets* (1950); others had been noticed by earlier commentators, and those of interest are pointed out in the commentary in this edition.
4. The knowledge of the law shown in the play was stressed by Cuningham (pp. xli–xlv) and others, but most Elizabethan dramatists seem to have been well-equipped with such knowledge.
5. The Inns of Court were then a kind of third university after Oxford and Cambridge, so described by W. Harrison in his *Description of England* prefixed to Holinshed's *Chronicles* (1587), pp. 148, 151; see J. D. Wilson, *Life in Shakespeare's England* (1926), p. 63.
6. The play was acted, however, in 1590, and Dromio in any case derives from the name, Dromo, given to a slave in several of the comedies of Terence. However, Shakespeare seems to have known *Mother Bombie* fairly well, see below, p. xxxiii.
7. The similarity is slight, and probably indicates no more than that Shakespeare had the same thin actor, John Sincklo, in mind for both parts; see note to v. i. 238–42; but T. W. Baldwin was sufficiently troubled by it to resurrect the old notion of a first version of *Romeo and Juliet* dating from 1591 in his *William Shakspere Adapts a Hanging*, pp. 10–12. The inadequacy of the evidence for this

His final argument turns on his observation that the elaborate wording of the title-page of William Warner's translation of *Menaechmi* (1595): 'A pleasant and fine Conceited Comædie, taken out of the most excellent wittie Poet *Plautus: Chosen purposely from out the rest, as least harmefull, and yet most delightfull*', is identical with the wording of the entry in the Stationers' Register of 10 June 1594. Many years ago G. B. Harrison drew attention to other examples of 'long-tailed' titles transcribed in the Register, and argued that such entries were made from printed copy.[1] So Thomas would suggest that Warner's book was in print in June 1594, and could have been used as a source for a play written late in that year. However, there is bibliographical evidence that the edition of 1595 was a small one, and probably the only one[2]; and the elaborate wording of the entry in the Register must have been copied from a manuscript. If Shakespeare used the translation in writing his play, he read it in manuscript,[3] but it is impossible to prove that he borrowed from it.[4]

It seems that reasons can be found for dating *The Comedy of Errors* in 1589, 1591–3, and 1594, but none of the evidence is very reliable. The affinities of *The Comedy of Errors* with other works by Shakespeare need to be taken into account at this point. Its connections with the narrative poems published in 1593 and 1594 have been noted. The play has particular links also with two other plays. One is *Love's Labour's Lost*, which is set at the court of the King of Navarre, and is generally thought to have been written when Henry of Navarre was engaged in civil war with the support of the English government and forces, that is, between 1591 and November 1593, when support for him was withdrawn on his becoming a Roman Catholic.[5] This play, however, has its own dating problem, for it seems to refer to the Gray's Inn Revels of Christmas 1594, in which, as in the play, there appears a mock-embassy of Russians,[6] and also shows signs of a later revision. The play which has the closest links with *The Comedy of Errors* is *The Two Gentlemen of Verona*; there are many phrases, jests, and relatively unusual words, such as 'hapless', 'timeless', 'overshoes', 'minion', 'peevish', 'ruin-

---

date has been drastically exposed by Chambers, *W.S.*, I. 345, and by G. I. Duthie in his Introduction to the New Cambridge edition of the play (1955), p. xvi.

1. 'Books and Readers, 1591–4', *The Library* (Fourth Series), VIII (December 1927), 273–302.

2. See G. W. Williams, 'Setting by Formes in Quarto Printing', *Studies in Bibliography*, XI (1958), 46–9.

3. As some editors, like Cuningham, p. xxiv, believe.

4. See below, pp. xxv–xxvi.   5. See R. W. David, *op. cit.*, p. xxviii.

6. *Ibid.*, pp. xxx–xxxi.

ous', and 'peasant' (used of a servant) common to the two plays,[1] and the 'vexing dialogue' of the clowns, Launce and Speed, has connections with, and is similar in kind to, that of the Dromios, notably in such passages as the mock-inventory of the virtues of Launce's mistress.[2] This play, again, is of uncertain date, but has signs of a maturing writer, and is usually thought to have been composed in 1594.[3] *The Taming of the Shrew* has in common with these plays a use of doggerel couplets, and has connections with *The Comedy of Errors* both in the theme of the shrewish wife, Katherina, who is a type similar to Adriana, and in its indebtedness to George Gascoigne's *Supposes* (1566) for many details[4]; Shakespeare seems to have known this play of errors and mistaken identities when he wrote his own play of errors. However, the date of *The Taming of the Shrew* is complicated by its doubtful relationship with *The Taming of a Shrew* published in 1594; it is usually assigned to the period 1592–4.[5]

These linkages tend to reinforce the supposition that *The Comedy of Errors* was written not long before or immediately after the long spell of plague which caused all acting to be prohibited in London throughout most of the year 1593, and which probably turned Shakespeare to writing his narrative poems. It is not possible to be more conclusive than this. There is no compelling reason why the play should not have been written for a special occasion— perhaps the Gray's Inn Revels of 1594; it is interesting that it is known to have been revived on Innocents' Day, that is, for the same festival, in 1604. On the other hand, its links with other works, the hints from internal evidence, and the stylistic features of the play all suggest an earlier date, and I prefer to think of it as written between 1590 and 1593. It is evidently an early play, showing a clever organization of its material, slight characterization, and a plain, competent style, occasionally distinguished by a richness suggestive of the mature Shakespeare; but it seems to me impossible to decide in what order Shakespeare's first four comedies were written, and in any case, *The Comedy of Errors* is a special kind of play, not easily compared with the other early exploratory works. Finally, all speculation returns to the one basic fact of the play's history, its earliest known performance at the very end of 1594.

ction footnotes:

1. See also the notes below to I. i. 20, I. ii. 35–8, II. ii. 48, II. ii. 81–2, III. ii. 4, 58, IV. i. 94–5, IV. iii. 51–2.
2. *Two Gentlemen of Verona*, III. i. 290ff.; cf. below, III. ii. 99ff.
3. So Greg, *First Folio*, p. 217; Chambers, *W.S.*, I. 331, suggests 1594/5.
4. See Bullough, *Sources*, I. 66–8 and 111ff.   5. See Greg, *First Folio*, p. 215.

III. THE SOURCES

The principal source of *The Comedy of Errors* was the *Menaechmi* of Plautus, which Shakespeare had enough Latin to read in one of the numerous editions of the sixteenth century.[1] The action of this play is here briefly summarized[2]: a Prologus explains how a Merchant of Syracuse once lost one of his twin sons (Menaechmus the Citizen) in Epidamnum, where he was adopted by a citizen of that town. Years later his brother, the Syracusan (Menaechmus Sosicles) comes to Epidamnum in search of him, and the play begins at this point. The first act shows Menaechmus the Citizen quarrelling with his wife, pursued by the parasite Peniculus, and arranging to have lunch with the courtesan Erotium. Menaechmus Sosicles arrives with his servant Messenio in Act II, and the confusion of identities begins when he meets Cylindrus, Erotium's cook, going to buy provisions, and then encounters Erotium, who welcomes him to lunch and to her bed. In Act III Peniculus mistakes him for the citizen, abuses him for excluding his parasite from the lunch, and goes to the citizen's unnamed Wife to complain; Erotium's maid then runs to him to give him her mistress's bracelet to take to a jeweller for alterations. The results of this sequence of errors for Menaechmus the Citizen are shown in Act IV; he has been busy with a client, and returns home to be attacked by his wife and Peniculus for consorting with Erotium, who enters to demand the bracelet, and a mantle she had also given to Menaechmus Sosicles. The Citizen goes to consult his friends, and in the last act Menaechmus Sosicles returns, to find himself confronted by the irate Wife, who thinks from his behaviour that he is mad, an opinion shared by her father and the doctor they fetch. Menaechmus Sosicles gets away before the doctor appears, but his brother then comes home to find that his wife's father and the doctor treat him as insane, and fetch slaves to carry him off. At this point, Messenio arrives to rescue his supposed master, before the final scenes in which the brothers are at last brought together, and all mistakes are cleared up.

1. See T. W. Baldwin, *Shakspere's Small Latine* (1944), vol. 2. It is now generally accepted that Shakespeare had an acquaintance with a wide range of Latin literature, and that by his school-training he was well-equipped to read in the language; see Virgil K. Whitaker, *Shakespeare's Use of Learning* (1953), pp. 25–35.

2. See Appendix I for further details concerning the sources. Shakespeare's treatment of his Latin sources has been studied exhaustively by Baldwin, *Shakspere's Five-Act Structure* (1947), pp. 665–90, and by Erma Gill in her articles, 'A Comparison of the Characters in *The Comedy of Errors* with those in *Menaechmi*', *University of Texas Studies in English*, v (1925), 79–95, and 'The Plot-Structure of *The Comedy of Errors* in Relation to its Sources', *University of Texas Bulletin*, Studies in English, No. 10 (1930), 13–65.

Shakespeare not only multiplied the twins and the possibilities of error in his play by creating the Dromios, he also altered the emphasis of the Plautine plot. In *The Comedy of Errors* the Courtesan loses prominence and has no name, while the wife not only gains in stature and acquires a name, Adriana, but has, too, a confidante in her sister Luciana. The parasite and the wife's father vanish altogether, while the courtesan's maid and cook are transferred to the wife, and changed into Luce, Adriana's servant, and Nell, the unseen 'kitchen-wench' (III. ii. 93).[1] In *Menaechmi*, thanks to the long interchange in Act I between Menaechmus of Epidamnum (who corresponds to Antipholus of Ephesus) and the parasite (who was cut out altogether by Shakespeare), and the sequence between him and his father-in-law at the end, of which only fragments are retained in *The Comedy of Errors*, this Menaechmus is the centre of dramatic interest. Considerably more prominence was given by Shakespeare to the other twin, and Antipholus of Syracuse has nearly a hundred lines more than his brother, as well as a more sympathetic rôle, which includes the wooing of Luciana. In addition, the characters of Shakespeare's play are given more humanity, and more distinctiveness, as even the rather flat Medicus of Plautus is transformed into the egregious Doctor Pinch.

It is possible that Shakespeare had seen the first English translation of *Menaechmi*, made by William Warner, and published in 1595.[2] In this edition a note from 'The Printer to the Readers' begins:

> The writer hereof (loving Readers) having diverse of this Poettes Comedies Englished, for the use and delight of his private friends, who in Plautus owne words are not able to understand them: I have prevailed so far with him as to let this one go farther abroad...

The translation was entered in the Stationers' Register on 10 June 1594, and presumably had circulated earlier in manuscript. It is written in lively prose, and reveals some parallels with *The Comedy of Errors*, for example, in echoes of words like patch, stale, and harlots; in an emphasis on madness[3]; in the suggestion that

1. These are assimilated into one figure towards the end of the play, cf. IV. iv· 72 and n., but the two names, Luce and Nell, may reveal Shakespeare's first thought of taking over into his play both the maid and a figure corresponding to the cook, Cylindrus.

2. This is reprinted in Geoffrey Bullough, *Narrative and Dramatic Sources of Shakespeare*, I (1957), 12–39. See also Appendix I below.

3. See Bullough, pp. 18–19, 21, 29, 31, 33–4, and cf. below, II. ii. 212ff., IV. iii and IV. iv, V. i. 33, etc.

Erotium is a witch (this is not in the Latin)[1]; and in the phrase
'birds that bear feathers, or fishes that have fins' (Latin 'avis squa-
mosas, piscis pennatos', l. 918; i.e. birds with scales, fish with
feathers), which could have suggested the line,

> For a fish without a fin, there's a fowl without a feather.

(III. i. 82)

Perhaps the most striking connection between the two texts is the
transformation in both of the 'spinter' (*Menaechmi*, l. 526), the
bracelet which Erotium asks Menaechmus of Syracuse to have
repaired, into a chain.[2] However, even those who have made as
much as possible of the verbal similarities have not been able to
build up a convincing case that Shakespeare knew Warner's translation[3]; indeed, the reverse could be true, that Warner echoed
Shakespeare.[4]

The most direct link between *The Comedy of Errors* and *Menaechmi*
is the use of the terms Surreptus (Sereptus) and Errotis (Erotes) to
describe respectively Antipholus of Ephesus and his twin of Syracuse. In sixteenth-century editions of Plautus the twin Menaechmi
were distinguished as Surreptus and Sosicles; the word Surreptus
(stolen, snatched away), was taken over into common reference as
part of the name of Menaechmus the citizen of Epidamnum,[5] and
was transferred to Antipholus of Ephesus at his first entry. The
term Errotis or Erotes (both spellings appear in the Folio) is not so
readily explained. It is tempting to seek for a source in Plautus, and
it has been suggested that Shakespeare derived the word from the
name of the Courtesan in *Menaechmi*, Erotium, and that he thought
initially of the Antipholus who was to be entertained in mistake for
his brother by Adriana as identified with Erotium's Menaechmus[6];

1. See Bullough, p. 21, and cf. IV. iii. 76 below; this has a thematic importance
in Shakespeare's play, which is examined in the Critical Introduction.
   2. See II. i. 106 and n., and Appendix I, p. 110.
   3. See, for instance, Cuningham, pp. xxv–xxviii, where he draws up a detailed
list of parallels, and also Appendix I below.
   4. This is Baldwin's opinion; see the Introduction in his edition of *The Comedy
of Errors*, section on the Sources.
   5. As for instance in Robert Greene's *The Card of Fancy* (1587), in *Shorter Novels
of the Sixteenth Century* (Everyman, 1929), p. 191, 'thou art *Castania* ... like Menechmus Subreptus his wife, thou dost not begin to love, ere again thou seekest to
hate'. This and another example are cited in Shakespeare, *Works*, edited W. G.
Clark and J. Glover (1863), I. 463. Dover Wilson seems not to have noticed the
connection with Plautus, and thought Shakespeare's terms were 'derived from
some play intermediate in development between the *Menaechmi* and *The Comedy
of Errors*' (p. 74), but Menaechmus of Epidamnum is called 'puerum surruptum'
and 'qui subruptus est' at the beginning of the play (ll. 38, 41).
   6. Bullough, *Sources*, I. 3.

or, alternatively, that the name of the Courtesan prompted Shakespeare to think of Eros, and to mark off Antipholus of Syracuse as the one who falls in love.[1] Errotis (Erotes), however, has no better connection with Eros as a Greek word than it has with any Latin word, and most scholars have preferred to find in it a corruption of a descriptive term in Latin parallel to Surreptus. It has usually been interpreted as distorted from Erraticus or Errans (wandering),[2] thus giving the twins labels (Surreptus and Erraticus) corresponding to the differentiation of the twin Menaechmi as 'civis' and 'advena' in the 'Argumentum' prefixed to Plautus's play—a distinction preserved in William Warner's translation in the terms 'Citizen' and 'Traveller'.[3] I prefer this last interpretation, but the word remains a puzzle, and it is difficult to account for corruption from Erraticus. Apart from Surreptus, and the possible connection of Errotis with Plautus, there is not much verbal connection between the Latin text and Shakespeare's play.[4]

In developing the action of *The Comedy of Errors*, Shakespeare borrowed from another play by Plautus, *Amphitruo*, which gave him material for III. i, the scene in which Adriana feasts Antipholus of Syracuse in the belief that he is her husband.[5] In *Amphitruo*, Jupiter takes the place of Amphitryon in his house, and sleeps with his wife, Alcmena, who believes she is with her husband. Meanwhile, Mercury adopts the appearance of Amphitryon's slave, Sosia, and first confuses, then drives away the real Sosia. A little later, Mercury, still Sosia in appearance, abuses Amphitryon when he knocks at the door of his own house and is not allowed to enter. In this play there are two pairs of twins, masters and servants, who cannot be distinguished by their friends or by Alcmena, and Shakespeare doubtless took a hint from this play for the development of the twin Dromios in addition to their twin masters, though Dromio of Syracuse is partly based on Messenio, the slave of Menaechmus of Syracuse. The other characters in the comic plot of Shakespeare's play, Luciana, the First and Second Merchants,

1. T. W. Baldwin, *Shakspere's Five-Act Structure*, p. 697.
2. Baldwin ingeniously suggested in his edition, p. 105, that Errotis might be corrupted from Erratus, a past participle constructed from the intransitive verb *errare* to match the adjective Surreptus.
3. See Bullough, *Sources*, I. 22, 24.
4. J. A. K. Thomson, *Shakespeare and the Classics* (1952), p. 49, states his belief that 'while the structure of the play [*The Comedy of Errors*] is Plautine, the superstructure is the work of a man who appears never to have looked at the Latin of Plautus at all.'
5. No translation of *Amphitruo* was in print at this time, but the plot had been used by at least one English dramatist, in the play *Jack Juggler* (1553).

and Balthasar,[1] seem to have been invented by him; a hint for the
creation of the Goldsmith, Angelo, was no doubt provided by
Erotium's proposal to send her bracelet to a goldsmith for re-
furbishing, and the two names, Luce and Nell, given to Adriana's
maid or kitchen-wench,[2] may reveal Shakespeare's first thought of
taking over into *The Comedy of Errors* Erotium's maid, and a figure
corresponding to Cylindrus, her cook.[3]

It is doubtful whether the edition of Plautus used by Shakespeare
can be certainly identified, but a strong claim has been made for
that of Lambinus (1576).[4] This claim rests chiefly on two features
of Lambinus's commentary.[5] One is his confused note about the
location of Epidamnum, on which, however, Shakespeare did not
need to rely for the geography of the play.[6] The other feature is
Lambinus's care in pointing out the various errors in *Menaechmi*,
drawing attention to them in his notes in phrases like 'coquus
errans', 'novus error', 'errat hic senex', and 'errat Messenio'. At
one point he also draws attention to a similar 'error' in *Amphitruo*,
'talis est error in Amphitr'.[7] This could have suggested Shakespeare's title to him, and his references to 'errors' in the text, as at
II. ii. 184 and III. ii. 35. It is also possible that he derived the idea for
his 'errors' from George Gascoigne's *Supposes* (1566), a play he
certainly knew, as it is one of the sources of *The Taming of the Shrew*,
and in which the various 'supposes' or mistakes are pointed out in
marginal notes.[8]

1. Erma Gill believes that Shakespeare's Balthasar is connected with Blepharo,
the pilot and friend of Amphitryon, but the link, if any exists, is most tenuous; see
'The Plot-Structure of *The Comedy of Errors* in Relation to its Sources', pp. 53ff.

2. See above, p. xxv.

3. Erma Gill, *loc. cit.*, p. 53, argues that Shakespeare was familiar with an early
reconstruction of the lost sequence of *Amphitruo*, Act IV; the only reconstruction
she can point to, however, is that in the English adaptation of the play, *The Birth
of Hercules* (? c. 1600), which is later than *The Comedy of Errors*, and is probably
indebted to it, for it gives Amphitryon another servant besides Sosia, named
Dromio.

4. Shakespeare could have seen other Lambinus editions than this first one;
I have examined the edition of 1577, published at Lyons, now in the Cosin
Library at Durham. The claim that Shakespeare used this edition was made by
T. W. Baldwin, in his edition of *The Comedy of Errors*, and, more fully, in *Shak-
spere's Five-Act Structure*, pp. 667–81, 688–94.

5. Baldwin is determined to find a source for everything in Shakespeare, and
he also argues that the playwright studied a note of Lambinus on the Latin
'Istros' (*Menaechmi*, l. 235) to find a suggestion for Egeon's travels through Asia
(I. i. 132–4; see note to this passage). There is no need to require a source for a
reference to Asia, but if one is sought, *Acts*, xix, supplies a close parallel for Egeon's
travels, as Baldwin himself observes, in its description of St Paul's travels.

6. See below, p. xxx.   7. Baldwin, *Shakespere's Five-Act Structure*, p. 692.

8. See Bullough, *Sources*, I. 114, 121, 125, 134–5, 142–6, etc.

Shakespeare altered the tone of his Latin sources considerably, not merely by putting an emphasis on marriage and courtship, rather than on the husband's relations with a courtesan, but also by giving his play a certain Christian colouring, and developing ideas of sorcery and witchcraft. It was perhaps natural for him to make his characters speak in Elizabethan terms of hell and heaven, devils and angels, with the common play on the coin called an angel,[1] and to have Antipholus of Syracuse say early on, 'Now as I am a Christian . . .' (i. ii. 77), but such things have a further relevance. For Shakespeare also transferred the setting of *The Comedy of Errors* from Epidamnum, the scene of *Menaechmi*, to Ephesus, re-calling for himself and his audience St Paul's Epistle to the Ephesians. This includes in chapters v. 22ff. and vi. 5ff. exhorta-tions on the relations of husband and wife and master and servant which have a bearing on the action of the play.[2] Furthermore, in the account of St Paul's visit to Ephesus in *Acts*, xix, the city is associated with magic, with those 'which used curious arts', and with 'exorcists',[3] hints which Shakespeare developed in making Antipholus of Syracuse think of it peopled with

> nimble jugglers that deceive the eye,
> Dark-working sorcerers that change the mind,
> Soul-killing witches that deform the body,
> Disguised cheaters, prating mountebanks. (i. ii. 98–101)

This passage owes something also to Messenio's description of Epidamnum at the beginning of Act II of *Menaechmi* as full of swind-lers, rakes, cheats, and harlots (sycophantae, voluptarii, palpa-tores, meretrices mulieres), lines slightly embroidered by Warner[4]; but Shakespeare elaborates the suggestions he found in the Bible and in Plautus into an atmosphere of strangeness, of witchcraft and deception in the Ephesus of *The Comedy of Errors*, which becomes a powerful element in the action.[5]

One motive in changing the scene to Ephesus may have been to give the play a setting more familiar to a London audience, for Ephesus was known not only through the Bible, but as a seaport, and the home of a famous temple of Diana. So, in *The Excellent and pleasant Works of Julius Solinus Polyhistor* (1587), Shakespeare might have read of Asia Minor that it was enclosed 'on the west wyth the Aegæan Sea. . . In it is the most famous Cittie *Ephesus*. The beauty of

1. See IV. iii. 19 and 38.
2. As was noted by Bullough, *Sources*, I. 9, who does not, however, point to all the links between *Ephesians* and the play; see Appendix I.
3. See verses 19 and 13 especially; the relevant passages are cited below, p. 114. Baldwin comments on this linkage in *Shakspere's Five-Act Structure*, pp. 681–2.
4. Bullough, *Sources*, I. 17.   5. See below, p. xlvi.

Ephesus is the Temple of *Diana*, buylded by the *Amazons*.'[1] There is no evidence that Shakespeare did read this book, but he probably knew of Solinus, whose name he gave to the Duke[2]; the name of the father in his play, Egeon, who suffered the loss of his wife and one son when the mast they floated on struck a 'mighty rock' (I. i. 101), seems to be derived from the name of the sea, which Solinus accounts for in this way: 'On the ryght hand, as men sayle to *Antandros,* there is a Rock...which...seemeth to have the shape of a Goate, which the Greekes call Æga... of this Rocke the *Aegaean* Gulfe taketh his name'.[3]

There is no reason to demand geographical accuracy in *Errors* of a playwright who elsewhere gave Bohemia a sea-coast, and made a port of Milan.[4] An audience is not likely to be troubled by inconsistencies of detail or inaccuracies in references to distant and unfamiliar places. The geography of Shakespeare's play is not fully explicable, and he no doubt arranged it to suit himself; at the same time, he is indebted to his reading for the locations he uses. Egeon's story in I. i begins from Epidamnum, the setting of *Menaechmi,* near which town he is shipwrecked, and spies

> Two ships from far, making amain to us,
> Of Corinth that, of Epidaurus this.   (I. i. 92–3)

The suggestion for Corinth may have come from *Acts,* xix. 1, 'whyle Apollos was at Corinth, Paul passed through the upper coastes, and came to Ephesus'. But this passage raises a difficulty, that Epidamnum (later Dyracchium, now Durazzo in Albania), was north-west of both Corinth and the Greek Epidaurus, not between them, as the text implies. It seems likely that Shakespeare relied for his information on the misleading entry in Cooper's *Thesaurus,* where Epidamnum is listed as 'A towne in the South-west part of Greece ... called afterwarde *Dyracchium*',[5] or else that

1. Signature Aa 3ᵛ. The work of this geographer, a description of the Mediterranean countries, was translated by Arthur Golding. Attention was drawn to it by Arthur Gray in the *Times Literary Supplement,* 17 February 1927, p. 108.

2. A character in John Lyly's *Campaspe,* printed 1584, is named Solinus.

3. Signature K4ᵛ; Shakespeare may have known the account of the origin of the sea's name given in Cooper's *Thesaurus;* this cites the legend of Aegeus, King of Athens, the father of Theseus, who stood on a cliff awaiting the return of his son from Crete, not knowing whether Theseus had survived the ordeal of the Minotaur. Theseus forgot to put up the prearranged white token of success on his ship, and his father, in grief, flung himself into the sea, which was named after him.

4. In *The Winter's Tale* and *Two Gentlemen of Verona* respectively.

5. *Thesaurus Linguae Romanae* (1565 etc.); the possibility that Shakespeare knew this is reinforced by the passages Bullough cites (I. 397–8, 404–5), in relation to *MND.* T. W. Baldwin, *Shakspere's Five-Act Structure,* p. 688, believes that Lambinus may be again involved. In his edition of Plautus (Lyons, 1577, p. 416),

he knew some such map of the ancient world as that included in Ortelius, *Theatrum Orbis Terrarum*, which shows another Epidaurus (later Ragusa, now Dubrovnik), north of Epidamnum on the Adriatic coast.[1] Egeon's wife, Emilia, seemed to Egeon to be picked up by 'fishermen of Corinth' (I. i. 111); but in Act V she tells us that she was returned to Epidamnum, and she does not explain how she eventually arrived in Ephesus. There is probably no point in raising the question, except that it perhaps illustrates that Shakespeare's concern was not with geographical accuracy, but was rather to stress names like Ephesus, which would be familiar to his audience, and which he could put to dramatic use.

In transferring the play's action to this city Shakespeare had in mind the story of Apollonius of Tyre, which he may well have learned from the version included by John Gower in his *Confessio Amantis*.[2] The location in *The Comedy of Errors* of Emilia at the Priory, which is descended from the 'famous temple of Diana, numbred among the seven woonders of the worlde' at Ephesus,[3] and the sea-storms and adventures endured by her and Egeon, were suggested by this tale. According to it, Lucina, the wife of Apollonius, in giving birth to a daughter while on board ship,

---

he has a note on 'Epidamnum devenit' in the Argumentum of *Menaechmi*, 'Dyracchium venit, Sed Steph. de urbibus docet duas Epidamnos esse, unam in Illyrico, alteram in sinu Ionio' (He came to Durazzo, but Stephanus teaches that there were two cities called Epidamnum, one in Illyria (the country north-west of Greece on the Adriatic), one on the Ionian gulf (the sea between Italy and Greece south of the Adriatic; but the Adriatic itself was once known as the Ionian gulf, whence arose, no doubt, the error in Stephanus). But I do not think Shakespeare puzzled over this note, and elsewhere Lambinus simply identifies Epidamnum as Dyracchium.

1. Probably the reference to Epidaurus was suggested to Shakespeare by one or both of these books; neither this city nor Corinth are mentioned in *Menaechmi* or *Amphitruo*. George B. Parks, 'Shakespeare's Map for *The Comedy of Errors*', *J.E.G.P.*, xxxix (1940), 93–7, argues that Shakespeare used Ortelius; he is right in claiming that in the maps of ancient Rome and of the travels of St Paul included in the *Theatrum Orbis Terrarum* (I have seen the edition of 1584), Epidamnus and Epidaurus are shown as 'virtually the only cities on the lower Adriatic'. Ortelius also displays the more familiar Epidaurus listed in Cooper as 'A citie in Greece, in the country called Achaia'. See the frontispiece to this edition.

2. This was printed in 1493 by Caxton, and reprinted in 1532 and 1554; the relevant section is included by Geoffrey Bullough in *Sources*, I. 50–4. Perhaps Shakespeare knew the version of this tale written by Laurence Twine as *The Pattern of Painful Adventures*, which was entered on the Stationers' Register in 1576, and survives in two editions, one of ? c. 1594, one of 1607. This was later used by the dramatist in writing *Pericles* (see the Arden edition, by F. D. Hoeniger, 1962, pp. xl–xlix), and parts of it were incorporated by G. Wilkins in *The Painful Adventures of Pericles* (1608; see the edition by Kenneth Muir, 1953, pp. 111–12).

3. T. Cooper, *Thesaurus* (1578).

C

appears to die, and is put in a chest which is cast into the sea; the chest floats to Ephesus, where Lucina is revived by a physician, Cerimon, and later becomes a priestess in the temple of Diana. Many years later, Apollonius, after surviving various stormy sea-journeys, is reunited with his daughter, whom he had left at Tarsus to be brought up, and finally with his wife. In Gower's version, Lucina is described as giving herself to 'religion', and then as becoming 'Abbesse there',[1] so that the change from temple to priory was already half-made.

Analogies for the story of Egeon and his family abound; another play by Plautus, the *Rudens*, has some of its elements, a shipwreck, a daughter lost by her father and eventually reunited with him, and a priestess, here at a temple to Venus, who helps the girl[2]; similar situations occur in a number of prose romances[3]; and some earlier Italian plays have parallel episodes. So *Gl'Inganni* by Nicolo Secchi (1549), well-known as an analogue for the plot of *Twelfth Night*, a play which owes something to *The Comedy of Errors*, contains a father of twins who is captured by pirates, taken into slavery, and many years later reunited with his children.[4] Another Italian play, *L'Ammalata* (1555), by Giovanni Cecchi, presents a mother, banished on suspected falsehood, who then becomes a nun in Florence, famous for her healing powers; she is rejoined by her husband when he comes to her to seek a cure for leprosy.[5]

In addition, there were a number of Italian adaptations of *Menaechmi* in the sixteenth century, which add to and complicate the Plautine intrigues and mistakes of identity, and a 'score or so of scenari' remain that 'in main or sub-plots make use of the *Menaechmi* theme'.[6] Though evidence is lacking that Shakespeare knew any of

1. Bullough, p. 53; *Confessio Amantis*, VIII. 1265, 1849. H. F. Brooks, writing on the concept of 'imitation' in *R.E.S.* XXV (1949), 124–40, points out that such 'naturalization' of literature goes back at least to Alfred; at first not deliberate, it becomes a principle after being a habit.

2. For an outline of this play, and comments on its relationship to Shakespeare's *Pericles*, see P. Simpson, *Studies in Elizabethan Drama* (1955), pp. 17–19.

3. See S. L. Wolff, *Greek Romances in Elizabethan Prose Fiction* (1912).

4. Bullough, *Sources*, I. 7; II. 339–40.

5. R. Warwick Bond argued strongly in *Studia Otiosa* (1938), pp. 43–50, that Shakespeare knew this play: 'The clinching point is that in both *L'Ammalata* and the *Errors* the long-lost wife or mother is a nun in a monastery famous for her medical skill' (pp. 49–50). However, Shakespeare may simply have transferred to the Abbess the marvellous healing powers of 'Maister Cerymon the leche' (l. 1874), the physician who finds and revives Lucina in Gower's story of Apollonius.

6. See K. M. Lea, *Italian Popular Comedy* (1934), I. 171–4; she shows that among the 'Plautine comedies that the actors of Renaissance Italy were never tired of playing the *Menaechmi* was the dominant note'. See also Bullough, *Sources*, I. 6–7.

them, he does seem 'to have been acquainted with the way in which the comedy of mistaken identity was exploited on the Italian stage'.[1] The extant scenari of the commedia dell' arte containing twin masters and twin servants date from the seventeenth century, but they almost certainly belong to a long acting tradition. In them are found such devices as the misdelivery of messages, or jewels, confusion over lost money, mistaken arrests, the fetching of a purse of money from a desk,[2] and the involvement of the zanni, or servant-fools, with maids, as Dromio of Syracuse runs into trouble with Nell (Luce), who is affianced to his twin, in III. ii of *The Comedy of Errors*. Furthermore, Luciana, an addition by Shakespeare to the characters he inherited from Plautus and Gower, 'might be compared to the second lady of a Commedia improvisa who is used as the confidante to the *prima donna* and the consolation prize for the deserving stranger'.[3]

There is no doubt that Shakespeare knew the elegant prose plays of John Lyly, written mostly on classical themes for boy actors of the choristers' school attached to St Paul's Cathedral. Of these plays, *Mother Bombie*, printed 1594, but acted probably in 1590, has closest affinities with *The Comedy of Errors*, as being modelled on Roman comedy, though its plot, in which a group of four gay and witty servants to four old men conspire against them in helping to forward the love-schemes of their masters' children, is Terentian, rather than Plautine. One of the servants is named Dromio, and Shakespeare may have borrowed the name from this play.[4] His debt to Lyly, especially in the exchange between the Dromios and their masters, is too general and pervasive, however, to be reduced to a list of borrowings. It is possible to point to a number of phrases or images in Lyly's works which recur or are echoed in Shakespeare's play; for instance, I have noticed the following in *Mother Bombie*: 'beg him for a foole' (I. i. 37; cf. *Errors*, II. i. 41); the images of the vine and elm (I. iii. 124; *Errors*, II. ii. 174); of pulling a crow (II. i. 82; *Errors*, III. i. 83); of the parrot crying 'rope' (III. iv. 57–8; *Errors*, IV. iv. 40); 'I had thought to have askt you' (IV. i. 36; *Errors*, III. i. 55); 'there's a time for al things' (v. iii. 15; *Errors*, II. ii. 63); 'sing til we catch cold on our feet' (v. iii. 88; *Errors*, III. i. 37); but some of these are proverbial, and some are to be found in other authors of the period also. The number of such echoes has a cumulative weight, especially when, in addition, Shakespeare employs

1. K. M. Lea, *op. cit.*, II. 438.
2. See IV. i. 103ff. below; this device is used in *Il Tradito*.
3. K. M. Lea, *op. cit.*, II. 442.
4. It should be noted, however, that this name is a variant of *Dromo*, a type-name for a slave in several of Terence's comedies.

formal devices he learned from Lyly, and in the mock dialectics of
II. ii, and again in the catechism of III. ii,[1] recalls similar passages in
Midas. Lyly's influence is felt finally in the tone of much of the
comic dialogue, the cadences, the cheerful quibbling insolence of
the servants, and the casual equality of speech between servant and
master, who may nevertheless turn sharply on his 'villain' at any
minute.

As noted earlier, Shakespeare was aware also of George Gascoigne's *Supposes* (printed 1575), a prose version of Ariosto's *I
Suppositi*, and a play performed at Gray's Inn in 1566, which deals
in 'errors' or confusions of identity, a 'mystaking or imagination of
one thing for an other'.[2] While neither Lyly's plays, nor *Supposes*,
may be regarded strictly as sources for *The Comedy of Errors*, they
illustrate the general derivation of the tone of this play.[3]

IV. THE STAGING

The Comedy of Errors is unique among Shakespeare's plays in the
way localities are indicated. It preserves a unity of place and of
time, for the entire action takes place within Ephesus and within
the space of one day; and, in addition, it seems to require only four
playing-areas, or at the most five, three of which were clearly
marked by signs. These localities are the 'street' (III. i. 36 etc.) or
'mart' (I. ii. 74, etc.), presumably the main playing area of the
stage; the house of Antipholus of Ephesus, called the Phoenix
(I. ii. 75); the house of the Courtesan, called the Porpentine (i.e.
Porcupine, III. i. 116); and the Priory which houses the Abbess
(v. i. 37). It is possible that an upper storey or gallery in the house of
Antipholus was also used (II. ii. 207 and n.; III. i. 47 S.D. and n.),

1. See II. ii. 54–109, III. ii. 99-143 and notes.
2. Bullough, *Sources*, I. 66–7, 112.
3. It is relevant to note here that Shakespeare perhaps borrowed the name
Menaphon (v. i. 368) either from Marlowe's *Tamburlaine*, a Persian nobleman in
this play, or from the name of the central figure in Robert Greene's pastoral
romance, *Menaphon*, subtitled *Camilla's Alarum to slumbering Euphues* (1589); and
that there is some analogy between the description of Nell's face and body at III.
ii. 112-49 and a passage in Rabelais, *Gargantua and Pantagruel*, Book III, Chapter
28, which was not available to Shakespeare in an English translation. D. T.
Starnes, 'Shakespeare and Apuleius', *PMLA*, LX (1945), 1021-50, argues that
Shakespeare could have derived ideas of sorcery and witchcraft for his play from
W. Adlington's translation of *The Golden Ass* (1566, etc.), as well as the talk of each
Dromio being transformed into an ass (II. i; III. i; IV. iv). But Shakespeare did not
need to go to this for ideas of sorcery, and the play on 'ass' is developed from a
stock joke; I can see no relevance to *The Comedy of Errors* here, not even in what
Starnes sees as an analogy to IV. iii. 69–73, a passage which may be found in the
edition of Adlington in Tudor Translations, edited by Charles Whibley (1893),
p. 73.

but it is not essential to the play's action. The evidence of the text points to one conclusion, that 'at the back of the stage three houses or doors represented to the right and left the Priory with some religious emblem over it, and the Courtesan's house with the sign of the Porpentine, and in the centre the house of Antipholus with the sign of the Phoenix'.[1]

Another peculiarity of the text is the direction at v. i. 9, 'Enter Antipholus and Dromio again', which suggests that there was no break on the stage between Acts IV and V, and that the division of the play into acts was made perhaps at the time of printing.[2] So the text indicates a continuous action on a stage with three fixed locations, which could have been 'houses', shallow structures from which characters could speak or make entries.[3] The use of 'houses' ('mansions' or 'domus') was common in Court productions, and standard practice in the dramaturgy of Lyly, from whom Shakespeare learned much in writing his play.[4] However, Shakespeare may also have had in mind the traditions of Gray's Inn, if *The Comedy of Errors* was written for performance there. For the educated gentlemen of the Inns of Court were familiar with the conventionalized arcade settings with which Renaissance editors illustrated editions of Terence and Plautus, apparently in the belief that they were imitating the Roman stage. In these arcades, each compartment would represent a house or 'domus',[5] and it seems that staging at the Inns of Court followed this pattern; George Kernodle describes the productions of the tragedies staged there for Queen Elizabeth's entertainment in this way:

> Several variations of a conventionalized façade were used for a series of tragedies. . . Their first classical tragedy, *Gorboduc*, produced in 1561, required only two entrance ways and a throne (or possibly two thrones) as a setting. . . The combination of throne and arcade screen was a commonplace of art from the time of the Hellenistic theatres.
>
> The next play, *Jocasta*, produced at Gray's Inn in 1566, had . . . a façade in the centuries-old pattern of a centre castle gate flanked by two side doors. . . Here the central castle was the palace doorway of Jocasta. . . At each side of the central palace was a gateway, one marked "Homolydes" and the other "Electrae" . . .

1. Chambers, *W.S.*, I. 307.   2. See above, p. xii.
3. See Chambers, *E.S.*, III. 42–3; I. 229. For accounts of the use of 'houses' on medieval and later stages, see Allardyce Nicoll, *The Development of the Theatre* (1952 edn), pp. 65–73, 82–5, and 119, and also Richard Southern, *Changeable Scenery* (1952), pp. 26–9.
4. See Chambers, *E.S.*, III. 32ff.; and above, p. xxxiii.
5. See George Kernodle, *From Art to Theatre* (1944), pp. 160–3.

For *The Misfortunes of Arthur*, produced at Gray's Inn in 1587 . . . two entranceways, after the medieval convention and the humanistic Terence conventions, served as the houses of Mordred and Arthur, though they were in actuality supposed to be many miles apart; and a third entrance is spoken of at one moment as the cloister of the nuns.[1]

All these had three fixed locations, and an arcade with three doors such as that used for *Jocasta* and possibly for *The Misfortunes of Arthur* would have served admirably for *The Comedy of Errors*, which seems to call for exactly this kind of setting.

Another feature of the play is a series of stage-directions suggesting that the author had doors or 'houses' in mind, the directions indicating entrances and exits 'from the Courtizans' (iv. i. 13), 'to the Priorie' (v. i. 37), and 'to the Abbesse' (v. i. 282). There is one more peculiar direction at iv. i. 85, 'Enter Dromio Sira. from the Bay'; this prompted Peter Alexander to think that there were two side entrances, one leading to the harbour from which Antipholus of Syracuse arrives on stage, and by which he plans continually to leave; the other leading to the city or court, the entrance from which the Duke and his procession would come in Act V:

One side entrance leads to the Bay, the other to the Town. This was the proper classic setting for the stage, since the Comedy, which was Shakespeare's model, was born at Athens between the Bay and the Town. And the courtesy of convention allowed Comedy to enjoy the advantages she was born to, even in cities where they were unsanctioned by the laws of nature. Plautus in his *Amphitruo* gives a harbour to Thebes. . .[2]

This is a reasonable suggestion, but I do not think we need suppose that Shakespeare had read Vitruvius, or realized what was a 'proper classic setting'; his reading of Plautus would have been enough, for *Menaechmi* and *Amphitruo* clearly indicate a harbour and a city. There is only the single direction 'from the Bay' to guide us and it is not clear from the rest of the play that Shakespeare thought of side-entrances as pointing to the harbour and to the city.

However, the indications in stage-directions and within the text all suggest a simple staging of a special kind. It is tempting to suppose that this short play, with its classical background, was designed for performance in a hall with no gallery, and for an audience used to 'houses' on stage, and perhaps familiar with the

1. Kernodle, *From Art to Theatre*, p. 133.
2. *Shakespeare's Life and Art* (1939), pp. 68–9. In the Greek theatre the side entrances in fact had a different significance; 'by one of them the characters entered as if coming from the city or harbor, by the other, as if from the country' (M. Bieber, *The History of the Greek and Roman Theater*, 1939, p. 141).

kind of arcade setting to be seen in illustrations to several early editions of Terence (see the examples reproduced on pp. xxxviii and xxxix). Perhaps the play was written for an Inns of Court performance, in 1594, or for some earlier occasion. It is also possible that Shakespeare had at some time, as John Aubrey recorded in the late seventeenth century, been a schoolmaster in the country[1] before he came to London, and was writing out of his own knowledge and experience of teaching, or even producing, plays by Plautus or Terence. But there is no need to push speculation too far, for as the text stands, it would, especially with the help of a gallery, go very conveniently on the stage of a public playhouse.

Some difficulty is presented by the scene (III. i) in which Adriana feasts the wrong Antipholus, while her husband clamours outside for entrance. Early editors mostly followed Rowe in assuming that the directions in F, 'Enter Luce' (III. i. 47), and 'Enter Adriana' (III. i. 60) could be interpreted as meaning that these characters speak from 'within'. More recently, there has been support for the idea that Luce appears on a balcony, and is there joined by Adriana.[2] Dover Wilson argued that Antipholus and Dromio of Ephesus are knocking on the door from which (through a wicket?) they are being answered by Dromio of Syracuse, and to put the women with him, he said, would be 'extremely awkward from the theatrical point of view, since the audience would be greatly puzzled by three unseen characters, more especially as one of them [i.e. Luce] appears nowhere else in the play'. So he concluded that this scene is arranged in the Folio text for the 'public playhouse'.

Since he wrote this, the evidence regarding the appearance and structure of the stages of the public theatres in Shakespeare's time has been reconsidered,[3] and we are not as certain as he was that the action here took place below a gallery, and in front of an 'inner stage' or alcove, with a door or curtain leading into it. There may not have been an inner stage at all, but rather a structure built out from the stage wall[4]; and we do not know what the doors referred to in the text of *The Comedy of Errors* were like, how big they were, or whether they included a wicket or aperture in the upper part, as seems to be suggested by the jesting cry of Dromio of Syracuse to his

1. A view supported by Peter Alexander, *op. cit.*, pp. 24–6; see Chambers, *W.S.*, II. 254.

2. This was proposed by Dover Wilson (*N.C.S.*, p. 98), and accepted by Chambers (*W.S.*, I. 307–8).

3. See A. M. Nagler, *Shakespeare's Stage* (1958), and *Shakespeare Survey*, 12 (1959).

4. As in illustrations in the 1493 and 1552 editions of Terence; see the reproductions on pp. xxxviii and xxxix and Kernodle, *op. cit.*, p. 161.

Acknow. University of Toronto Library

*Illustrations in the edition of the Comedies of Terence published by Johann Trechsel
at Lyons in* 1493, *reproduced from the copy in Toronto University Library: that
above is from the* Andria, *sig. d4ʳ, the one opposite from the* Adelphoe, *sig. C1ʳ.*

twin, 'Either get thee from the door, or sit down at the hatch' (III.
i. 33; see the note to this line). The aperture may have been a half-
door, or at least large enough for several figures to be visible to the
audience, and Luce certainly appears from the dialogue to be
located within the door, for Antipholus calls to her 'you'll let us in
I trow', and 'Thou baggage, let me in' (III. i. 54, 57). In addition,
there is little evidence for the use of a gallery here; at II. ii. 207
Adriana says

> Husband, I'll dine above with you to-day,
> And shrive you of a thousand idle pranks,

but it is doubtful whether this can be taken literally as referring to
the stage[1]; and it may be an accidental slip in the Folio that

1. S. A. Tannenbaum, *Shaksperian Scraps and other Elizabethan Fragments* (1953),
pp. 87–8, felt that 'above' here must be an error for 'alone', since it does not apply
to III. i, and the idea of shriving suggests that Adriana intends to dine alone with
Antipholus; but see v. i. 207.

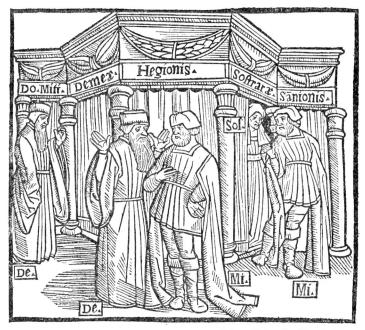

Acknow. University of Toronto Library

Dromio of Syracuse is given no entry when he speaks at III. i. 32, whereas Luce's entry is marked at III. i. 47. The evidence is finally inconclusive, and does not compel belief in one kind of staging rather than another, or require us positively to affirm or deny that Shakespeare had in mind a gallery or upper stage. However, it seems to me that Luce and Adriana are meant to be visible to the audience in this scene, while apparently, or in supposition, remaining concealed from Antipholus of Ephesus and his companions, and that this could be more easily and convincingly staged by using a structure on stage than by placing the mistress and her maid on a balcony.[1]

2. CRITICAL INTRODUCTION

Any developed account of *The Comedy of Errors* is likely to seem portentous in relation to the complexities of Shakespeare's mature drama, and extravagant in relation to the usual classification of the play as an early farce. Clearly it is important to keep a critical balance; but it is also important to recognize that, from the beginning of his career, Shakespeare was an artist of unusual power, and

1. See below, III. i. 47, S.D. and n.

that all his work deserves serious attention. Such attention has been given to patently serious plays, like *Richard III* and *Titus Andronicus*; the exploration of levels of action or meaning in these does not clash with common assumptions about the kind of play each is, history or tragedy, or conflict with common expectations about the kind of experience they afford. The critic can be, and often is, solemn in his account of them. Let him, however, probe beneath the vocabulary commonly used to describe the comedies, gay, warm, enchanting, romantic, lively, and so forth, and he is at once liable to invite the scorn of the many who believe interpretation to be unnecessary, and provoke the hostility of those for whom the experience afforded by the comedies is a sort of inviolate glow, sacred and not to be profaned. He may well seem to murder to dissect, to set bounds to Illyria, to turn the forest of Arden into a formal garden, in short, to destroy the dream.[1]

There is health in such responses, which should warn the critic to avoid what, in relation to the comedies, would be a killing solemnity; but they owe much to a long tradition of regarding comedy in general as inferior to 'serious' plays, and Shakespeare's comedies in particular as entertainments, plays of escape into a careless world.[2] If Shakespeare's mature comedies are often regarded in this way, how much more difficult it would seem to be to discuss *The Comedy of Errors*, which has so often been thought of in the way Coleridge saw it, as a farce, to be distinguished from comedy: 'A proper farce is mainly distinguished from comedy by the license allowed, and even required in the fable in order to produce strange and laughable situations.'[3] In such a view, ingenuity alone matters, and the virtue of the play lies in its clever adaptation of Roman comedy, and in its neatness of structure as the 'best plotted of Shakespeare's early comedies'[4]; the first and last scenes

1. Some psychologists have no inhibitions of this kind, and *The Comedy of Errors* has been interpreted, by A. Bronson Feldman in the *International Journal of Psycho-Analysis*, xxxvi (1955), 114–33, as Shakespeare's expression of an unconscious desire for incest with his mother.

2. See J. R. Brown, *Shakespeare and his Comedies* (1957), pp. 11–13 for a fuller record and discussion of criticism of the comedies.

3. *Coleridge's Shakespearean Criticism*, ed. T. M. Raysor, 2 vols. (1930), I. 99.

4. T. M. Parrott, *Shakespearian Comedy* (1949), p. 105. The play seems to have been conceived as a unit, and the act-division of the Folio is imposed on the text (see v. i. 9 and n.); its design is best thought of in terms of the skilful development of the central action in relation to the frame-plot, which provides a starting-point and a point of resolution. The claim elaborated by T. W. Baldwin, *William Shakspere's Five-Act Structure*, pp. 703ff., that it is based upon a five-act structure derived from Terence, has been attacked by Henry L. Snuggs, who demonstrates the flimsiness of Baldwin's evidence in his *Shakespeare and Five Acts* (1960), pp. 32–4, 59–67; see also W. T. Jewkes, *Act Division in Elizabethan and*

may serve the purpose of relaxing the mood of the audience with an appeal to sentiment, but the rest is to be taken simply as laughable. Even Adriana, Luciana, and the Courtesan, who 'form a dreary procession through the quick twists of the plot', are part of the farce, and 'it would ruin everything to take the wife's troubles, or Dromio's many beatings at all seriously.'[1] Alternatively, the play has been seen as an attempt to combine romance and farce, with disastrous results:

> It might (though we doubt it) have come near to deserve such praise [as the 'high water-mark of elaborate farce'] had Shakespeare not set his artificial farce between the romantic-realism of the distressed merchant, with which he opens, and of the long-lost wife reclaimed, with which he concludes ... as yet, farce and romance were not one 'form' but two separate stools; and between them in *The Comedy of Errors* he fell to the ground.[2]

In introducing Luciana, Egeon, and Emilia, Shakespeare, it is argued, brought in a 'range of sentiment utterly incompatible with the atmosphere of *The Comedy of Errors*', a play in which the general temper of life is 'crude, coarse and brutal'.[3]

A different view has been taken of the play, more especially in recent years. Perhaps Dowden was the first to be so moved by the plight of Egeon as to think of it as embryonic tragedy, and to notice that 'the human sorrow and affliction cannot wholly pass from our view; before the close it must give place to some consolation'.[4] What he recognized is that in spite of the implausibility and fantastic coincidences of Egeon's tale of the shipwreck, we are directly affected by his wretchedness, his dramatic presence on stage as a lonely, pathetic figure, lacking money and friends, and sentenced to die at the day's end. His state is not, of course, tragic; the fantastic nature of his extraordinary adventures prevents us from being deeply troubled by his predicament, or the doom hanging over him; but even though we know that for one

> whom the fates have mark'd
> To bear the extremity of dire mishap,   (i. i. 140–1)

Jacobean Plays, 1583–1616 (1958), p. 98. It is, of course, a commonplace of criticism to point out that the play is unusual among Shakespeare's in preserving the unities of place and time, and in its imitation of classical models, but there is little reason to suppose that he planned it in five acts.

1. Francis Fergusson, '*The Comedy of Errors* and *Much Ado About Nothing*', *Sewanee Review*, LXII (1954), 24–37. The quotations are from p. 28.

2. A. Quiller-Couch, Introduction in the New Cambridge edition of the play (1922), pp. xxi–xxii.

3. H. B. Charlton, *Shakespearean Comedy* (1943), p. 70.

4. Cited by Quiller-Couch, *op. cit.*, p. xxi.

some sort of restoration is due, the sombre tone established in Act I is never entirely dispelled until the end of the play, and is carried over immediately into Act II in the suggestions of sorcery and witchcraft in Ephesus.

The note of weirdness and bewitchment that runs through the comic action is one of the features of the play that has received serious attention. In particular, G. R. Elliott has observed what he calls the 'comic horror' of the subject of mistaken identity: 'real horror attaches to the notion of the *complete* identity of two human beings', because we set so much store by individuality, and Shakespeare exploits this in a way that makes the comedy congruent with the romance elements of the play.[1] Another feature that has been well brought out is the interplay between personal and commercial relationships, in which 'giving' ultimately triumphs over 'taking and keeping'[2]—and, one might add, over paying. At the end the difficulties raised through the need for money, to pay Egeon's ransom, to pay the goldsmith for his chain, to pay the Second Merchant the sum owed to him, are resolved in the harmony of love. The discords and final harmony in human relationships are reflected in images of disorder and order, and the sense of witchcraft in Ephesus has a bearing here as related to disorder.[3]

The recognition of these aspects of the play has led to the just claim that 'it is a play of greater promise than the mere dexterity of its plotting suggests'[4]; one might go further and argue that it is a work of some achievement. What have sometimes been regarded as disparate elements, romance and farce, or tragic envelope and central comic action, unite most harmoniously in the final effect.[5] As is well known, Shakespeare altered the tone of his immediate sources for the comedy, *Menaechmi* and *Amphitruo*, by introducing an element of romantic love in the jealousy of Adriana and in the

1. 'Weirdness in *The Comedy of Errors*', *University of Toronto Quarterly*, LX (1939), 95–106.

2. J. R. Brown, *Shakespeare and his Comedies*, pp. 54–7.

3. *Ibid.*, pp. 128–9. A good brief study of the play is also provided by Derek Traversi in his booklet, *Shakespeare: The Early Comedies* (1960), pp. 8–14. Bertrand Evans, in *Shakespeare's Comedies* (1960), concentrates on dramatic technique, and thinks of Shakespeare in *The Comedy of Errors* as 'trying a dramatic method that at once became a principle of his dramaturgy'; this method is one of creating a structure of discrepant awarenesses so as to obtain from the audience 'conflicting responses simultaneously' (p. 8).

4. J. R. Brown, *op. cit.*, p. 57.

5. The play's remarkably skilful variations and contrasts of style and pace well illustrate this controlled development and final integration of comic and serious elements—blank verse, quatrains, couplets, doggerel, prose, are all used purposefully in a total stylistic shaping. This aspect of the play is discussed in the commentary; see especially the headnotes to each scene.

passion of Antipholus of Syracuse for Luciana, and also by enclos-
ing the comic plot within the story of the pathetic Egeon; he also
enlarged and complicated the element of farce by giving the twin
masters twin servants, so multiplying the possibilities of comic confusion. These two developments of source-material do not really
tug in different directions, and Shakespeare had a larger purpose
than merely to soften the harsh world of Plautine comedy, or
exploit more fully the ancient comic device of mistaken identity.
His modifications of the sources are used to develop a serious concern for the personal identity of each of the main characters, and
for the relationships between them; and the jesting of the Dromios,
and the 'errors' or mistakes of the complicated action continually
support this main development.[1]

So Antipholus of Syracuse arrives in Ephesus with a feeling that
in searching for his mother and brother he has lost his identity, as
if he will only find himself when he finds them:

> I to the world am like a drop of water
> That in the ocean seeks another drop,
> Who, falling there to find his fellow forth,
> (Unseen, inquisitive) confounds himself.
> So I, to find a mother and a brother,
> In quest of them, unhappy, lose myself.   (I. ii. 35–40)

Ephesus holds a shock for him, mistaking him for his twin, and
fastens an identity on him, so that he is invited to dine with Adriana
as her husband, and feels that he is

> Known unto these, and to myself disguis'd.   (II. ii. 214)

Here he seizes on the status of intimacy given to him in the household to make love to Luciana, and in her finds a new self, as he
discovers a true passion for her. When he says,

> would you create me new?
> Transform me then, and to your power I'll yield,
>   (III. ii. 39–40)

he is already transformed through love, in the recognition that she
is

> mine own self's better part,
> Mine eye's clear eye, my dear heart's dearer heart.
>   (III. ii. 61–2)

Luciana thinks he is her brother-in-law gone mad, and, in the face

---

1. See in the commentary the notes to I. ii. 40, II. ii. 142, III. ii. 45–66, 76, 161–6,
IV. iii. 40–2, and V. i. 405.

of her inability to recognize him for what he is, he finally claims, 'I am thee' (III. ii. 66).

Even as Antipholus of Syracuse discovers a new self, he is also bewildered by the assumptions of the people he meets, including Luciana, that they know him, that he is another person. Meanwhile, his brother, Antipholus of Ephesus, a more strongly determined character, more certain of himself, is angered when his wife refuses to acknowledge his identity; and Adriana, by nature jealous of him, and misled by his twin's attempt to woo Luciana, comes to think the worst of her husband, until she is ready to transform him in her mind[1]:

> He is deformed, crooked, old and sere,
> Ill-fac'd, worse bodied, shapeless everywhere;
> Vicious, ungentle, foolish, blunt, unkind,
> Stigmatical in making, worse in mind.   (IV. ii. 19–22)

It is but a step from this for her to treat him as if he were mad or possessed, make him endure the ministrations of Doctor Pinch, and have him locked away in a dark cellar.

The serious force of the presentation of the Antipholus twins is paralleled by a more comic treatment of their servants. Each is puzzled at being mistaken for the other, and each comes to feel that he is being transformed—but into an ass, rather than another person. So Dromio of Ephesus suffers like an ass from the blows of his master (III. i. 18), and, finding that another has assumed his office and identity as servant in Adriana's household, and that for his service he is rewarded with still more blows as his master grows angrier, he resigns himself to his topsy-turvy world with a humorous acceptance of it:

> *Eph. Ant.* Thou art sensible in nothing but blows, and so is an ass.
> *Eph. Dro.* I am an ass indeed; you may prove it by my long ears. I have served him from the hour of my nativity to this instant, and have nothing at his hands for my service but blows . . .   (IV. iv. 25–30)

At the same time, Dromio of Syracuse shares something of his master's sense of being subjected to witchcraft, and when Luciana, whom he has never seen before, addresses him by name, he speaks as if he has been 'transformed':

1. Adriana and her husband are alike in their proneness to anger, their 'impatience', or lack of 'patience', words used in relation to them several times; see II. i. 9ff., III. i. 85, IV. ii. 16, IV. iv. 18–19, 78–99 and notes.

Syr. Dro. I am transformed, master, am I not?
Syr. Ant. I think thou art in mind, and so am I.
Syr. Dro. Nay, master, both in mind and in my shape.
Syr. Ant. Thou hast thine own form.
Syr. Dro.   No, I am an ape.
Luc.   If thou art chang'd to aught, 'tis to an ass.
Syr. Dro. 'Tis true, she rides me, and I long for grass;
           'Tis so, I am an ass. . . .   (II. ii. 195–201)

His sense of change or loss of identity is confirmed when the
kitchen-maid Nell treats him as her man, and he bursts out, 'I am
an ass, I am a woman's man, and besides myself' (III. ii. 76). Each
Dromio applies the term 'ass' in relation to the beatings he is made
to suffer, and to the way he is made to seem a fool; but the idea of
being made a beast operates more generally in the play, reflecting
the process of passion overcoming reason, as an animal rage, fear,
or spite seizes on each of the main characters.[1]

For the sense of loss or change of identity in these figures goes
together with a disruption of family, personal, and social relationships. Antipholus of Syracuse loses himself in the search for his
mother and brother, but is hailed by all in Ephesus as if they knew
him well; even as he thinks he is subject to 'imaginary wiles' (IV.
iii. 10), he is, unwittingly, causing a rift in the marriage of Adriana
and his brother, and stirring discord between Antipholus of
Ephesus and, on the one hand Angelo the goldsmith, on the other
hand the Courtesan, over the matter of the chain. In the confusion
which follows upon his dining with Adriana, the new self he had
found in his passion for Luciana is frustrated; confirmed in his
belief that he wanders in 'illusions' (IV. iii. 41), he comes on at the
end of Act IV, sword in hand, to drive her and Adriana off as
'witches'. At the same time, Antipholus of Ephesus, denied entry to
his own house, comes to believe that he is the victim of a plot, and
that his wife is a 'strumpet' (IV. iv. 122). In addition, the normal
relationship of master and servant is broken as each Antipholus
meets the other's Dromio, and then beats his own servant for failing
to carry out orders given to someone else. The normal intercourse
of the city in its friendly, commercial relationships is also disturbed,
to the extent that the Second Merchant, believing himself wronged,

1. The process is summed up in the Duke's cry as he is faced with conflicting
claims at the end, 'I think you all have drunk of Circe's cup'; see below, p. xlviii,
and see also III. ii. 39–40, 76, 145, IV. iv. 26–8 and notes. The same kind of process
is at work in the transformation of the sergeant into a devil in Dromio's mind
(IV. ii), and of the Courtesan into a fiend in the mind of Antipholus of Syracuse
(IV. iii).

puts both Angelo and Antipholus under arrest, and the long-standing trust between these two is destroyed. The confusions of identity, involving for Antipholus of Syracuse and the two Dromios a sense especially of loss or transformation, and for Antipholus of Ephesus a need defiantly to assert his identity in a world that seems to go mad, thus lead to a breakdown of the social order through the frustration of normal relationships. Quarrels and arrests follow; Antipholus of Ephesus is bound and locked up; Doctor Pinch is harshly treated, and suffers the painful loss of a beard; the Dromios are mercilessly beaten[1]; and Antipholus of Syracuse and his Dromio usurp the office of the law when they rush in with 'naked swords'.

The growth of this disorder is reflected in two other strands in language and action which reinforce the serious undertones of the comedy. One is the establishment of Ephesus as a place associated with witchcraft. Antipholus of Syracuse arrives there with a prejudice about the city[2]:

> They say this town is full of cozenage,
> As nimble jugglers that deceive the eye,
> Dark-working sorcerers that change the mind,
> Soul-killing witches that deform the body,
> Disguised cheaters, prating mountebanks,
> And many such-like liberties of sin.   (I. ii. 97–102)

As he becomes involved with the Merchant, Adriana, Luciana, and the Courtesan, so his belief that the city is a nest of sorcerers grows stronger. He wonders if his love for Luciana results from bewitchment, and calls her 'mermaid' and 'siren' (III. ii. 45, 47); soon he is ready to think 'There's none but witches do inhabit here' (III. ii. 155), or 'Lapland sorcerers' (IV. iii. 11); he comes to regard the Courtesan as a 'fiend' and a 'sorceress' (IV. iii. 63, 64), and finally achieves a state of mind so distraught that he feels safe only with a sword in his hand, and, pursued by Adriana's men, takes refuge in the priory. The prejudice which he has on reaching Ephesus provides a ready explanation for all the strange things that happen to him, and becomes a settled conviction; he is more and more dis-

---

1. It is true that Dromio of Ephesus says of his master, 'I have served him from the hour of my nativity to this instant, and have nothing at his hands for my service but blows' (IV. iv. 28–30), and both servants cheerfully expect beatings as part of their lot; at the same time, the anger of Antipholus of Ephesus is abnormal, and it is the sight of him beating Dromio in this scene that confirms Adriana in her belief that her husband is mad: 'His incivility confirms no less' (IV. iv. 44).

2. See above, p. xxix; Shakespeare deliberately set the scene of his play in Ephesus because of the city's biblical associations with sorcery. *Menaechmi* has its setting in Epidamnum.

abled from distinguishing between what is real and what is not, until the whole city seems to him to be in the grip of an evil power:

This fellow is distract, and so am I,
And here we wander in illusions—
Some blessed power deliver us from hence! (iv. iii. 40-2)

Antipholus of Ephesus, by contrast, regards himself as alone sane in a world gone mad. He is given some force of character, and a tendency to violence,[1] so that when he is shut out of his own house, he is driven to bewilderment and to passionate exclamation; though calmed for a moment by Balthasar, he thinks of punishing his wife by going at once to the Courtesan's, and by bestowing a 'rope's end' (iv. i. 16), i.e. a whipping, upon Adriana and her 'confederates'. He invents an explanation of her treatment of him with this word; he decides he is the victim of a conspiracy. This private interpretation of his experience is confirmed for him when he is arrested in error, meets Dromio of Syracuse at cross-purposes, in his anger is himself regarded as mad, bewitched, or possessed, and is at last imprisoned in a 'dark and dankish vault'.

The confusions of identity and consequent disruptions of normal relationships force the characters to judge events according to their own private ordering of experience, as Adriana, too, is ready, at the suggestion of the Courtesan, to think her husband mad, and treat him as a dangerous lunatic. Out of the clashes of these private worlds of experience emerges another strand in language and action which is of some importance, a sense of evil at work in Ephesus. Dromio of Syracuse jests about the Officer who arrests Antipholus of Ephesus, calling him a devil,

One that, before the judgment, carries poor souls to hell;
(iv. ii. 40)

he is quibbling on the last judgment, and on a common term for prison,[2] but his jest, as is characteristic of the word-play of the Dromios, quickly becomes earnest when he meets his own master in the next scene.[3] For Antipholus of Syracuse really thinks of the Courtesan as a 'fiend', and uses to her Christ's words, 'Satan,

---

1. As Erma Gill noted, 'A Comparison of the Characters in *The Comedy of Errors* with those in the *Menaechmi*', pp. 79ff., Shakespeare transferred this tendency to violence from the traveller brother in *Menaechmi* to the citizen Antipholus.

2. See note to this line.

3. Compare the jokes on mistiming (i. ii. 41ff., ii. ii. 54ff.), which turn out to have a bearing on the disorder later in the play (see ii. ii. 54-109 and n.; iv. i. 41-80 and n.), and the way in which Dromio of Syracuse both parodies and reinforces his master's prejudices in his account of the kitchen-wench, Nell (iii. ii. 143 and n.).

D

avoid', spoken in rejection of the devil's temptations in the wilder-
ness[1]; and if the Officer was a 'devil in an everlasting garment' to
Dromio, the Courtesan now becomes 'the devil's dam'. A little
later, Adriana puts her husband, as a man possessed by the 'fiend',
into the hands of an exorcist, who chants,

> I charge thee, Satan, hous'd within this man,
> To yield possession to my holy prayers.   (IV. iv. 52–3)

These hints of the devil at work mark a stage in the play when the
appearance of normal order breaks down, and the action erupts
into violence, as one Antipholus is bound, and the other rushes in
to attack a group he believes are 'witches'—a group that includes
the Officer of the law.

In Act V the scene transfers to the Priory, which is the setting for
the resolution of all difficulties, and which lends a faintly holy and
redeeming colour to the end of the play. Here the enveloping action
concerning Egeon is resumed. His hopeless condition, stranded
friendless in a hostile city where the law condemned him to death,
had been presented in a simple and dignified way in the opening
scene. The Duke, representative of justice, had listened to the tale
of his long search for his family, and had given him a day in which
to seek, vainly as we see, for money to pay a ransom that would save
him from execution. The end of the day comes just when one Antipholus lies bound as a madman, and the other has taken refuge in
the Priory. At this point (v. i. 129), a solemn procession enters,
headed by the Duke, and bringing on Egeon, bound, guarded, and
accompanied by the executioner. Adriana, who is anxiously trying
to persuade the Abbess to release the man she thinks to be her husband, stops the Duke to beg for 'Justice, most sacred Duke, against
the Abbess', and, shortly afterwards, Antipholus of Ephesus arrives
to cry, 'Justice, most gracious Duke, O, grant me justice', this time
against Adriana. Each clamours for an idea of justice based on a
private ordering of experience, and the conflicting evidence of
witnesses and supporters sets a problem too difficult for the law to
solve; the Duke cries,

> Why, what an intricate impeach is this?
> I think you all have drunk of Circe's cup.   (v. i. 270–1)

His words nicely suggest the kind and degree of transformation that
has taken place in the citizens of Ephesus; they are behaving madly,
and there is no order or coherence in what they allege against one
another.

To make matters worse, Egeon seizes the opportunity to appeal

1. *Mathew*, iv. 10 (Geneva version).

for help to the son he sees before him, but Antipholus of Ephesus does not know him. The law cannot deal with this situation, and it is time for the Abbess to reappear, with the second Antipholus; the twins are brought face to face for the first time, Adriana's mistake is revealed, and Egeon is saved as the Abbess turns out to be his long-lost wife Emilia. It is as if, through her intervention, the harsh justice embodied in the Duke is tempered by a Christian grace and mercy. Bitterness gives way to harmony, a harmony celebrated in a feast that marks a new beginning, a new life, a baptismal feast, from which Antipholus of Ephesus will not be excluded. Here the characters recover or discover their real identity, order is restored, and the two pairs of twins follow the others off stage, the masters embracing, the servants hand in hand. Violence is replaced by mildness and love, and the sense of witchcraft, evil, and Circean transformation is dispelled.

In this account of the play, I have laid stress on its serious elements, but not out of any desire to minimize its comic appeal, its clever exploitation of mistakes, of repartee, and talk at cross-purposes. The fact is that the serious elements are in some danger of going unobserved, while no one is likely to miss the fun, especially in the distorted and jazzed-up versions of the play which are commonly staged.[1] Some writers on comedy have recently re-affirmed its important functions by drawing attention to its origins in ritual, or to its social nature and purpose. On the one hand the 'authentic comic action' may be described thus:

If the authentic comic action is a sacrifice and a feast, debate and passion, it is by the same token a Saturnalia, an orgy, an assertion of the unruliness of the flesh and its vitality. Comedy is essentially a Carrying Away of Death, a triumph over mortality by some absurd faith in rebirth, restoration and salvation.[2]

On the other hand, a conception of comedy has been developed as a form in which

The normal individual is freed from the bonds of a humorous society, and a normal society is freed from the bonds imposed on it by humorous individuals.[3]

The terms of the first description are too large for *The Comedy of Errors*, but clearly they have some relevance; there is the hint of a sacrifice in Egeon, the hero-victim brought to the point of death, and the comic action leads in its vitality to a kind of resurrection, a rebirth, the baptismal feast of the end. The second description

1. See below, p. liv.   2. Wylie Sypher, *Comedy* (1956), p. 220.
3. Northrop Frye, 'The Argument of Comedy' *English Institute Essays* (1948), p. 61.

too applies in some degree; in this view, 'the moral norm is not morality, but deliverance', so that comedy is seen to be both radical and conservative. It may make the outsider, the man who does not fit into our society or its conventions, into a victim, exposing him or driving him out, like Doctor Pinch; and it may also expose the hollowness of a society's pretensions by setting them against the exuberance of a figure like Dromio of Syracuse.

Shakespeare's comedies, even his earliest ones, offer something more perhaps than this deliverance from moral bondage, the release from a self-imposed pattern of behaviour, or the rigidity of convention that Bergson speaks of; they also go beyond Wylie Sypher's analysis of comedy as a 'momentary and publicly useful resistance to authority and an escape from its pressures . . . a free discharge of repressed psychic energy or resentment through laughter'.[1] For the sense of deliverance in them is a means to an end —the end being a re-establishment of responsibility among individuals in a society in the light of a test undergone, or a penance endured, an acceptance of moral bondage in the full understanding of what this means. In other words, the ritual origin of comedy is buried in them under the groupings and sophistication of a high civilization, and the deliverance from rigidities serves to purge errors and evils from a society that is warmly and generously approved by the plays.

These general considerations may help to illustrate the particular quality of *The Comedy of Errors*. The play has farcical comedy, and it has fantasy, but it does more than merely provoke laughter, or release us temporarily from inhibitions and custom into a world free as a child's, affording delight and freshening us up. It also invites compassion, a measure of sympathy, and a deeper response to the disruption of social and family relationships which the action brings about. Our concern for the Antipholus twins, for Adriana and Luciana, and our sense of disorder are deepened in the context of suffering provided by the enveloping action. The comedy proves, after all, to be more than a temporary and hilarious abrogation of normality; it is, at the same time, a process in which the main characters are in some sense purged, before harmony and the responsibility of normal relationships are restored at the end. Adriana learns to overcome her jealousy, and accepts the reproof of the Abbess; her husband is punished for his anger and potential brutality by Doctor Pinch's drastic treatment; and Antipholus of Syracuse is cured of his prejudices about Ephesus. Behind them stands Egeon, a prototype of the noble sufferer or victim in later

1. *Op. cit.*, pp. 241–2.

plays by Shakespeare, of Antonio in *The Merchant of Venice*, and of Pericles, central figure in a play which uses more profoundly the story on which Egeon's adventures are based. The extra perspective afforded by the enveloping action enriches the play; the restoration of love and harmony derives force from a context not only of potential violence and disorder, but of real suffering; great joy is felt the more for being set against great pain. *The Comedy of Errors*, then, differs from its Plautine models in a characteristically Shakespearian way; later on Shakespeare was to absorb the pole of violence or suffering into his comedies, as in *Twelfth Night* and *Much Ado*, or to make the enveloping action, as in *As You Like It*, slide so smoothly into the central plot that it is hardly noticed as a frame at all. To invoke these masterpieces is not to deny the slender nature of our play; it has no great characters, little memorable verse, and a great deal of buffoonery, but it shows a playwright already beginning to generate, out of clashes between suffering and joy, disorder and order, appearance and reality, the peculiar character and strength that is found in his mature work. In this sense Shakespeare's comedies are true to life as we know it, and *The Comedy of Errors* is fascinating as revealing the young Shakespeare formulating the terms of his kind of comedy, and transcending the farce which a lesser writer might have been satisfied to make.[1]

3. STAGE HISTORY

The Christmas Revels at Gray's Inn in 1594 included a performance of 'a Comedy of Errors' similar to the *Menaechmi* of Plautus, and related in some way to witchcraft, sorcery, and enchantment; the description of this night of revels preserved in *Gesta Grayorum* (1688) leaves little doubt that the play staged was Shakespeare's.[2] Ten years later *The Comedy of Errors* was presented at Court, also as part of the Christmas festivities, and on the same day, 28 December, Innocents' Day, 1604. No other early performance is recorded.

Francis Meres, in his *Palladis Tamia* (1598), lists the play among other comedies of Shakespeare as 'his *Errors*', and there are a num-

1. In writing this essay, I have benefited greatly by the advice of H. F. Brooks, whose excellent discussion of the play, 'Themes and Structure in *The Comedy of Errors*', has appeared in *Early Shakespeare* (Stratford-upon-Avon Studies 3, edited J. R. Brown and Bernard Harris, 1961), pp. 55–71. His argument is in many ways complementary to what I have written, and analyses in more detail Shakespeare's 'handling of the lesser units of structure' within the individual scene, as well as the themes of mistiming and of family relationships in the play.
2. See the extracts from *Gesta Grayorum* printed below in Appendix II.

ber of allusions to it in the seventeenth century. Most of these simply cite the title, which seems to have become something of a catch-phrase, used by Thomas Dekker no less than three times, and also by Robert Burton.[1] A verse satire of 1616 includes in an attack on the theatre the line:

What *Comedies* of *errors* swell the stage,

again suggesting an almost proverbial use of the title.[2] As all these references precede the play's publication, they at least suggest that it made some impact, and, indeed, two dramatists seem to have remembered and used material from it, one in *The Birth of Hercules* (? *c*.1600), an English adaptation of the *Amphitruo* of Plautus, which adds a character named Dromio,[3] the other in *How a Man may choose a Good Wife from a Bad* (1602). This comedy has among its characters a thin schoolmaster called Aminadab, who is described in terms that recall Antipholus's depiction of Doctor Pinch (*The Comedy of Errors*, v. i. 238–42): 'that lean chittiface, that famine, that leane Envy, that all bones, that bare anatomy, that Jack a Lent, that ghost, that shadow . . .'[4]

However, no other production of Shakespeare's play in the seventeenth century is known,[5] and when it was revived in 1716, it was altered into the farce *Every Body Mistaken*. The later history of the play on the stage is largely a tale of adaptation, for *The Comedy of Errors* has too often been regarded as a short apprentice work in need of improvement, or as a mere farce, 'shamelessly trivial' as one reviewer in *The Times* put it,[6] and not worth serious treatment. In 1734 another version was called *See if You Like It*, and then, in 1762, the play, as altered by Thomas Hull and renamed *The Twins*, proved a great success. This held the stage into the nineteenth century, when it was taken over and refurbished by J. P. Kemble in 1808.[7] Hull added extra scenes, and inserted a number of songs,

1. *Shakspere Allusion-Book* (1932), I. 66, 107, 181, 282. Dekker used the phrase 'comedy of errors', evidently with Shakespeare's play in mind, in *Satiromastix* (1602), *The Honest Whore* (1604), and *A Knight's Conjuring* (1607). For the allusion in *The Anatomy of Melancholy* (1621), see A. R. Shillitoe's edition (1904), I. 54.

2. Robert Anton, *The Philosopher's Satyrs; Shakspere Allusion-Book*, I. 262.

3. See above, p. xxviii, n. 3.

4. Sig. E1ᵛ; the play was reprinted in the series 'The Tudor Facsimile Texts' by J. S. Farmer (1912).

5. Further allusions to it occur in R. Whitlock, *Zootomia* (1654), and in *Poor Robin's Visions* (1677). The first of these is noted in George Williamson, *Seventeenth Century Contexts* (1960), p. 183, the other in *Shakspere Allusion-Book*, II. 230.

6. On 7 September 1937, in a review of an open-air production.

7. Hull's version was played year after year at Covent Garden; see C. B. Hogan, *Shakespeare in the Theatre, 1701–1800*, 2 vols. (1952, 1957).

providing also a singer in the person of Hermia, Adriana's cousin.[1] Another adaptation, entitled *The Twins*, or *Which is Which?*, by W. Woods, was played in Edinburgh and published in 1780, and ten years later a new three-act version, perhaps a revision of Hull's work, was staged at Covent Garden. These versions emphasized the farce, added a sentimental interest, and cut out much of the word-play of the original.

The next major adaptation was that of Frederick Reynolds, who turned some of Shakespeare's comedies into operas, his second being *The Comedy of Errors* (1819). He added and altered freely, inserting numerous songs 'selected entirely from the Plays, Poems and Sonnets of Shakespeare', and set to music by a variety of composers, including Mozart.[2] New scenes included a hunting-scene and a drinking-scene; and Adriana, after rendering the willow song from *Othello*, joined Luciana in a duet, 'Tell me, where is fancy bred', words from *The Merchant of Venice*. For one scene the setting was a river surrounded by mountains covered with snow.[3]

Later in the century Shakespeare's play was restored to the stage by Samuel Phelps in 1855, and the most notable production of the century followed in 1864 at the Princess's Theatre, when Charles and Harry Webb appeared as almost identical Dromios. The play was acted continuously without scene-breaks, and Shakespeare's text was followed but for some cuts. There was another London production in 1883, and in 1905 F. R. Benson put on *The Comedy of Errors* at the Coronet Theatre, himself playing the part of Antipholus of Syracuse. In 1915 the play was presented at the Old Vic in a production that is notable because Sir Philip Ben Greet introduced a new actress to Lilian Baylis and the company for the part of Adriana, her name, Sybil Thorndike.[4] The Old Vic again staged the play, in a spirit of clowning, in 1927, with the twins sporting false noses, two turned up and two turned down. In 1934 it was put on in Regent's Park as part of a double bill with Milton's *Comus*.

The reviewers usually enjoyed the fun in these productions, but were inclined to find fault with Shakespeare; so *The Times* adopted a reproving tone in commenting on Benson's 1905 production:[5]

We . . . find certain things in *The Comedy of Errors* out of place in what is mainly, after all, a farce—the impending death of

1. G. C. D. Odell, *Shakespeare from Betterton to Irving*, 2 vols. (1920), II. 45–8.
2. Odell, II. 131ff.   3. *Ibid.*, II. 161–2.
4. See Sybil and Russell Thorndike, *Lilian Baylis* (1938), pp. 28ff.
5. Unsigned review in the issue of 27 February 1905.

Ægeon, for instance, the love-making of Antipholus of Syracuse to Luciana, and the scene between the Abbess and Adriana before the steps of the priory. These things are not of farce as we understand it. . .

If farce was what they wanted, Theodore Komisarjevsky brilliantly obliged them with his outstanding production at Stratford in 1938.[1] He used a stylized set reminiscent of Serlio's *scena comica*, with a large clock as its centrepiece, and mixed costumes of many ages, giving many of his male characters, including the two Dromios, bowler hats of various colours to wear. One reviewer described the scene as follows[2]:

> Against a romantic huddle of pink and green and grey and yellow houses which may be Ephesian, but in fact suggest an amused memory of Italy, he sets the characters capering . . . in costumes that seem to have been drawn by happy accident out of an inexhaustible miscellaneous wardrobe.

The emphasis was on fun, and the citizens of Ephesus burst into song or moved into ballet whenever tedium threatened; the music was by Handel and Anthony Bernard. The grace and liveliness of this production brought it wide acclaim, but there were some who noticed that, in turning *The Comedy of Errors* into a box-office success, Komisarjevsky had shown his contempt for Shakespeare's play, and had simply burlesqued it.[3]

Modern productions have, on the whole, followed Komisarjevsky's lead, or have looked back to his predecessors, Hull and Reynolds. At the end of 1938, a musical comedy, *The Boys from Syracuse*, was performed at the Alvin Theatre in New York, and a film was later made of this. A little later, in 1940, *A New Comedy of Errors*, or *Too Many Twins*, a hotch-potch of Plautus, Shakespeare, and Molière in modern dress, was staged at the Mercury Theatre in London. Since then the play has been presented as a Victorian musical comedy, set in the north of England (Cambridge, 1951); as an Edwardian extravaganza, with music by Sullivan, set in the Levant about 1910 (Canterbury and London, 1952); as an operetta in the style of *The Beggar's Opera*, music by Julian Slade, with costumes of the Regency period (televised 1954, played at the Arts Theatre, London, 1956); as a modern American musical set on the waterfront of New Orleans (Oxford Playhouse, 1956); and as a

1. Not 1939, as, by an oversight, it is dated in *Early Shakespeare*, p. 69 (see above, p. li, n. 1).

2. In *The Times*, 7 April 1938. A photograph of his set is reproduced as Plate VII in *Shakespeare Survey*, 2 (1949).

3. See the reviews in *The Yorkshire Post*, and by Lionel Hale in the *News Chronicle*, on 13 April 1938.

pendant to the singing of Cy Grant, who acted as a sort of minstrel narrator, using songs from other plays, and music of 'intercontinental origin'[1] (Bristol, Theatre Royal, 1960).

There have also been some straightforward productions, notably by the Birmingham Repertory Theatre (director, Douglas Seale) in 1948, when Donald Pleasance made an excellent Dromio; by the Bristol Old Vic (director, Denis Carey) in 1953; and by the London Old Vic (director, Walter Hudd) in 1957. For this last production the play was severely cut in order to reduce it to an hour's length, as the second part of a double bill with *Titus Andronicus*. In it Robert Helpmann mimed and expanded the part of Doctor Pinch to such good effect that he almost stole the show.

1. The phrase is borrowed from the review by Peter Rodford, *Western Daily Press*, 29 June 1960.

THE COMEDY OF ERRORS

DRAMATIS PERSONAE[1]

SOLINUS, *Duke of Ephesus.*
EGEON, *a Merchant of Syracuse.*
ANTIPHOLUS *of Ephesus* \ \ *twin brothers, and sons*
ANTIPHOLUS *of Syracuse* \ \ *of Egeon and Emilia.*
DROMIO *of Ephesus* \ \ *twin brothers, and servants*
DROMIO *of Syracuse* \ \ *to the Antipholus twins.*
BALTHASAR, *a merchant.*
ANGELO, *a goldsmith.*
DOCTOR PINCH, *a schoolmaster.*
First Merchant.
Second Merchant.[2]
EMILIA, *Abbess at Ephesus, and Egeon's wife.*
ADRIANA, *wife of Antipholus of Ephesus.*
LUCIANA, *her sister.*
LUCE,[3] *her maid.*
Courtesan.

Jailor, Officers, Headsman, and other attendants.

SCENE: *The play is set in Ephesus. The scene throughout represents an unlocalized street or 'mart' in front of three 'houses', structures or doors marked with the signs of the Courtesan's house (a Porcupine), the house of Antipholus of Ephesus (the Phoenix), and the Priory (a cross or some religious emblem).*

1. Not in F; first listed by Rowe. The derivation of some of the characters' names is noted in the Introduction or the commentary. Solinus is the name of a minor character in Lyly's *Campaspe*, and also of a geographer, see p. xxix; Egeon is probably derived from the name of the Ægean Sea, see p. xxx; for comment on Dromio, a name borrowed from Lyly, and ultimately from Terence, see p. xxxiii. Antipholus appears to stem from the Greek 'Antiphilos', listed as a proper name for a lover in H. Estienne (Stephanus), *Thesaurus Græcae Linguae* (1572), but we do not know where Shakespeare found it; see Baldwin, *Shakspere's Five-Act Structure*, pp. 695-6. The name Pinch may be related to the physical appearance of the actor John Sincklo, for whom the part was probably written, cf. v. i. 238–42 and n., but the word had special associations for Shakespeare, discussed in E. A. Armstrong, *Shakespeare's Imagination* (1946), pp. 42–7.

2. First distinguished by Dyce, who noticed that the merchants who appear in I. ii and IV. i must be different figures; see headnotes to these scenes.

3. Luce, who enters in III. i, is later identified with Nell, a kitchen-maid, who does not appear on stage; see Introduction, p. xxv, and III. ii. 107 and n.

2

THE COMEDY OF ERRORS

ACT I

SCENE I

Enter [SOLINUS] *the Duke of Ephesus, with* [EGEON] *the Merchant of Syracuse, Jailor, and other attendants.*

Egeon. Proceed, Solinus, to procure my fall,
    And by the doom of death end woes and all.
Duke. Merchant of Syracusa, plead no more.
    I am not partial to infringe our laws;
    The enmity and discord which of late   5
    Sprung from the rancorous outrage of your Duke
    To merchants, our well-dealing countrymen,
    Who, wanting guilders to redeem their lives,

ACT I
Scene 1
ACT I SCENE I] *Actus primus, Scena prima. F.*   S.D. SOLINUS] *not in F.*
EGEON] *not in F.*   Syracuse] Siracusa *F.*   1. *Egeon*] *Marchant | F.*

SCENE I] This corresponds in function, though not in style or content, with the Prologue to *Menaechmi*, which recounts the events leading up to the opening of the action; here Egeon, the narrator (*narratio* was the term used in Renaissance commentary on Latin comedy, see M. T. Herrick, *Comic Theory in the Sixteenth Century* (1950), pp. 28–9, 116–18) is under sentence of death, and his resignation is marked by the couplets of his first two speeches. The measured dignity of the verse in this scene, with its single-moulded lines, finely conveys the present plight of Egeon, and his fantastic story, told

with such simple gravity, becomes almost credible.

1. S.H. Egeon] In F the initial heading *Marchant* is given a line to itself. Throughout the rest of the scene the S.H. *Mer(ch)* is used for Egeon, whose name occurs only in l. 140.

1. *Solinus*] The name appears nowhere else in the play.

2. *doom*] sentence.

4. *partial to*] biased so as to; *partial* here means the opposite of *impartial*.

6. *outrage*] violence, cf. IV. iv. 114 below.

8. *guilders*] gold coins current at one time in the Netherlands and part of

3

Have seal'd his rigorous statutes with their bloods,
Excludes all pity from our threat'ning looks;   10
For since the mortal and intestine jars
'Twixt thy seditious countrymen and us,
It hath in solemn synods been decreed,
Both by the Syracusians and ourselves,
To admit no traffic to our adverse towns;   15
Nay more, if any born at Ephesus
Be seen at Syracusian marts and fairs;
Again, if any Syracusian born
Come to the bay of Ephesus, he dies,
His goods confiscate to the Duke's dispose,   20
Unless a thousand marks be levied
To quit the penalty and to ransom him.
Thy substance, valued at the highest rate,
Cannot amount unto a hundred marks;
Therefore by law thou art condemn'd to die.   25

16–17. Nay more, if . . . Ephesus / Be seen at Syracusian] *as Pope;* Nay more, if
. . . *Ephesus* / Be seene at any *Siracusian F;* Nay more, / If . . . Ephesus be seen / At
any Syracusan *Steevens.*

Germany, or Dutch silver coins worth about 1s. 8d. (*O.E.D.*); they are not referred to elsewhere by Shakespeare, except at IV. i. 9 below, but the word had passed into English as one of several terms for money. Many foreign coins were in continual circulation in England during Elizabeth's reign. Shakespeare seems to have changed his mind later about what name to use for coins in the play; see IV. i. 30 and n.

11. *intestine jars*] internal quarrels, but also, as at *1H4*, I. i. 12, 'in the intestine shock / And furious close of civil butchery', giving effect to the body metaphor, in connection with 'mortal'.

15. *admit . . . towns*] allow no trade between our hostile towns; this is the usual sense of 'traffic' in Shakespeare, cf. *Shr.*, I. i. 12, 'A merchant of great traffic through the world'.

17. *at Syracusian*] The intrusive *any* in F was no doubt caught up, as Cuningham suggested, from the lines above

or below by the compositor as he was setting the type. But Abbott, 512, noting many similar instances, provides support for Malone's treatment of these lines, keeping *any*, and taking *Nay more* as a separate interjectional line.

20. *confiscate*] here accented on the second syllable, as at *Cym.*, v. v. 323, but cf. I. ii. 2 below.
dispose] disposal, control, cf. *Gent.*, II. vii. 86.

21. *marks*] As in the case of *guilders*, l. 8, Shakespeare is using a term familiar to his English audience, as equivalent in England to 13s. 4d. (there was no coin of this amount), but representing also 'the various continental forms of the same word, as a name of foreign moneys of account' (*O.E.D.*, sb.² 2c). The word originally signified a measure of weight, usually of gold or silver, equivalent to eight ounces.

22. *quit*] pay.

23. *substance*] wealth, possessions.

Egeon. Yet this my comfort; when your words are done,
My woes end likewise with the evening sun.
Duke. Well, Syracusian; say in brief the cause
Why thou departedst from thy native home,
And for what cause thou cam'st to Ephesus.   30
Egeon. A heavier task could not have been impos'd,
Than I to speak my griefs unspeakable;
Yet that the world may witness that my end
Was wrought by nature, not by vile offence,
I'll utter what my sorrow gives me leave.   35
In Syracusa was I born, and wed
Unto a woman happy but for me,
And by me,—had not our hap been bad.
With her I liv'd in joy; our wealth increas'd
By prosperous voyages I often made   40
To Epidamnum, till my factor's death,
And the great care of goods at random left,

---

26. *Egeon*] *Mer* / *F* (*Mer or Merch throughout scene*).   41, 62. Epidamnum] *Pope;*
Epidamium *F.*   42. the . . . random] *Theobald;* he . . . randone *F.*

---

26. *this my comfort*] *is* omitted, as
commonly; Abbott, 461.
27. *evening sun*] Cf. ll. 150–4; this
establishes the confinement of the
action to one day, as in *Menaechmi.*
28–32.] The echo in l. 32 of Virgil,
Aeneid, II. 3, 'Infandum, Regina, jubes
renovare dolorem', was observed by
Theobald, but, as T. W. Baldwin has
shown, *Shakespeare's Small Latine,* II.
485–7, there is some general similarity
between Dido's command to Aeneas
to relate his misfortunes, and the
Duke's conversation with Egeon here;
see also ll. 67–9, 88–91 and n. below.
34. *nature*] natural affection (i.e.
which made me seek my son; so
Malone), cf. *2H4,* IV. v. 39, 'Nature,
love and filial tenderness / Shall, O
dear father, pay thee plenteously'.
38. *by me*] *by me too* (F2 and edd.)
has no authority, and merely regular-
izes the line; a pause after *me* (*me;* F)
seems appropriate, and lines short by
a syllable are not uncommon, cf. l. 54
(Abbott, 508). The verse of this scene

is very regular, but its flow is broken
to good effect here, and occasionally
elsewhere, as at ll. 54 and 61.
hap] fortune.
41. *Epidamnum*] The setting of
Menaechmi, later called Dyracchium
by the Romans, then Durazzo: the
town was located on the Adriatic in
what is now Albania; but Shakespeare
may have believed it was in southern
Greece, see Introduction, p. xxx. F
consistently prints *Epidamium,* but
Epidamnum is the form used by Warner,
and derived from Plautus. According
to Baldwin, *Errors,* p. 71, early editions
of Plautus often emend to *Epidamnium*
for smoother metre, and this may be
what Shakespeare wrote. A confusion
of minim letters is the commonest kind
of compositorial error, and it is not
likely that Shakespeare left out *n* as F
does.
42. *at random*] untended; the phrase
occurs several times in Shakespeare's
early works, and the common form
randon may be Shakespeare's spelling.

Drew me from kind embracements of my spouse;
From whom my absence was not six months old
Before herself (almost at fainting under   45
The pleasing punishment that women bear)
Had made provision for her following me,
And soon, and safe, arrived where I was.
There had she not been long, but she became
A joyful mother of two goodly sons,   50
And, which was strange, the one so like the other,
As could not be distinguish'd but by names.
That very hour, and in the self-same inn,
A mean woman was delivered
Of such a burden male, twins both alike;   55
Those, for their parents were exceeding poor,
I bought, and brought up to attend my sons.
My wife, not meanly proud of two such boys,
Made daily motions for our home return;
Unwilling I agreed; alas, too soon   60
We came aboard.
A league from Epidamnum had we sail'd
Before the always-wind-obeying deep
Gave any tragic instance of our harm,
But longer did we not retain much hope;   65
For what obscured light the heavens did grant,

54. mean] F (meane); poor mean *Malone*; meaner *Walker*.   55. burden male,
twins] *As F*; burthen, male twins *F2*.   60–1.] *As Pope; one line in F.*

43. *kind*] loving.
51–2. *so like ... As*] = so like ... that
they (see Abbott, 280).
52. *distinguish'd . . . names*] In fact
they are distinguished on their first
appearance as 'Erotes' and 'Sereptus'
(see the entries to I. ii and II. i), but not
by name; possibly Shakespeare was
thinking here of the 'Argumentum' of
Menaechmi, which names the brothers
Menaechmus and Sosicles. Cf. l. 128,
where they are spoken of as having
the same name, and the note to this
line.
54. *mean*] *meaner* (S. Walker and
edd.) is an unnecessary regularization.
The point is not that the woman is of
lower rank than Egeon's wife, but that

she is very base indeed, and 'exceeding
poor'. See l. 38 and n.
55. *male*] N.C.S. sees here a quibble
on 'mail' = baggage.
58. *not meanly*] considerably, in no
small degree.
59. *motions*] urgings, requests, cf.
Shr., I. ii. 276.
61. *We . . . aboard*] Cuningham sees
a hiatus here, and takes the liberty of
conjecturing the rest of the line, while
N.C.S. finds the broken line a sign of a
cut. But a pause for Egeon to recover
from his emotion is entirely appropriate, and common in Shakespeare; see
Abbott, 511–12.
64. *instance*] sign, evidence; cf. *Lucr.*,
1511.

Did but convey unto our fearful minds
A doubtful warrant of immediate death,
Which though myself would gladly have embrac'd,
Yet the incessant weepings of my wife,   70
Weeping before for what she saw must come,
And piteous plainings of the pretty babes,
That mourn'd for fashion, ignorant what to fear,
Forc'd me to seek delays for them and me,
And this it was (for other means was none):   75
The sailors sought for safety by our boat,
And left the ship, then sinking-ripe, to us.
My wife, more careful for the latter-born,
Had fasten'd him unto a small spare mast,
Such as sea-faring men provide for storms;   80
To him one of the other twins was bound,
Whilst I had been like heedful of the other.
The children thus dispos'd, my wife and I,
Fixing our eyes on whom our care was fix'd,

75. was (for . . . none):] *As F4;* was: (for . . . none) *F.*

67–9, 88–91.] This account of the storm may echo Virgil, *Aeneid,* I. 88–91. 142–3; the parallel is not close, but Shakespeare certainly refers to Book II of the *Aeneid* in l. 32 above; see ll. 28–32 and n.

67. *fearful*] frightened; the most common sense of the word in Shakespeare.

68. *doubtful*] dreadful, causing fear, cf. *Mer. V.,* III. ii. 109.

72. *plainings*] wailings.

73. *for fashion*] i.e. because the others did.

74. *seek delays*] i.e. find reasons for staying aboard, and putting off as long as possible the death they saw 'must come' (l. 71).

75.] thus it was (this is what happened), for there were no other means than those we took. For *this,* cf. *R3,* I. i. 62, 'Why, this it is when men are ruled by women'. The punctuation in F, 'was; (for . . . none)', may indicate that we should understand 'thus it was: for (i.e. because, as at l. 56 above) there were no other means, the sailors

sought', etc. I much prefer the interpretation presented here, but the passage from l. 74 on is a characteristically Shakespearian sequence of thoughts linked emotionally, not logically, and other arrangements of the sense are possible: I take it that Egeon's 'this it was' introduces a general account of what happened, but he seems to promise to describe the 'delays' he sought, slides to what the sailors did, and, instead of returning to himself, relates first what action his wife took, and only then what he did himself. So another legitimate way of taking the passage would be to regard the parenthesis in F as closed too soon, and to extend it to include all the sailors did, '(for . . . to us)'.

77. *sinking-ripe*] for similar forms, cf. *LLL.,* v. ii. 274, *3H6,* I. iv. 172.

78. *latter-born*] second-born; as Cuningham notes, there is some confusion over which of the twins is the elder. See l. 124 and n.

84. *on whom*] on him on whom, cf. *Cæs.,* II. i. 331 (Abbott, 251).

E

Fasten'd ourselves at either end the mast,   85
And floating straight, obedient to the stream,
Was carried towards Corinth, as we thought.
At length the sun, gazing upon the earth,
Dispers'd those vapours that offended us,
And by the benefit of his wished light   90
The seas wax'd calm, and we discovered
Two ships from far, making amain to us,
Of Corinth that, of Epidaurus this,
But ere they came—O, let me say no more;
Gather the sequel by that went before.   95
Duke. Nay forward, old man, do not break off so,
For we may pity, though not pardon thee.
Egeon. O, had the gods done so, I had not now
Worthily term'd them merciless to us:
For ere the ships could meet by twice five leagues,   100
We were encounter'd by a mighty rock,
Which being violently borne upon,
Our helpful ship was splitted in the midst;
So that in this unjust divorce of us,
Fortune had left to both of us alike   105
What to delight in, what to sorrow for;
Her part, poor soul, seeming as burdened
With lesser weight, but not with lesser woe,

93. Epidaurus] *F* (Epidarus).   94. came—O, ... more;] *As Pope;* came, oh ...
more, *F.*   102. upon] *Pope;* vp *F.*

85. *end the*] end of the; Abbott, 202.
86. *straight*] straightway, at once.
87. *Was ... we*] Such disagreements
in number are common in Shakespeare (Abbott, 333).
89. *vapours that offended us*] clouds that
assailed us; 'vapours' more commonly
refer to mists, but cf. *2H4*, II. iv. 351.
90. *by the benefit of*] through the
agency of.
92. *amain*] at full speed, as at *LLL.,*
v. ii. 542.
93. *Epidaurus*] Probably Shakespeare had in mind the Epidaurus on
the Adriatic coast (later Ragusa, now
Dubrovnik), rather than the town on
the east coast of Greece; for the former,

shown prominently in the atlas of Ortelius, was north of Epidamnum, while
Corinth was well to the south and east.
The appearance of the ships coming
towards Egeon at Epidamnum from
apparently opposite directions would
thus be most easily explained; but
see l. 41 and n., and Introduction,
p. xxx.
95. *that*] that which; common, as at
Gent., II. iv. 10.
99. *Worthily*] justly.
103. *ship*] i.e. the mast to which they
were lashed.
splitted] a common form into the
17th century, cf. v. i. 308; Abbott, 344.
107. *as*] as if.

Was carried with more speed before the wind,
And in our sight they three were taken up   110
By fishermen of Corinth, as we thought.
At length another ship had seiz'd on us,
And knowing whom it was their hap to save,
Gave healthful welcome to their ship-wrack'd guests,
And would have reft the fishers of their prey,   115
Had not their bark been very slow of sail;
And therefore homeward did they bend their course.
Thus have you heard me sever'd from my bliss,
That by misfortunes was my life prolong'd
To tell sad stories of my own mishaps.   120

Duke. And for the sake of them thou sorrowest for,
Do me the favour to dilate at full
What have befall'n of them and thee till now.

Egeon. My youngest boy, and yet my eldest care,
At eighteen years became inquisitive   125
After his brother, and importun'd me
That his attendant, so his case was like,
Reft of his brother, but retain'd his name,

116. bark] *F2;* backe *F.*   119. That] *F;* Thus *Rann.*   123. have . . . thee]
Alexander; haue . . . they *F;* hath . . . thee *F2+.*

111. *as we thought*] This prepares for
Egeon's discovery of his mistake.

113. *hap*] chance, cf. l. 38.

114. *healthful*] health-restoring,
beneficent.

shipwrack'd] the regular spelling and
pronunciation in Shakespeare; cf. the
rhyme with 'back', *Mac.,* v. iv. 51.
'Wrack' is, in origin, a different word
from 'wreck', but their meanings over-
lap, and the former has passed out of
common use.

116. *bark*] backe (F) is probably due
to a misreading of *r* as *c;* the two letters
are easily confused in English secretary
hand.

122. *dilate*] amplify, cf. *Oth.,* I. iii.
153; the word was used in their in-
structions about composing a *narratio*
by writers of textbooks of rhetoric,
such as Aphthonius, whose *Progym-
nasmata* Shakespeare probably used
at school; see T. W. Baldwin,

Shakspere's Small Latine, II. 315–16.

123. *have befall'n of*] has become of;
for a similar false concord between
verb and subject, cf. l. 87 above
(Abbott, 333).

thee] *they* (F); did the compositor
wrongly expand MS. *the?*

124. *youngest*] According to l. 78, the
mother took the younger boy, the
'latter-born'; but such conflict in details is not uncommon in Shakespeare,
and is not noticed on the stage.

125. *inquisitive*] Cf. I. ii. 38 and n.

126. *importun'd*] accented, as commonly, on the second syllable.

127. *so . . . like*] so similar was his
case; an odd construction.

128. *Reft . . . name*] Again, the construction is odd; N.C.S. thinks it implies that the boy and his attendant
take the names of their twin brothers,
but this seems to be forcing the sense
in order to do away with the apparent

Might bear him company in the quest of him;
Whom whilst I labour'd of a love to see,   130
I hazarded the loss of whom I lov'd.
Five summers have I spent in farthest Greece,
Roaming clean through the bounds of Asia,
And coasting homeward came to Ephesus,
Hopeless to find, yet loth to leave unsought   135
Or that or any place that harbours men:
But here must end the story of my life,
And happy were I in my timely death,
Could all my travels warrant me they live.
Duke. Hapless Egeon, whom the fates have mark'd   140
To bear the extremity of dire mishap;
Now trust me, were it not against our laws,
Against my crown, my oath, my dignity,
Which princes, would they, may not disannul,
My soul should sue as advocate for thee;   145

130. labour'd] *Pope* (laboured *F*).   143, 144.] *lines transposed by Theobald.*

contradiction between this line and
l. 52 above (see n. to this line). Shakespeare is often inconsistent in minor
details, cf. l. 124 and n.; here it becomes important to give the pairs of
twins identical names; this is a condition of the action to follow, which
turns on 'errors', but Shakespeare did
not need to trouble about this in de-
scribing their birth at l. 52.

130–1. *Whom . . . lov'd*] i.e. while he
strove to see the lost twin out of love
for him, he hazarded the loss of the
other, whom he also loved. With 'of a
love' = from, impelled by love, cf.
3H6, III. i. 13, 'From Scotland am I
stol'n, even of pure love / To greet
mine own land . . .'.

132–4. *Five . . . Ephesus*] adapted
from *Menaechmi*, where Messenio says,
in Warner's words, 'six yeares now
have we roamde about thus, *Istria,
Hispania, Massylia, Ilyria*, all the upper
sea, all high *Greece*, all Haven Towns
in Italy' (Bullough, I. 17). Shakespeare
has altered the setting to Ephesus, and
so substitutes Asia (Ephesus—'A noble
auncient city in Asia the lesse', Tho-

mas Cooper, *Thesaurus*, 1578) for some
of the names, and 'farthest Greece'
for 'Graeciamque exoticam' (*Menaechmi*, l. 236), which refers to Magna
Graecia, an area in southern Italy.
See v. i. 400 and n. He may have had
in mind also the travels of St Paul,
cf. *Acts*, xix. 1, 'Paul when he passed
through the upper coastes, came to
Ephesus.'

133. *bounds*] territories, cf. *Lr.*, I. i.
62.

135. *Hopeless to find*] For the construction, cf. *Cym.*, IV. iv. 27.

136. *Or that or*] a common construction, cf. *MND.*, II. i. 171.

harbours] accommodates, cf. *John*,
II. i. 262.

139. *travels*] and *travails*, labours; the
two spellings represent in origin the
same word, and were 'not differentiated in Shakespeare's day' (N.C.S.);
cf. *Lucr.*, 1543.

143. *crown*] 'duke', as commonly in
Shakespeare, is a generic word for a
prince or ruler.

dignity] high office.

144. *disannul*] cancel, abolish.

But though thou art adjudged to the death,
And passed sentence may not be recall'd
But to our honour's great disparagement,
Yet will I favour thee in what I can;
Therefore, merchant, I'll limit thee this day 150
To seek thy health by beneficial help;
Try all the friends thou hast in Ephesus,
Beg thou, or borrow, to make up the sum,
And live; if no, then thou art doom'd to die.
Jailor, take him to thy custody. 155
Jailor. I will, my lord.
Egeon. Hopeless and helpless doth Egeon wend,
But to procrastinate his lifeless end. *Exeunt.*

151. health] *N.C.S.;* helpe *F, Alexander (subst.);* life *Rowe 3;* hope *Staunton, conj. Collier;* fine *Singer 2;* pelf *Cuningham.* help] *F;* hap *Alexander.* 157. Egeon] *F* (Egean).

146. *adjudged*] sentenced.

147. *recall'd*] revoked.

148. *disparagement*] disgrace.

150.] The Duke thus indicates the duration of the play's action; cf. I. ii. 26 and n.

Therefore, merchant] Shakespeare nowhere accents *merchant* on the second syllable, and there is no need to suppose, with Capell and Cuningham, that he does so here; the change of rhythm marks the climax of the Duke's speech, the transition from comment to decision; cf. Abbott, 453, for further examples.

limit] appoint, cf. *R3*, v. iii. 25.

151. *health*] the most satisfactory correction of *helpe* (F), which appears to be an anticipation of the last word of the line; Shakespeare elsewhere uses *health* to mean safety or prosperity, cf. *Ham.*, I. iv. 40, and 'healthful', l. 114 above. The jingle too is appropriate. N.C.S., in first proposing the present emendation, explained the error as due to a compositor mishearing a line that was dictated to him; at that time (1922), it was usual to regard compositorial errors as misreadings or mishearings, but now scholars are less inclined to be so categorical, and recognize that

the silent associations in the compositor's mind of words alike in sound may have led him to substitute one word for another, or assimilate words.

155. *Jailor*] Most edd. add 'go' or some such word to give the line ten syllables, and N.C.S. suspects abridgement; but the short line, like that at l. 150, marks a change of tone, and here, of address.

156. *I ... lord*] Such phrases, standing outside the metrical pattern, are frequent in Shakespeare, and are often, by their abruptness or brevity, very effective; cf. I. ii. 16 (Abbott, 511–12). There is no need to suspect abridgement with N.C.S., or to regard them as broken lines.

158. *procrastinate*] postpone; not elsewhere in Shakespeare.

lifeless] *liuelesse* (F) is a mere variant spelling. Kellner, pp. 7–9, proposes emending to 'timeless', a good Shakespearian word, used of death to mean 'untimely', cf. *Gent.*, III. i. 21, on the analogy of 'time', *2H4*, IV. iv. 39, usually emended to 'line', and 'lamely', *Lr.*, II. iv. 275 (Q), 'tamely' (F). This is tempting, but the tautology of the present text effectively enough suggests Egeon's despair.

SCENE II

Enter ANTIPHOLUS [*of Syracuse, First*] Merchant, *and* DROMIO.

First Mer.   Therefore give out you are of Epidamnum,
          Lest that your goods too soon be confiscate;
          This very day a Syracusian merchant
          Is apprehended for arrival here,
          And not being able to buy out his life,   5
          According to the statute of the town
          Dies ere the weary sun set in the west.
          There is your money that I had to keep.

Scene II

SCENE II] *Pope; not in* F.   S.D. *of Syracuse*] *Erotes* / F.   *First*] *not in* F.
1. *First*] *not in* F.   Epidamnum] *Pope;* Epidamium *F.*   4. arrival] *F2* (a riuall
F).

SCENE II] The opening lines continue the mood of I. i, economically establish that another merchant from Syracuse has arrived in Ephesus, and give him a motive for concealing his identity. Shakespeare remembered this scene in *Tw. N.*, III. iii, where the newly-landed Sebastian goes off to view the city while Antonio waits at an inn for him. The whole scene is in verse, including Dromio's speeches, maintaining a flow into Act II; we are released gently into the comic world of Ephesus, where we never lose touch with the tone of the first scene.

S.D. of Syracuse] F has *Erotes*, which is usually thought to be a corruption of *Erraticus* (wandering), *Errans*, or *Erratus*, formed from the verb *errare*, to wander, by analogy with *Surreptus* (see II. i. S.D. and n.); but it may refer to Erotium, the Courtesan of *Menaechmi*, distinguishing the brother favoured by her from the one stolen away as an infant and resident in Epidamnum. See Introduction, p. xxvi.

S.D. First] In F no distinction is made between this merchant, who knows what is going on in Ephesus, and the other merchant, who appears in IV. i and later, and seems to be a

stranger to the city. They are clearly different characters, but this one vanishes before the other enters, and Shakespeare simply calls each 'a Merchant'; cf. IV. i. Entry and note. The whole play is notable for the author's casual treatment of names and speech-headings. See Introduction, p. xi.

1. S.H. First Mer.] In the previous scene the speech-headings for Egeon are *Marchant*, *Mer*, and *Merch*.; this scene begins in F with *Mer.* for the anonymous merchant, but, as if the author noticed the possibility of confusion, it continues with *E.* (Ephesian?) *Mar.*

4. arrival] *a riuall* (F) shows a splitting not uncommon in words beginning with *a*; Kellner cites *Shr.*, IV. v. 40, 'Allots thee', where F reads 'A lots', and cf. the spelling 'a levenpence' in the Shakespearian portion of *Sir Thomas More*, f.8ʳ.

5. *buy out*] redeem.

7. *weary . . . west*] something of a poetical cliché in Shakespeare's early works, deriving from the personification of the sun as Phaethon; cf. *Ven.*, 529, *Sonn.* VII. 9; Cuningham also compares *R3*, V. iii. 19, and *John*, V. iv. 35.

8–9. *money . . . bear it*] The money which is to be the source of much con-

Syr. Ant. Go, bear it to the Centaur, where we host,
  And stay there, Dromio, till I come to thee;   10
  Within this hour it will be dinner time;
  Till that I'll view the manners of the town,
  Peruse the traders, gaze upon the buildings,
  And then return and sleep within mine inn,
  For with long travel I am stiff and weary.   15
  Get thee away.
Syr. Dro. Many a man would take you at your word,
  And go indeed, having so good a mean.   *Exit.*
Syr. Ant. A trusty villain, sir, that very oft,
  When I am dull with care and melancholy,   20
  Lightens my humour with his merry jests.
  What, will you walk with me about the town,
  And then go to my inn and dine with me?
First Mer. I am invited, sir, to certain merchants,
  Of whom I hope to make much benefit.   25
  I crave your pardon; soon at five o'clock,

9. *Syr. Ant.*] *Ant.* / F (*so throughout scene*).   17. *Syr. Dro.*] *Dro.* / F.   18. *Exit.*]
F (*Exit Dro.*).   24, 32. *First Mer.*] *E.Mar.* / F.

fusion is thus emphasized in stage
action; cf. ll. 54-84 below, and especially l. 81 and n.
  9. *Centaur*] Possibly a London inn
bore this sign, but I have not found a
reference to one.
  host] lodge, as at *All's W.*, III. v. 91,
the only other instance in Shakespeare
(Cuningham). Cf. v. i. 410 and n.
  11. *dinner time*] that is, between 11
a.m. and 12 noon; see below, l. 45
and n.
  13. *Peruse*] survey; cf. *2H4*, IV. ii. 94,
'that we may peruse the men'.
  16. *Get . . . away*] Cf. I. i. 156 and n.
  18. *mean*] opportunity, cf. *Lucr.*,
1045, 'seek . . . / Some happy mean to
end a hapless life'. Dromio holds the
bag of money, and may, as Baldwin
thinks, be suggesting 'means'=wealth,
as at *Meas.*, II. ii. 24, the first appearance of this sense noted in *O.E.D.*
  19. *villain*] used playfully, as often,
cf. *Gent.*, IV. i. 41, *Wint.*, I. ii. 136,
'sweet villain' (of a woman), but also,

as N.C.S. notes, citing *Lucr.*, 1338,
'The homely villain curtsies to her
low', with the sense of bondman or
villein.
  21. *humour*] disposition, but still perhaps used here with reference to
melancholy as one of the four humours,
or vital fluids in the body, which, it
was thought, determined temperament; hence too the use of 'Lightens'
in allusion to the blackness of melancholy, cf. *LLL.*, I. i. 225, 'besieged with
sable-coloured melancholy, I did commend the black oppressing humour to
the most wholesome physic'.
  25. *benefit*] profit, cf. *2H6*, I. iii. 96.
  26. *soon . . . five o'clock*] the first indication of the hour when the action will
be completed; cf. I. i. 150 and IV. i. 10.
Baldwin cites Gil, *Logonomia Anglica*
(1619), p. 28, ' "soon", hodie apud
plurimos significat ad primam vesper-
am', i.e. early in the evening. It is used
perhaps in this way by Shakespeare
here and in the phrase 'soon at night

Please you, I'll meet with you upon the mart,
And afterward consort you till bed-time;
My present business calls me from you now.
Syr. Ant. Farewell till then: I will go lose myself,   30
    And wander up and down to view the city.
First Mer. Sir, I commend you to your own content.   *Exit.*
Syr. Ant. He that commends me to mine own content
    Commends me to the thing I cannot get.
    I to the world am like a drop of water   35
    That in the ocean seeks another drop,
    Who, falling there to find his fellow forth,
    (Unseen, inquisitive) confounds himself.
    So I, to find a mother and a brother,

32. S.D. *Exit*] Rowe; *Exeunt.* F.

(supper, etc.)', cf. *Mer. V.*, II. iii. 5, *Rom.*, II. v. 76. See also III. ii. 173 and IV. i. 10 below, and n.

o'clock] *a clocke* (F), the common Elizabethan form, represents what is still a normal pronunciation.

28. *consort*] attend, cf. *LLL.*, II. i. 177, 'fair desires consort your grace'.

30. *lose myself*] roam at random, but perhaps suggesting also the sense 'lose my wits', cf. l. 40 and n.

35–8. *drop . . . himself*] This image perhaps grew by association from Egeon's account of his shipwreck, and parallels his story of searching by sea (cf. 'coasting' and 'harbours', I. i. 134, 136) for his lost sons. It is a prominent and potent image in a play much concerned with identity (see Introduction, p. xliii), and links with the conceit Adriana uses at II. ii. 125–9 to describe her feeling for Antipholus. As H. F. Brooks points out, images of water or melting connected with dissolution of reality or loss of identity recur in Shakespeare's work and seem to spring from deep feelings; cf. *Gent.*, II. iv. 196–8; III. ii. 6–9, 'This weak impress of love . . . Dissolves to water and doth lose his form', and in later plays Richard II's desire to melt himself 'away in waterdrops' (*R2*, IV. i. 260–2), Hamlet's 'O, that this too, too solid flesh

would melt' (*Ham.*, I. ii. 129–30), and Antony's 'even with a thought / The rack dislimns, and makes it indistinct, / As water is in water' (*Ant.*, IV. xiv. 9–11). See also Tilley, D 613.

36–7. *That . . . Who*] For the construction, see Abbott, 259, 264; 'who' is frequently used by Shakespeare in relation to inanimate objects, especially where there is personification.

37. *find . . . forth*] seek his fellow out; cf. *Mer.V.*, I. i. 143.

38. (*Unseen, inquisitive*)] 'Unseen' may mean 'unknown' or 'unnoticed', cf. *LLL.*, v. ii. 358, *Sonn.* cxviii, 3, or 'ignorant' (a sense not otherwise recorded in Shakespeare, but cf. *Shr.*, I. ii. 131, 'a schoolmaster / Well seen in music'). For 'inquisitive' = eager for knowledge, cf. I. i. 125 and n. The punctuation of F, here retained, shows that the two adjectives go together; and they must apply to the speaker, for the Ephesian Antipholus, who is unaware of his brother's existence, cannot be termed 'inquisitive'.

confounds himself] mingles indistinguishably with the rest (Onions, who compares *R2*, IV. i. 141, 'Shall kin with kin and kind with kind confound'), but also carrying the sense of mental confusion, cf. 'lose myself', l. 40.

In quest of them, unhappy, lose myself.   40

Enter DROMIO *of Ephesus.*

Here comes the almanac of my true date:
What now? How chance thou art return'd so soon?
Eph. Dro. Return'd so soon? rather approach'd too late;
The capon burns, the pig falls from the spit;
The clock hath strucken twelve upon the bell;   45
My mistress made it one upon my cheek;
She is so hot because the meat is cold;
The meat is cold because you come not home;
You come not home because you have no stomach;
You have no stomach having broke your fast;   50
But we that know what 'tis to fast and pray,
Are penitent for your default to-day.
Syr. Ant. Stop in your wind, sir, tell me this I pray:
Where have you left the money that I gave you?
Eph. Dro. O, sixpence that I had o' Wednesday last,   55

40. unhappy] *F2;* vnhappie a *F;* unhappier *N.C.S. (conj. Clark and Glover).*

40.] foreshadowing main themes of the play, confusion of mind, produced by the 'errors' of meeting the wrong twin, cf. l. 95 below, II. ii. 11, 184, etc., and confusion of identity (see Introduction, p. xliii). Antipholus, who feels he has no identity, is given one in Ephesus, where everyone claims acquaintance of him, and discovers another in falling in love with Luciana (see III. ii. 39–40 and n.), before 'finding' himself at the end of the play in meeting his parents and brother. For the extension of the sense of 'lose' here, cf. *Ant.,* I. ii. 114, 'Or lose myself in dotage'.

unhappy] unlucky.

41. *almanac . . . date*] Dromio, born at the same time as Antipholus, fixes the term of his life like a calendar; cf. v. i. 404, 'the calendars of their nativity'. For the sense of 'date' here, cf. *1H6,* IV. vi. 9.

43, 68. *too late . . . out of season*] Mistiming is a feature of the sequence of 'errors' in the play, and here is nicely

ironical in relation to Antipholus's confidence in Dromio as his 'almanac', l. 41.

45. *strucken*] an unusual form, cf. *LLL.,* IV. iii. 220 (Abbott, 344).

twelve] The common Elizabethan dinner-hour was about 11 a.m. to 12 noon, as indicated by the proverb, 'My stomach has struck twelve' (Tilley, S 872); see also *Shakespeare's England,* I. 15 and II. 134–5. Dinner was the biggest meal of the day.

49. *stomach*] appetite.

52. *penitent*] a quibble: they are chastised, suffering the punishment inflicted by their mistress, and they are having poor fare, like men fasting in penance (as in the phrase 'take penance', *O.E.D.,* sb. 3b).

default] offence.

53. *wind*] breath; perhaps alluding to the emptiness of Dromio's chatter; cf. III. i. 75 below, and *O.E.D.,* sb. 14.

55. *sixpence*] an indication that Shakespeare was thinking in contem-

To pay the saddler for my mistress' crupper:
The saddler had it, sir, I kept it not.

Syr. Ant. I am not in a sportive humour now:
Tell me, and dally not, where is the money?
We being strangers here, how dar'st thou trust   60
So great a charge from thine own custody?

Eph. Dro. I pray you jest, sir, as you sit at dinner:
I from my mistress come to you in post;
If I return I shall be post indeed,
For she will scour your fault upon my pate.   65
Methinks your maw, like mine, should be your clock,
And strike you home without a messenger.

Syr. Ant. Come Dromio, come, these jests are out of season,
Reserve them till a merrier hour than this;
Where is the gold I gave in charge to thee?   70

Eph. Dro. To me, sir? why, you gave no gold to me.

Syr. Ant. Come on, sir knave, have done your foolishness,
And tell me how thou hast dispos'd thy charge.

Eph. Dro. My charge was but to fetch you from the mart
Home to your house, the Phoenix, sir, to dinner;   75
My mistress and her sister stays for you.

56. crupper:] *F;* crupper? *Pope.*   64. indeed,] *Capell;* indeed. *F.*   65. scour]
F (scoure); score *Pope.*   66. clock] *Pope;* cooke *F.*

porary terms, while writing on a classical theme.

58. *sportive*] no earlier example is recorded by *O.E.D.*

62. *jest*] each thinks the other speaks in jest.

63-4. *in post . . . post*] i.e. he comes in great haste (post = a courier, cf. 'posthaste'), and if he returns without Antipholus, he will be brought to account for it (post = the door-post on which a tavern reckoning was scored). See next note.

65. *scour*] beat, punish, cf. *H5*, II. i. 55, and quibbling on 'score', to keep account by cutting notches in a post or tally.

66. *clock*] Pope's emendation of *cooke* (F) is fortified by the proverbial allusion here, cf. Tilley, B 287a, 'The belly is the truest clock', and also B 301,

S 872. The error is presumably due to a simple misreading.

73. *dispos'd*] deposited, cf. *Tit.*, IV. ii. 174.

75. *Phoenix*] the sign of the shop of Antipholus of Ephesus, who is a merchant (N.C.S.); see l. 88 and II. ii. 11 for further allusions. The image of this mythical bird, rising out of its own ashes to renewed youth, is appropriate to the story of Antipholus and Adriana, whose love is finally renewed out of the break-up of their marital relationship. The Phoenix was the sign of a London tavern, and also of a shop in Lombard Street, according to Sugden, *Dictionary*, p. 409. The tavern is referred to in the prologue of Ben Jonson's *Staple of News.*

76. *stays*] See I. i. 87 and n.

Syr. Ant. Now as I am a Christian, answer me
        In what safe place you have bestow'd my money,
        Or I shall break that merry sconce of yours
        That stands on tricks when I am undispos'd;   80
        Where is the thousand marks thou hadst of me?
Eph. Dro. I have some marks of yours upon my pate;
        Some of my mistress' marks upon my shoulders;
        But not a thousand marks between you both.
        If I should pay your worship those again,   85
        Perchance you will not bear them patiently.
Syr. Ant. Thy mistress' marks? what mistress, slave, hast
        thou?
Eph. Dro. Your worship's wife, my mistress at the Phoenix;
        She that doth fast till you come home to dinner,
        And prays that you will hie you home to dinner.   90
Syr. Ant. What, wilt thou flout me thus unto my face
        Being forbid? There, take you that, sir knave.
Eph. Dro. What mean you, sir? for God's sake hold your
        hands.
        Nay, and you will not, sir, I'll take my heels.   *Exit.*
Syr. Ant. Upon my life, by some device or other   95
        The villain is o'er-raught of all my money.
        They say this town is full of cozenage,

93. God's] *F3;* God *F.*   94. S.D. *Exit.*] *F2; Exeunt Dromio Ep. | F.*   96. o'er-
raught] *Capell;* ore-wrought *F.*

77. *as . . . Christian*] a common as-
severation, cf. *Oth.*, IV. ii. 83. See note
to 'sixpence', l. 55 above.
    79. *sconce*] head; cf. II. ii. 34 below.
    80. *stands on*] devotes itself to.
    undispos'd] not in the mood for it.
    81. *thousand marks*] This is the very
sum needed to ransom Egeon (I. i. 21),
and the emphasis on Antipholus's
money, and his anger at his supposed
loss of it, together with Dromio's quibbling on 'marks', are perhaps designed
to enforce the irony of the situation—
Egeon's son has the money which
could redeem his father, but is unaware of his father's presence in
Ephesus.
    85. *pay*] quibbling on the sense 'beat,
flog' (*O.E.D.*, v¹. 3c); cf. IV. iv. 10.

94. *take my heels*] i.e. take to my heels;
formerly a common form, and Tilley,
H 394, has an example from as late as
1721. In this and the preceding line
there is a nice opposition between
'hold' and 'take' in the two common
phrases.
    96. *o'er-raught*] *ore-wrought* (F) is ex-
plained by N.C.S. as 'probably a mishearing', but cf. I. i. 151 and note. It
may be the compositor's misunderstanding of what he saw, or even a
Shakespearian spelling, for at *LLL.*,
IV. ii. 38, 'raught' is spelt 'rought' in
the quarto, printed probably from
Shakespeare's own 'foul papers' (Greg,
First Folio, p. 222).
    97. *cozenage*] cheating.
    97–102. *They say . . . sin*] No doubt

As nimble jugglers that deceive the eye,
Dark-working sorcerers that change the mind,
Soul-killing witches that deform the body,   100
Disguised cheaters, prating mountebanks,
And many such-like liberties of sin:
If it prove so, I will be gone the sooner.
I'll to the Centaur to go seek this slave;
I greatly fear my money is not safe.   *Exit.*   105

102. liberties] *F;* libertines *Hanmer.*   104. to go] *F;* go to *Rowe.*

this passage owes something to *Acts,*
xix, where St Paul's visit to Ephesus,
and his dealings with those who used
'curious arts' is reported (so Baldwin,
and see Noble, pp. 106–7); and Ephesus would be known to an Elizabethan
audience as associated with magic
through this passage. But in the main
it echoes the beginning of Act II of
Menaechmi, where Messenio reports,
in Warner's translation, 'this towne
Epidamnum, is a place of outragious
expences, exceeding in all ryot and

lasciviousnesse: and (I heare) as full
of Ribaulds, Parasites, Drunkards,
Catchpoles, Cony-catchers, and Sycophants, as it can hold: then for Curtizans, why here's the currantest stamp
of them in the world' (Bullough, I. 17).
Shakespeare emphasizes sorcery and
witchcraft for his own purposes, see
Introduction, p. xlvi; the whole question of the alteration of location from
Plautus's Epidamnum to Ephesus is
also further discussed in the Introduction, p. xxix.

ACT II

SCENE I

Enter ADRIANA, *wife to Antipholus* [*of Ephesus*], *with* LUCIANA *her sister.*

Adr. Neither my husband nor the slave return'd,

ACT II
Scene I
ACT II SCENE I] *Pope; Actus Secundus F.*   S.D. *of Ephesus*] *Sereptus F.*

SCENE I] The exchange between Adriana and Luciana takes the form, after the opening lines in blank verse, of a set disputation on the relations of husband and wife, and is a kind of dialectic Shakespeare inherited from the Euphuistic novel; see L. Borinski, 'The Origin of the Euphuistic Novel and its Significance for Shakespeare', *Studies in Honor of T. W. Baldwin*, ed. D. C. Allen (1958), 38–52. From l. 10 to l. 43 they speak in rhyme, at first in stichomythia, Luciana 'answering' each line of Luciana by completing a couplet; this is followed by Luciana's speech, another exchange in stichomythia, and a speech by Adriana roughly corresponding to that of Luciana, who closes the sequence with a couplet. The same manner, and the rhyme, are resumed at l. 86, but there Adriana's argument turns to complaint, punctuated only by three sharp one-line comments on her from Luciana; who, however, attempts to renew the discussion in the same style with Antipholus in III. ii. The mixed sequence of prose and verse during Dromio's presence on stage interrupts the pattern, being directly concerned with forwarding the action, but though

less formal, it is notable that Dromio speaks in schemes and employs the colours of rhetoric, as in the repetitions of his speech ll. 60–8; see Thomas Wilson, *Arte of Rhetorique 1560*, ed. G. H. Mair (1909), pp. 176–7, 201.

Entry. of Ephesus] F has *Sereptus*, i.e. *surreptus*, stolen away, an epithet applied several times by Plautus to the Menaechmus who was snatched away from his home at Tarentum in infancy, taken to Epidamnum, and grew up there—and who thus corresponds to Antipholus of Ephesus. The word was taken over into ordinary literary reference in Shakespeare's time, and this character was generally known as 'Menaechmus Subreptus'; see Introduction, p. xxvi.

1. *slave*] a common term of abuse, and often used jocularly meaning 'fellow' (cf. I. ii. 104 above), this word is employed here, and perhaps elsewhere in *Errors*, with overtones of the technical Latin meaning; in *Menaechmi*, Messenio, the comic servant, is the slave of Menaechmus Sosicles, cf. l. 251, 'illoc enim verbo esse me servom scio' (Warner translates this as 'now it appeares what it is to be a servant').

That in such haste I sent to seek his master?
Sure, Luciana, it is two o'clock.
Luc. Perhaps some merchant hath invited him,
And from the mart he's somewhere gone to dinner.   5
Good sister let us dine, and never fret;
A man is master of his liberty;
Time is their master, and when they see time,
They'll go or come; if so, be patient, sister.
Adr. Why should their liberty than ours be more?   10
Luc. Because their business still lies out o'door.
Adr. Look, when I serve him so, he takes it ill.
Luc. O, know he is the bridle of your will.
Adr. There's none but asses will be bridled so.
Luc. Why, headstrong liberty is lash'd with woe.   15
There's nothing situate under heaven's eye
But hath his bound in earth, in sea, in sky.
The beasts, the fishes, and the winged fowls
Are their males' subjects, and at their controls;

11. o'door] *F* (adore).   12. ill] *F2;* thus *F.*

3. *two o'clock*] Cf. I. ii. 26 and n.; it was twelve noon in the previous scene, see I. ii. 45.

7-25.] This passage has several echoes of the Old Testament (see ll. 16-24 and n.), but in its general theme on the duty of wives to husbands, it reflects *Ephesians*, v. 22ff., 'Wives, submit your selves unto your husbands...'

7. *A ... liberty*] This sounds proverbial (Luciana's 'if so', l. 9, seems to point this), and Tilley records comparable phrases, but not this one, see A 88, M 474.

12. *when ... so*] i.e. when I treat him as he is treating me (H.F.B.).

ill] *thus* (F) may be, as H.F.B. suggests, an error of mental association on the part of the compositor, pairing the word with *so*; cf. III. i. 54-6 and n. It is certainly wrong, for not only the stychomythia of repartee, but the general pattern of the verse here demands a rhyme.

14-15. *asses ... woe*] This links with the images of loss or transformation of

identity in the play, change into a beast, especially an ass, being the most common form these take, cf. II. ii. 199, III. ii. 39-40 and n. Here the passage implies that Adriana's 'headstrong liberty' is more beastly than accepting the bridle of a husband's authority, since even the beasts are 'masters to their females'.

15. *lash'd*] scourged, continuing the image from *bridle* and *asses.*

16-24. *There's ... lords*] This passage is derived from *Genesis*, i. 26, 28, or *Psalm* viii. 4-8. In *Genesis* God gives Adam and Eve jointly 'dominion over the fish of the sea, and over the fowl of the air, and over the cattle'; in the Psalm, more specifically, man and 'the son of man' have power, and God has 'put all things in subjection under his feet'. So Luciana is putting the passages to special use in applying them to the relations of husband and wife. Cf. also *Ecclesiastes*, iii. 19, where the word 'pre-eminence' is used (Noble, p. 107).

Man, more divine, the master of all these,   20
Lord of the wide world and wild wat'ry seas,
Indued with intellectual sense and souls,
Of more pre-eminence than fish and fowls,
Are masters to their females, and their lords:
Then let your will attend on their accords.   25
Adr. This servitude makes you to keep unwed.
Luc. Not this, but troubles of the marriage bed.
Adr. But were you wedded you would bear some sway.
Luc. Ere I learn love, I'll practise to obey.
Adr. How if your husband start some other where?   30
Luc. Till he come home again I would forbear.
Adr. Patience unmov'd! no marvel though she pause;
They can be meek that have no other cause.
A wretched soul bruis'd with adversity,
We bid be quiet when we hear it cry;   35
But were we burden'd with like weight of pain,
As much, or more, we should ourselves complain:
So thou that hast no unkind mate to grieve thee,
With urging helpless patience would relieve me;
But if thou live to see like right bereft,   40
This fool-begg'd patience in thee will be left.

20-1. Man ... master ... / Lord] *F;* Men ... masters ... / Lords *Capell.*   22-3.
souls, / ... fowls,] *F;* soule, / ... fowle, *F2.*   39. would] *F;* wouldst *Rowe.*

30. *How ... where?*] How if your husband fly off in pursuit of some other
woman? (Cuningham). With this use
of 'start' he compares Marlowe, *Dido,*
IV. ii. 37, 'Mine eye is fixed where
fancy cannot start'; it is probably derived from the idea of a horse 'starting',
or swerving off its course. For 'where',
cf. l. 104 below.

32. *pause*] take time for consideration (i.e. before getting married); cf.
MND., I. i. 83.

33. *cause*] ground of action; or perhaps, as Abbott, 12, explains, 'no
cause *otherwise* than for meekness'.

34-7. *A ... complain*] an expansion
of the proverb, 'All commend patience,
but none can endure to suffer', Tilley,
A 124.

38. *grieve*] vex, hurt.

39. *helpless*] unavailing, cf. *R3,* I. ii.
13. These lines, 38-41, have some
reference to the proverb 'Patience is
a remedy for every grief', Tilley,
P 108, R 71. See also Introduction,
p. xliv n.

40. *like ... bereft*] Adriana is saying,
'If you live to see your rights as a wife
stripped from you . . .'; for 'right', cf.
IV. ii. 7 below, and *MND.,* I. i. 97.

41. *This ... left*] This patience of
yours, branded as foolish, will be aban-
doned. *Fool-begg'd,* apparently Shakespeare's combination, derives from the
phrase 'To beg a person for a fool' (cf.
Lyly, *Mother Bombie,* I. i. 37), i.e. to set
him down for a fool; this in turn arises
from the procedure of petitioning in
the Court of Wards (begging a person),
which deals with the estates of minors

Luc. Well, I will marry one day but to try.
Here comes your man, now is your husband nigh.

Enter DROMIO *of Ephesus.*

Adr. Say, is your tardy master now at hand?
Eph. Dro. Nay, he's at two hands with me, and that my   45
two ears can witness.
Adr. Say, didst thou speak with him? knowst thou his mind?
Eph. Dro. Ay, ay, he told his mind upon mine ear,
Beshrew his hand, I scarce could understand it.
Luc. Spake he so doubtfully, thou couldst not feel his   50
meaning?
Eph. Dro. Nay, he struck so plainly I could too well feel
his blows; and withal so doubtfully, that I could
scarce understand them.
Adr. But say, I prithee, is he coming home?   55
It seems he hath great care to please his wife.
Eph. Dro. Why, mistress, sure my master is horn-mad.
Adr. Horn-mad, thou villain?
Eph. Dro.   I mean not cuckold-mad,
But sure he is stark mad.
When I desir'd him to come home to dinner,   60
He ask'd me for a thousand marks in gold;
"'Tis dinner-time", quoth I; "my gold," quoth he;

43. S.D. *of Ephesus.*] *Eph.* / *F.*   45. two] *F2*; too *F.*   61. thousand] *F4* (1000. *F2*); hundred *F.*

who were Wards of the Crown, and of
lunatics, for the custody of one of its
charges. The guardian had complete
control over the ward's property, and
could marry an heiress to anyone of
equal rank (see *Shakespeare's England,*
I. 386). There are many allusions to
this practice in the drama; the subplot
of Middleton's *Women Beware Women*
turns upon it. See also Tilley, F 496.
      45. *at two hands*] a quibble on 'at
hands', fighting at close quarters, and
a reference to Dromio's beating at I.
ii. 92–3.
      48. *told*] quibbling on 'tell' and 'toll'
—Dromio's ear has been struck like a
bell.

      49, 54. *understand*] playing on 'stand
under', a common quibble, cf. *Gent.,*
II. v. 25–31.
      50, 53. *doubtfully*] ambiguously, and,
in the second instance, dreadfully,
quibbling on the sense of 'doubtful', at
I. i. 68.
      57. *horn-mad*] furious (as bulls and
other beasts attack with their horns
when enraged), but quibbling too on
the imaginary horns cuckolds were
said to wear.
      61. *thousand*] *hundred* (F) must be an
error, cf. l. 65 and I. ii. 81; perhaps
due, as N.C.S. observes, 'to the use of
figures in the copy' from which the
text was set up.

"Your meat will burn", quoth I; "my gold", quoth he,
"Will you come?", quoth I; "my gold", quoth he,
"Where is the thousand marks I gave thee, villain?"   65
"The pig", quoth I, "is burn'd"; "my gold", quoth he;
"My mistress, sir...", quoth I; "hang up thy mistress;
I know not thy mistress, out on thy mistress..."
Luc. Quoth who?
Eph. Dro. Quoth my master;   70
"I know", quoth he, "no house, no wife, no mistress",
So that my errand due unto my tongue,
I thank him, I bare home upon my shoulders;
For in conclusion, he did beat me there.
Adr. Go back again, thou slave, and fetch him home.   75
Eph. Dro. Go back again, and be new beaten home?
For God's sake, send some other messenger.
Adr. Back slave, or I will break thy pate across.
Eph. Dro. And he will bless that cross with other beating;
Between you I shall have a holy head.   80
Adr. Hence, prating peasant, fetch thy master home.
Eph. Dro. Am I so round with you, as you with me,
That like a football you do spurn me thus?

64. come] *F;* come home *Capell.*   71–4.] *As Pope; prose in F.*   72. errand] *F4*
(arrant *F*).   76, 79, 82. Eph. Dro.] *Dro. | F.*

67. *hang up*] an imprecation (= to hell with!), from hanging on a gibbet, cf. *Rom.*, III. iii. 57.

68. *not... mistress*] usually emended to 'thy mistress not', in order to make the verse regular; but the force of the passage lies in the echoing 'mistress' at the end of each phrase. Dromio embroiders considerably on what Antipholus actually said, cf. I. ii. 83–90.

72. *errand*] The spelling *arrant* (F) occurs again, for instance at *Troil.*, v. iv. 11.

73. *bare*] The form 'bore' for the past tense only became common after 1600; F has both *bare* and *bore*, the Bible of 1611 only *bare* (*O.E.D.*).

79. *bless*] consecrate, quibbling on *bless* = beat (*N.C.S.*). Dromio affects to understand Adriana's words, 'break across', as meaning that his head will

be cut open in such a way as to make the sign of the cross on it.

80. *holy*] full of holes, and marked with a cross.

81. *peasant*] often used to mean 'servant' (cf. v. i. 231), and also as a term of abuse (cf. *Gent.*, v. ii. 35); the usage here includes both senses.

82. *round*] harsh, with a quibble on spherical.

83. *football*] a popular, rough game, played between teams of any number, football was very different from the relatively refined modern 'soccer'. James I warned his son in *Basilikon Doron* (1599) against 'all rough and violent exercises, as the foot-ball; meeter for laming then making able the users thereof' (ed. J. Craigie, *Scottish Text Society*, Series 3, Vol. XVI, 1944, p. 189).

F

You spurn me hence, and he will spurn me hither;
If I last in this service you must case me in leather.   85
                                                        [*Exit.*]
Luc. Fie, how impatience loureth in your face.
Adr. His company must do his minions grace,
Whilst I at home starve for a merry look.
Hath homely age th'alluring beauty took
From my poor cheek? then he hath wasted it.   90
Are my discourses dull? barren my wit?
If voluble and sharp discourse be marr'd,
Unkindness blunts it more than marble hard.
Do their gay vestments his affections bait?
That's not my fault, he's master of my state.   95
What ruins are in me that can be found
By him not ruin'd? Then is he the ground
Of my defeatures; my decayed fair
A sunny look of his would soon repair;
But, too unruly deer, he breaks the pale   100
And feeds from home; poor I am but his stale.

85. S.D. *Exit.*] *F2; not in F.*

87. *do . . . grace*] give pleasure to his paramours; for 'minion' used contemptuously in this way, cf. *Tit.*, II. iii. 124, 'This minion stood upon her chastity', and IV. iv. 58 below.

88. *starve . . . look*] For similar images, cf. *Sonn.* XLVII, 3, and LXXV, 10, 'clean starved for a look'.

89. *homely age*] i.e. old age which brings plainness or ugliness; for *age* in this sense, cf. v. I. 329 below.

90. *wasted*] squandered and worn away, laid waste to. Shakespeare was no doubt conscious of both senses, cf. *R2*, v. v. 49, 'I wasted time, and now doth time waste me'.

91. *discourses*] conversation, cf. *Rom.*, III. v. 53.
wit] power of invention; cf. *Gent.*, II. iv. 37, 'If you spend word for word with me, I shall make your wit bankrupt'.

92. *sharp*] witty; but the primary sense of the word is dominant in the image of a sharp instrument made

blunt by being struck on marble.

94. *bait*] offer bait to, entice.

95. *state*] condition of life, and the representation of it in her appearance. She implies that he could provide for her more splendid array than that of his 'minions'.

98. *defeatures*] literally, ruins, but passing here into the sense 'loss of beauty', 'disfigurement', as at v. i. 300 below, and *Ven.*, 736, the only other places where Shakespeare uses the word.
fair] beauty, cf. *MND.*, I. i. 182, 'Demetrius loves your fair'.

100–1. *deer . . . home*] Cf. *Ven.*, 229–31; the play on 'dear' is common.

101. *stale*] tool or stalking-horse (the basic meaning is 'decoy-bird'), and hence, 'A lover or mistress whose devotion is turned into ridicule for the amusement of a rival' (*O.E.D.*, sb.³ 6, where it is suggested that the word may have an as yet unexplained connection with 'deer').

Luc. Self-harming jealousy! fie, beat it hence.

Adr. Unfeeling fools can with such wrongs dispense;
     I know his eye doth homage otherwhere,
     Or else what lets it but he would be here?   105
     Sister, you know he promis'd me a chain;
     Would that alone a toy he would detain,
     So he would keep fair quarter with his bed:
     I see the jewel best enamelled

107. alone a toy] *This ed., after Kellner;* alone, a loue *F;* alone, alone *F2+ ;* alone alas! *Hanmer;* alone o'love *N.C.S., conj. Cuningham.*

103. *with . . . dispense*] pardon or put up with, cf. *Lucr.*, 1070, 'And with my trespass never will dispense'.

104. *otherwhere*] elsewhere; a common usage, cf. l. 30 above.

105. *lets . . . here*] i.e. prevents him from being here.

106. *chain*] Like Warner, Shakespeare changes the 'spinter', or bracelet of *Menaechmi* (ll. 527, 530), which Erotium asks Menaechmus to take to a goldsmith for repair, into a chain. This is probably a coincidence, and due to the popular fashion of the time of wearing chains of gold or jewels round the neck (see *Shakespeare's England*, II. 115–17), as well as to the greater prominence of a chain on the stage; cf. v. i. 10, where Antipholus of Syracuse comes on stage wearing it.

107. *alone a toy*] an emendation suggested by Kellner, p. 75; *toie* is close enough to *loue* in secretary hand for confusion to be possible, since a looped *t* may easily look like *l* (cf. *lime* for *time*, *H8*, v. i. 37), and minim letters are rarely clear. I take it that there is a play on 'detain' and 'keep' in the next line (see note), 'detain' meaning 'to keep back what is due' (*O.E.D.*, v.2).

108. *keep fair quarter with*] have a proper regard to; Cuningham compares II. ii. 145.

109–13. *I see . . . shame*] not satisfactorily explained. The passage seems to be corrupt, and though Theobald's *Wear* for *Where* improves the sense, it leaves obscure the phrase 'no man . . .

shame'. N.C.S. supposes that two lines are omitted between 'gold, and' and 'no man', and Baldwin, who also keeps *Where*, would emend 'gold, and' to 'gold abides' or some such phrase. But it seems better to accept the rich implications offered by the reading *Wear*. The 'jewel', linking with 'chain', l. 106, indicates, as commonly, not a precious stone, but an ornament of some sort; cf. 'wear this jewel for me, 'tis my picture', *Tw.N.*, III. iv. 198. So the passage contrasts an enamelled surface which wears away in use, with the gold underneath, which still 'wears gold', i.e. remains; the implication is a double one, for as 'jewel' refers to herself, Adriana laments that she has lost her beauty (cf. l. 89 above), and goes off (ll. 114–15) to weep away what's left of it, while feeling that her true worth remains intact; as 'jewel' refers to Antipholus, Adriana seems to say that although he wears away his outward attractions in the service of other women, his true value as her husband cannot be violated by falsehood or corruption, or, as Baldwin puts its, 'the enamel of reputation may indeed be tarnished, but the gold of character will not be affected'. I assume that 'shame' is a noun, used here in the phrase 'to do shame', to inflict injury, as at *Tw.N.*, III. iv. 350, 'Thou hast, Sebastian, done good feature shame'.

This lengthy explanation still does not do justice to the ambiguity of syntax in ll. 110–12, where 'often touch-

Will lose his beauty; yet the gold bides still   110
That others touch, and often touching will
Wear gold, and no man that hath a name
By falsehood and corruption doth it shame.
Since that my beauty cannot please his eye,
I'll weep what's left away, and weeping die.   115
Luc. How many fond fools serve mad jealousy?   *Exeunt.*

SCENE II

Enter ANTIPHOLUS [*of Syracuse*].

Syr. Ant. The gold I gave to Dromio is laid up
Safe at the Centaur, and the heedful slave

110. yet the] *F;* and the *Theobald;* and tho' *Hanmer;* yet though *Collier.*   111.
and] *F, Collier;* yet *Theobald, Hanmer.*   111–12. will / Wear] *Theobald;* will, /
Where *F.*   112. and no man] *F;* and so no man *Theobald;* and e'en so, man
Capell.   113. By] *F;* But *Theobald*+.   115. what's . . . away] *Pope;* (what's
. . . away) *F.*   116. S.D. *Exeunt.*] *F2; Exit. | F.*

Scene II

SCENE II] *Capell, after Pope; not in F.*   S.D. *Antipholus of Syracuse*] *Antipholis*
Errotis F.   1. *Syr. Ant.*] *Ant. | F.*

ing will Wear gold' could mean that
gold does wear away; Tilley cites this
passage in relation to a phrase, 'Gold
by continual wearing wasteth' (I 92),
and Malone quotes from *Damon and*
Pithias (1571) by Richard Edwards,
'Gold in time do wear away'. This
contradiction of the obvious sense re-
gisters Adriana's doubt even as she
tries to reassure herself about her
husband.

116. *fond*] infatuated, and hence,
silly; cf. *Ven.,* 1021.

Scene II

SCENE II] This scene begins in
blank verse, lowering the tone after
the couplets of the previous scene, and
leading into the comic prose dialogue
of ll. 35ff. The entry of Adriana and
Luciana at l. 110 sharply counters this
with a return to the formal blank verse

of Adriana's attack on Antipholus; as
her affection overcomes her anger, so
her speech changes to rhymed couplets
(ll. 171ff.), which persist to the end
except for her directions about dinner
(ll. 203–11). The first few lines mark
a point of rest in the play's mounting
confusion, as Antipholus discovers his
gold is safe, but the conflict of purposes
begins again when Dromio enters.
There is a second point of rest in the
exchange of couplets between Adriana
and Antipholus, when they agree together, and Antipholus accepts his
new status, his 'transformation'; and
again Dromio interrupts (l. 188), being much less ready to accept his
change of identity.

Entry. of Syracuse] F has *Errotis;*
see above, I. ii. S.D. and n.

2. *Centaur*] See I. ii. 9 and n.

slave] See II. i. 1 and n.

Is wander'd forth in care to seek me out
By computation and mine host's report.
I could not speak with Dromio since at first   5
I sent him from the mart; see, here he comes.

Enter DROMIO *of Syracuse.*

How now, sir, is your merry humour alter'd?
As you love strokes, so jest with me again.
You know no Centaur? you receiv'd no gold?
Your mistress sent to have me home to dinner?   10
My house was at the Phoenix? Wast thou mad
That thus so madly thou didst answer me?
Syr. Dro. What answer, sir? when spake I such a word?
Syr. Ant. Even now, even here, not half an hour since.
Syr. Dro. I did not see you since you sent me hence,   15

3–4. out / . . . report.] F; out. / . . . report, *Rowe*+.   6. S.D. *of Syracuse*] *Rowe;*
Siracusia F.   12. didst] *F2;* did didst F.   14. *Syr. Ant.*] *E. Ant.* / F.

3. *Is . . . out*] This passage refers back
to I. ii. 9ff.; Antipholus had told
Dromio to wait for him at the inn, but
his servant disobeyed him, and has
gone off in search of him.

4. *By . . . report*] Neither the meaning
nor the syntax are clear; Antipholus
may be saying that he cannot find
Dromio, who has not stayed at the
inn (cf. I. ii. 10), but has gone to seek
him, working out where he might be
on the host's advice (as the punctuation of F suggests); or he may be finding out that he cannot have spoken
with his own Dromio since I. ii. 18 (as
Rowe's punctuation, shown in the
collation, suggests).

6, 14. *here . . . even here*] N.C.S. argues
that l. 14 indicates that this scene, like
I. ii, takes place in 'the Mart of Ephesus', and this location is given at the
head of the scene. But 'here' is ambiguous as referring to the stage where
all the action takes place; and if there
was a multiple setting (see Introduction, p. xxxiv), then this scene belongs
to that unlocalized area of the platform stage which served for street or
mart, and allows an easy transference

of the action later in the scene to the
outside of Adriana's house. See l. 164
and n.

12. *didst*] N.C.S. suggests that F's
'did didst' shows correction of the
sheets in proof, 'the correction "didst"
being inserted into the forme without
the removal of the original error
"did" '. It may equally well have been
a correction in MS.

14. S.H. Syr. Ant.] F has *E. Ant.*,
i.e. Antipholus Errotis, which is confusing as representing Antipholus of
Syracuse, and which does not corre-
spond with *E. Dro.*, i.e. Dromio of
Ephesus. It may be for this reason that,
except for this one instance, there is no
differentiation of the Antipholuses in
speech-headings before Act III, and
then only sporadically until Act V,
when both are on stage together, and
have to be distinguished. In Act III
they are distinguished as *E.* or *Eph.*
(Ephesian), and *S.* (Syracusan). The
Dromios, whose identity is not confused by the labels *Errotis* and *Surreptus*
given to their masters, are distinguished from the start as of Ephesus or Syracuse. See Introduction, p. xii.

Home to the Centaur with the gold you gave me.

Syr. Ant. Villain, thou didst deny the gold's receipt,
And told'st me of a mistress and a dinner,
For which I hope thou felt'st I was displeas'd.

Syr. Dro. I am glad to see you in this merry vein;   20
What means this jest; I pray you master, tell me?

Syr. Ant. Yea, dost thou jeer and flout me in the teeth?
Think'st thou I jest? hold, take thou that, and that.

                            Beats Dromio.

Syr. Dro. Hold sir, for God's sake; now your jest is earnest,
Upon what bargain do you give it me?   25

Syr. Ant. Because that I familiarly sometimes
Do use you for my fool, and chat with you,
Your sauciness will jest upon my love,
And make a common of my serious hours;
When the sun shines let foolish gnats make sport,   30
But creep in crannies when he hides his beams.
If you will jest with me, know my aspect,
And fashion your demeanour to my looks,
Or I will beat this method in your sconce.

Syr. Dro. Sconce call you it? so you would leave batter-   35
ing, I had rather have it a head; and you use these

---

17. *Syr. Ant.*] *Ant.* / *F. (Ant., An., Anti., Antip.,* or *Antiph. throughout scene).*   20. I
am] *F;* I'm *Pope.*   23. S.D. *Dromio.*] *F (Dro.).*   28. jest] *F;* jet *Dyce.*

19. *felt'st*] See I. ii. 92, where he had beaten Dromio of Ephesus.

22. *flout . . . teeth*] insult me to my face; a common expression (cf. Tilley, T 429).

24. *earnest*] as the next line indicates, a quibble on earnest money, money paid as a deposit to secure a bargain; cf. Tilley, J 46.

28. *jest upon*] mock, trifle with; as Dyce thought, this might well be the compositor's adjustment to a familiar word of the author's: 'jet', i.e. encroach, which also caused difficulty at *Tit.,* II. i. 64, 'how dangerous / It is to jet (Qq.; *set* F) upon a prince's right'. But 'jest' is used several times in this passage, ll. 21, 23, 24, 32.

29, 47.] Antipholus thinks Dromio's jests ill-timed, and Dromio thinks he is beaten at the wrong time; cf. I. ii. 43 and n.

29. *common*] figuratively from common or waste land; Herford paraphrases the line, 'treat my hours of business as common property in which every man is free to indulge his humour'.

32. *aspect*] i.e. as it is friendly or unfriendly; in astrology the 'aspects' of the planets were their relative positions, and hence came to represent their favourable or unfavourable influence on man. As commonly in Shakespeare, the word is accented on the second syllable.

34–7. *sconce . . . sconce*] quibbling on the senses 'head', 'a small fort' ('so you would leave battering'), and 'a protective screen or shelter' ('I must get a sconce for my head').

blows long, I must get a sconce for my head, and in-
sconce it too, or else I shall seek my wit in my
shoulders; but I pray, sir, why am I beaten?
Syr. Ant. Dost thou not know?   40
Syr. Dro. Nothing, sir, but that I am beaten.
Syr. Ant. Shall I tell you why?
Syr. Dro. Ay, sir, and wherefore; for they say, every why
hath a wherefore.
Syr. Ant. Why, first, for flouting me, and then wherefore,   45
for urging it the second time to me.
Syr. Dro. Was there ever any man thus beaten out of
season,
When in the why and the wherefore is neither rhyme
nor reason.
Well, sir, I thank you.
Syr. Ant. Thank me, sir, for what?   50
Syr. Dro. Marry, sir, for this something that you gave me
for nothing.
Syr. Ant. I'll make you amends next, to give you nothing
for something. But say, sir, is it dinner-time?
Syr. Dro. No, sir, I think the meat wants that I have.   55

45–6.] *As F; verse, Capell* (First, why . . . wherefore, / . . . me).   45. Why, first,]
F; First, why *Capell.*   47–8.] *As Rowe 3; prose in F.*

38–9. *seek . . . shoulders*] i.e. because
his head so battered will be useless; cf.
Tilley, W 548.

43–4. *every . . . wherefore*] proverbial;
see Tilley, W 331, and Abbott, 75.

48. *neither . . . reason*] *rhyme* is used in
its old sense of 'measure' in this common phrase (Tilley, R 98), though we
may be intended to notice that Dromio
now speaks in rhymed verse after a few
lines of prose; cf. a similar passage in
Gent., II. i. 132, 'Nay, I was rhyming:
'tis you have the reason'.

53–4. *nothing for something*] i.e. to pay
him nothing for his services.

54–109.] This passage of burlesque
dialectics is germane to the action of
the play as it relates to the constant
mistiming which is a part of the sequence of 'errors', cf. I. ii. 43 and n.,
and ll. 29 and 47 above. The argument
leads to two main points; one is Anti-

pholus's 'learn to jest in good time;
there's a time for all things' (l. 63), a
comment which suggests how inti-
mately proper timing is linked with
good order; the other is Dromio's
mock-proof that 'there is no time for
all things' (l. 99), which comes home
to Antipholus when he becomes deeply
involved with the affairs of Ephesus,
finds his normal sense of order and
time disturbed, and believes himself
the victim of witchcraft and illusions.
Shakespeare was immediately indebted to Lyly for this kind of 'vexing dialogue', as L. Borinski calls it in his
'Shakespeare's Comic Prose', *Shakespeare Survey*, 8 (1955), pp. 63–5; see,
for example, *Midas*, II. ii. 15ff.

55–7. *meat . . . Basting*] Dromio says
the meat lacks what he has had, quibbling on the special sense of basting =
a thrashing.

Syr. Ant. In good time, sir; what's that?

Syr. Dro. Basting.

Syr. Ant. Well, sir, then 'twill be dry.

Syr. Dro. If it be, sir, I pray you eat none of it.

Syr. Ant. Your reason?   60

Syr. Dro. Lest it make you choleric, and purchase me
another dry basting.

Syr. Ant. Well, sir, learn to jest in good time; there's a
time for all things.

Syr. Dro. I durst have denied that before you were so   65
choleric.

Syr. Ant. By what rule, sir?

Syr. Dro. Marry, sir, by a rule as plain as the plain bald
pate of Father Time himself.

Syr. Ant. Let's hear it.   70

Syr. Dro. There's no time for a man to recover his hair
that grows bald by nature.

Syr. Ant. May he not do it by fine and recovery?

Syr. Dro. Yes, to pay a fine for a periwig, and recover the
lost hair of another man.   75

56, 63. *In good time*] in l. 56 used as an ejaculation = Indeed!, as at *Shr.*, II. i. 193, 'Myself am mov'd to woo thee for my wife. / Mov'd! in good time!'; put Shakespeare must have had in mind the sense 'at the appropriate time', which emerges in l. 63.

61. *choleric*] choler, or yellow bile, as one of the four humours or liquids which were thought to circulate in a man's body and nourish him, was assigned the property of being hot and dry; and since it was believed that the humours were distilled directly out of the food and drink a man consumed, so his temperament or balance of humours depended on his diet; cf. *Shr.*, IV. i. 153–6, 'The meat was well . . . 'twas burnt and dried away, / And I expressly am forbid to touch it; / For it engenders choler, planteth anger'.

62. *dry basting*] severe beating; for 'dry' in this sense, cf. *Rom.*, IV. iv. 121, 'I will dry-beat you with an iron wit'. The usual sense of basting, i.e. moist-

ening, is ironically brought into play.

63–4. *there's . . . things*] See l. 54 and n.; the phrase is proverbial (Tilley, T 314).

68–9. *plain . . . Time*] As commonly personified, Time was bald except for a forelock, cf. *John*, III. i. 324, 'that bald sexton Time', and Tilley, T 311.

73. *fine and recovery*] terms for processes based on legal fictions whereby a property not normally transferable might be obtained or conveyed from one party to another, and, in particular, an entail might be broken and converted into fee simple; for another quibbling use of the phrase, cf. *Ham.*, v. i. 99, and see also *Shakespeare's England*, I. 404–6. Besides the play on the various meanings of *recover(y)* in this passage, there may be a quibble on *hair* and *heir* (N.C.S.), and on *fine* and *foin* = the fur used for trimming gowns (Kökeritz, p. 107).

75. *lost . . . man*] Hair was bought and sold to make wigs; cf. *Mer.V.*, III. ii. 88ff.

Syr. Ant. Why is Time such a niggard of hair, being (as it
    is) so plentiful an excrement?

Syr. Dro. Because it is a blessing that he bestows on
    beasts, and what he hath scanted men in hair, he
    hath given them in wit.   80

Syr. Ant. Why, but there's many a man hath more hair
    than wit.

Syr. Dro. Not a man of those but he hath the wit to lose
    his hair.

Syr. Ant. Why, thou didst conclude hairy men plain   85
    dealers without wit.

Syr. Dro. The plainer dealer, the sooner lost; yet he
    loseth it in a kind of jollity.

Syr. Ant. For what reason?

Syr. Dro. For two, and sound ones too.   90

Syr. Ant. Nay, not sound, I pray you.

Syr. Dro. Sure ones, then.

Syr. Ant. Nay, not sure in a thing falsing.

79. men] *Pope 2 (Theobald); them F.*

77. *excrement*] outgrowth from the
body; cf. *LLL.*, v. i. 85, 'Dally with my
excrement, my mustachio'.

79. *men*] Theobald's emendation of
F is generally accepted; Malone noted
a similar error in *2H4*, Induction, 8,
where the correct *men* (Q) becomes
them in F.

81–2. *more . . . wit*] a proverbial
phrase, cf. Tilley, B 736, 'Bush natural,
more hair than wit'. See also *Gent.*, III.
i. 349ff., where the same phrase is used
in a similar context.

83–4. *lose his hair*] probably an
allusion to one of the consequences of
syphilis, as Dr Johnson noted. So
Timon hopes the prostitutes Phrynia
and Timandra will 'Make curl'd pate
ruffians bald' (IV.iii. 159), and Quince,
thinking of the French disease, jests,
'Some of your French crowns have no
hair at all' (*MND.*, I. ii. 100). The hint
of bawdy here may explain *jollity*, l. 88.

85–6. *plain dealers*] i.e. free from deceit, the usual sense, and, here, lacking
wit.

87. *plainer . . . lost*] The old sense of
'deal', to divide or share out, may be
implied here. There seems also to be
an allusion to the proverb, 'The pro-
perer (honester) man the worse luck'
(Tilley, M 360). It is possible that the
bawdy suggestion of l. 84 is carried
over, if 'dealer' means 'dealer with
women', cf. *Per.*, IV. vi. 24, 'Have you
that a man may deal withal, and
defy the surgeon?', and *O.E.D.*, deal,
v 11b.

88. *jollity*] i.e. through sexual intercourse. Cuningham's emendation
policy is ingenious, as linking with the
discussion about reasons which follows, but it is unnecessary, and ignores
the undercurrent of bawdy. Cf. next
note.

90–1. *sound . . . sound*] quibbling on
the senses 'valid' (of reasons) and
'healthy' (morally and physically);
the latter sense continues from the
bawdy suggestions noted above, ll. 84,
87, 88.

93. *falsing*] deceptive.

Syr. Dro. Certain ones then.

Syr. Ant. Name them.   95

Syr. Dro. The one, to save the money that he spends in
    tiring; the other, that at dinner they should not drop
    in his porridge.

Syr. Ant. You would all this time have proved, there is
    no time for all things.   100

Syr. Dro. Marry, and did, sir: namely, e'en no time to
    recover hair lost by nature.

Syr. Ant. But your reason was not substantial, why there
    is no time to recover.

Syr. Dro. This I mend it: Time himself is bald, and   105
    therefore to the world's end will have bald follow-
    ers.

Syr. Ant. I knew 'twould be a bald conclusion; but soft,
    who wafts us yonder?

Enter ADRIANA *and* LUCIANA.

Adr. Ay, ay, Antipholus, look strange and frown,   110
    Some other mistress hath thy sweet aspects;
    I am not Adriana, nor thy wife.
    The time was once when thou unurg'd wouldst vow

97. tiring] *Pope; trying F.*   101. e'en] *Malone, conj. Capell; in F; omitted F2+.*

97. *tiring*] dressing his hair; *trying* (F)
is a simple compositor's error, a trans-
position of letters. The reasons which
Dromio at last produces are of course
quite trivial.

98. *porridge*] soup; the original
meaning, cf. *Troil.*, i. ii. 234.

99. *there*] As N.C.S. notes, the *t* is
very faint in F, and appears broken;
the comma before it is huge and of a
wrong fount, and perhaps prevented
the letter from registering properly.

99–100. *there . . . things*] See l. 54 and
n., and l. 63; cf. also Tilley, T 314.

101. *e'en*] Capell's emendation of *in*
(F) was adopted by N.C.S., which explains *in* as a mishearing, on the theory
that the text was dictated to a scribe
at some time, but cf. i. i. 151 and n. It
is conceivable that Shakespeare sometimes spelt *e'en* this way, and possible

parallels are afforded by *Meas.*, iv. iv.
7, 'proclaim it *in* an hour before his
ent'ring', and *Troil.*, i. iii. 354, where F
reads 'Limbes are in his instruments, /
In no lesse working, then are Swords
and Bowes'. The latter is discussed by
Alice Walker, *Textual Problems*, p. 75.

105. *bald*] Cf. ll. 68–9 above.

108. *bald*] trivial; cf. *1H4*, i. iii. 65,
'This bald, unjointed chat of his'.

108–9.] so F; many edd. print as
two lines of verse, with a break after
conclusion, so emphasizing the change
of tone in the final phrase.

109. *wafts*] beckons, as at *Mer.V.*,
v. i. 11.

110. *look strange*] i.e. as if you did
not know me; cf. *Sonn.* LXXXIX. 8, 'I
will acquaintance strangle and look
strange'.

111. *aspects*] Cf. l. 32 and n. above.

That never words were music to thine ear,
That never object pleasing in thine eye,   115
That never touch well welcome to thy hand,
That never meat sweet-savour'd in thy taste,
Unless I spake, or look'd, or touch'd, or carv'd to thee.
How comes it now, my husband, O, how comes it,
That thou art then estranged from thyself?—   120
Thyself I call it, being strange to me,
That undividable, incorporate,
Am better than thy dear self's better part.
Ah, do not tear away thyself from me;
For know, my love, as easy mayst thou fall   125
A drop of water in the breaking gulf,
And take unmingled thence that drop again
Without addition or diminishing,
As take from me thyself, and not me too.
How dearly would it touch thee to the quick,   130
Shouldst thou but hear I were licentious?
And that this body, consecrate to thee,
By ruffian lust should be contaminate?
Wouldst thou not spit at me, and spurn at me,
And hurl the name of husband in my face,   135

120. then] *F;* thus *Rowe+.*

115. *in thine eye*] in your range of
vision, cf. *3H6,* v. vi. 16, 'Have now
the fatal object in mine eye'.
  120-3. *That . . . part*] Adriana says
Antipholus must be alienated from
himself in behaving coldly towards
her, for she is so indissolubly knit to
him that she is more essential to him
than his soul. The phrase 'better part'
could refer both to the soul or most
intimate part of a man, and to his best
qualities, and both senses are often
brought into play in contexts relating
to love; cf. *Sonn.* XXXIX. 2, and the note
to ll. 123-9 below.
  123-9.] See I. ii. 35-8 and n. The
repetition of the striking image of
waterdrops lost in the ocean relates
Antipholus's concern for a reunion
with his family to Adriana's anxiety
for a proper union with her husband.

And as Antipholus does not see the full
application of his words (he goes into
the city to lose himself, but also to find
himself and his family), so Adriana
does not realize that her claim upon
her husband is too possessive, see v. i.
98-101 and n. This passage also con-
nects directly, through the repetition
of the idea of l. 123, with Antipholus's
wooing of Luciana in III. ii. 39-66,
which echoes in the terms of its appeal
Adriana's plea here to him.
  125-7. *fall . . . again*] developed from
the proverb, 'As lost as a drop of water
in the sea' (Tilley, D 613).
  125. *fall*] let fall, as at *MND.,* v. i.
141, 'her mantle she did fall'.
  130. *dearly*] grievously; a Shakespearian usage, cf. *AYL.,* I. iii. 29, 'My
father hated his father dearly'.
  touch . . . quick] Tilley, Q 13.

And tear the stain'd skin off my harlot brow,
And from my false hand cut the wedding-ring,
And break it with a deep-divorcing vow?
I know thou canst; and therefore, see thou do it!
I am possess'd with an adulterate blot,   140
My blood is mingled with the crime of lust;
For if we two be one, and thou play false,
I do digest the poison of thy flesh,
Being strumpeted by thy contagion.
Keep then fair league and truce with thy true bed,   145
I live unstain'd, thou undishonoured.

136. off] F (of), Hanmer.   141. crime] F; grime Warburton+.   145, 146.]
transposed by N.C.S.   146. unstain'd] Hanmer, conj. Theobald; distain'd F; dis-
stain'd Theobald; undistain'd Keightley.

136. stain'd . . . brow] cf. Ham., IV. v.
115, 'brands the harlot / Even here,
between the chaste unsmirched brows /
Of my true mother'; the forehead proverbially stood for the face or character
as signalling shame or guilt, cf. Tilley,
F 590, and 1H4, I. i. 85.
    off] of F; see Abbott, 165.
    141. crime] sin, offence, as common-
ly, cf. Oth., v. ii. 27. Many editors, including N.C.S. and Cuningham, accept Warburton's emendation to grime,
which is plausible, but unnecessary;
this word would certainly provide a
smooth link with 'blot', l. 140, and
'unstain'd', l. 146, but Adriana's horror at the thought of being involved in
adultery is strikingly reflected in the
less obvious word of F.
    142. we two be one] Adriana seems to
desire to absorb her supposed husband's identity into her own, a desire
which is shown finally to be jealous and
possessive, and earns the rebuke of the
Abbess at v. i. 68ff.; see note to ll. 123–
9 above. Compare also III. ii. 62–6,
where Antipholus woos Luciana with
the same violence of language, claiming that he is Luciana ('I am thee').
The whole sequence relates to what is
a central theme of the play, the nature
of personal identity and its place in
proper family and social relationships.
See Introduction, p. xlv.

144. strumpeted] the earliest use
known to O.E.D.; cf. Sonn. LXVI. 6.
    145. Keep] conditional, = 'If you
keep . . .'.
    146. unstain'd] Hanmer's emenda-
tion of distain'd, which could easily
have arisen as a compositor's error by
attraction from undishonour'd. N.C.S.
keeps distain'd, on the plea that it is a
good Shakespearian word, occurring
for instance at R3, v. iii. 322, and
meaning 'defiled', 'dishonoured'; but
in order then to make sense, N.C.S.
transposes ll. 145 and 146. The result
is still not good sense, for if Adriana is
dishonoured by Antipholus's sin, surely he is also. This, indeed, is the force
of what Adriana has been saying in the
previous 15 lines. Baldwin also keeps
distain'd, finding an 'ironic application'
here: Adriana advises Antipholus 'to
keep fair league . . . with his bed by
punishing or distaining her. So he will
clear his own honour'. This is over-
ingenious, strains the meaning of distain, and again disregards the stress of
Adriana's pleading on the indivisibi-
lity of husband and wife—his honour
is her honour too. Theobald is followed
by Alexander in inventing dis-stain'd
(= unstained), which would be tempting if it could be differentiated from
distain'd (= stained), but I do not see
how an actor could put across a coin-

Syr. Ant. Plead you to me fair dame? I know you not.
  In Ephesus I am but two hours old,
  As strange unto your town as to your talk,
  Who, every word by all my wit being scann'd,   150
  Wants wit in all one word to understand.
Luc. Fie, brother, how the world is chang'd with you.
  When were you wont to use my sister thus?
  She sent for you by Dromio home to dinner.
Syr. Ant. By Dromio?   155
Syr. Dro. By me?
Adr. By thee, and this thou didst return from him,
  That he did buffet thee, and in his blows
  Denied my house for his, me for his wife.
Syr. Ant. Did you converse, sir, with this gentlewoman? 160
  What is the course and drift of your compact?
Syr. Dro. I, sir? I never saw her till this time.
Syr. Ant. Villain, thou liest, for even her very words
  Didst thou deliver to me on the mart.
Syr. Dro. I never spake with her in all my life.   165
Syr. Ant. How can she thus then call us by our names?—
  Unless it be by inspiration.
Adr. How ill agrees it with your gravity
  To counterfeit thus grossly with your slave,
  Abetting him to thwart me in my mood;   170
  Be it my wrong, you are from me exempt,

151. Wants] *F;* Want *Johnson.*   156. *Syr. Dro.*] *Drom.* / *F.*   me?] *Rowe 2;* me. *F.*   166–7. names?— / ... inspiration.] *As F;* names, / ... inspiration? F*4.*

age identical in sound but opposite in meaning to a common word; in any case the parallelism of the line seems to require a word beginning with *un-*. Keightley made good sense with *undis-tain'd*, a known word, but this wrecks the metre. After all, *unstain'd* seems best; it is clearly required by the sense, it satisfies the metrical demand, and it is a reading based on a common sort of compositor's mistake; moreover, it follows naturally from the use of *stain'd*, l. 136, and is a Shakespearian word.
  150. *Who*] = and I; see Abbott, 263.
  161. *course and drift*] hendiadys; both words have roughly the same meaning,

of 'scope', 'gist'. Antipholus and Adriana (l. 169) each thinks that Dromio is confederate with the other.
  164. *mart*] Antipholus and Dromio have presumably moved from somewhere on the platform stage, the unlocalized street or mart (cf. ll. 6, 14 above, and n.), to meet Adriana and Luciana issuing from their house, marked with the sign of the Phoenix; see Introduction, p. xxxiv.
  167. *inspiration*] to be read as five syllables; cf. *succession*, III. i. 105.
  169. *grossly*] obviously.
  171–2. *Be ... contempt*] Adriana says, in effect, 'if I must suffer the injustice

But wrong not that wrong with a more contempt.
Come, I will fasten on this sleeve of thine;
Thou art an elm, my husband, I a vine,
Whose weakness married to thy stronger state,   175
Makes me with thy strength to communicate:
If aught possess thee from me, it is dross,
Usurping ivy, briar, or idle moss,
Who all for want of pruning, with intrusion,
Infect thy sap, and live on thy confusion.   180

Syr. Ant. [*Aside.*] To me she speaks, she moves me for her
        theme;
    What, was I married to her in my dream?

---

175. stronger] *F3;* stranger *F.*   181. S.D. *Aside*] *Capell; not in F.*

---

of your alienation from me, do not
make the wrong harder to bear by
inflicting it with a contemptuous dis-
regard for my feelings'; for *exempt*
cf. *AYL.,* II. i. 15, 'exempt from
public haunt'; for *more* = greater,
cf. *John,* II. i. 34, and Abbott, 17; and
for *contempt* in the sense shown in this
passage, cf. *Tit.,* IV. iv. 34. Note the
commencement of rhymed couplets
here, marking Adriana's abandon-
ment of anger, Antipholus's transition
from hostility to acceptance of a fantastic situation.

173–80.] J. R. Brown, *Shakespeare
and his Comedies,* pp. 54–7, draws attention to the jealous and possessive nature of Adriana's love, concerned with
claiming, with fastening on him, not
with giving; cf. v. i. 98–101 and n.

173. *sleeve*] Was Shakespeare thinking of the doublet of his own time?

174. *elm . . . vine*] alluding to the
practice of training vines on elm trees.
The figure was biblical (Noble, p. 107,
Psalm cxxviii, 3), and proverbial, cf.
Tilley, V 61; but Shakespeare may
have had Ovid in mind, as Steevens
thought. The relevant lines are *Meta-
morphoses,* XIV. 665–6, which occur in
a passage relating to marriage, in
which the vine represents the woman;
Arthur Golding translates them (1567
edition, p. 183), 'if that the vyne which

ronnes upon the Elme had nat / The
tree too leane untoo, it should upon
the ground ly flat'. See also Introduction, p. xxxiii.

175. *stronger*] *a* and *o* were liable to
confusion in English secretary hand,
and *stranger* (F) is probably due to a
simple misreading by the compositor.

176. *with . . . communicate*] share in;
not used elsewhere by Shakespeare in
this sense.

177. *possess*] occupy, or infect, cf.
l. 140 above, and *Shr.,* III. ii. 44, 'possess'd with the glanders' (i.e. a disease
horses suffer from).

from] = apart from, other than
(Abbott, 158).

178. *idle*] useless, barren; cf. *Oth.,* I.
iii. 140, 'Antres vast and deserts idle'
(cited Steevens).

179. *with intrusion*] by forced entry;
cf. III. i. 103 below, and *Lucr.,* 848.

180. *confusion*] destruction, ruin; the
usual sense in Shakespeare.

181–6.] Cf. *Tw.N.,* IV. i. 59–62,
where Sebastian, addressed by Olivia
as if he were almost her husband, accepts what is to him a fantastic situation in terms that echo these lines of
Antipholus, 'If it be thus to dream,
still let me sleep!'

181. *moves . . . theme*] appeals to me
as the subject of her discourse; cf. *All's
W.,* I. ii. 6.

Or sleep I now, and think I hear all this?
What error drives our eyes and ears amiss?
Until I know this sure uncertainty,   185
I'll entertain the offer'd fallacy.
Luc. Dromio, go bid the servants spread for dinner.
Syr. Dro. O for my beads; I cross me for a sinner.
This is the fairy land; O spite of spites,
We talk with goblins, elves and sprites;   190
If we obey them not, this will ensue—
They'll suck our breath, or pinch us black and blue.
Luc. Why prat'st thou to thy self and answer'st not?

186. offer'd] *Capell;* free'd *F;* favour'd *Rowe 3.*   190. goblins, elves and]
Cuningham, conj. Lettsom, Cartwright; Goblins, Owles and *F;* Goblins, Owles and
Elves *F2;* goblins, owls and elvish *Pope;* goblins, ouphs and *Theobald;* ghosts and
goblins, owls and *conj. Lettsom;* none but goblins, elves and *Dyce 2;* fairies, goblins
elves and *Cuningham.*

184. *error*] picking up the title of the
play; cf. III. ii. 35.

186. *offer'd*] As N.C.S. suggests, *the
free'd* (F) probably arose as a compositor's misreading of MS. *thofred* (=
th'offer'd) or *the ofred*, and Capell's
emendation seems well justified. In
secretary hand, *o* and *e*, like *a* and *e*,
cf. l. 175 and n. above, are not always
distinguishable.

fallacy] delusion.

188. *beads . . . sinner*] Dromio's
thought of praying keeps in mind
the Christian undertone of the
play.

190. *We . . . sprites*] The line has only
eight syllables, and numerous guesses,
such as 'fairies', 'ghosts and', have
been made as to what word or words
may have been omitted. My own suggestion would be *urchins* (= elves), a
good Shakespearian word; the repetition of *ins* from *goblins* might have
caused the compositor to overlook this
word; the reconstructed line would
then be, 'We talk with goblins, urchins,
elves, and sprites'.

elves] Halliwell-Phillips and Baldwin cite passages to show that
Owles (F) could belong to the same
category of beings as goblins and
spirits, with which it is conceivable

that one might talk; so, for instance,
J. Baret, *Dictionary* (1580), explains a
screech-owl as a 'witch that chaungeth
the favor of children, an hagge or
fairie' (this sense is not recorded by
O.E.D., which merely has *owl-blasted=*
bewitched). However, Shakespeare
nowhere else writes of owls in this way,
and he explicitly dissociates owls from
the 'fairy land' of *MND.* (see II. ii. 6);
moreover, as N.C.S. argues, Dromio
is clearly thinking of spirits in human
form. So, feeling, like many editors,
that owls are incongruous in this passage, I have adopted *elves* (F2), as
being a more natural word in the context, a common Shakespearian word,
and also a form from which the reading of F might easily derive. I assume
the compositor saw *olues* in MS., an
initial *e* looking like *o* (cf. l. 186 and n.),
and made sense of it by transposing
letters.

192. *breath*] i.e. life; cf. 'breath of
life', *Genesis,* vii. 22.

pinch] A traditional idea about
fairies, see E. A. Armstrong, *Shakespeare's Imagination* (1946), p. 48n., and
Tilley, B 160. In view of other reminis-
cences of Lyly in the play, it is possible
that Shakespeare had *Endimion,* IV. iii.
28–36, in mind.

Dromio, thou drone, thou snail, thou slug, thou sot.
Syr. Dro. I am transformed, master, am I not?   195
Syr. Ant. I think thou art in mind, and so am I.
Syr. Dro. Nay, master, both in mind and in my shape.
Syr. Ant. Thou hast thine own form.
Syr. Dro.   No, I am an ape.
Luc. If thou art chang'd to aught, 'tis to an ass.
Syr. Dro. 'Tis true, she rides me, and I long for grass;   200
 'Tis so, I am an ass, else it could never be
 But I should know her as well as she knows me.
Adr. Come, come, no longer will I be a fool,
 To put the finger in the eye and weep
 Whilst man and master laughs my woes to scorn.   205
 Come, sir, to dinner; Dromio, keep the gate.
 Husband, I'll dine above with you to-day,
 And shrive you of a thousand idle pranks.
 Sirrah, if any ask you for your master,
 Say he dines forth, and let no creature enter.   210

194. drone] *Theobald; Dromio F.*

194. *drone*] Theobald's emendation has been generally accepted on metrical grounds; it is also reasonable palaeographically, and makes good sense. But F may be correct if Luciana calls and is ignored: 'Dromio—thou Dromio [Dromio becoming for the moment a generic term for a lazy servant] —thou snail', etc. (cf. 'Thou drunkard, thou', III. i. 10 below, and also IV. iv. 58).

sot] idiot.

195–9. *transformed . . . chang'd*] On the thematic importance of this jesting, see Introduction, p. xliv.

198–9. *ape . . . ass*] Two meanings of *ape* are brought into play. Dromio intends to say, 'I am a counterfeit, imitating my real self' (cf. *Cym.*, II. ii. 31, 'O sleep, thou ape of death'), but Luciana seems to catch up another sense, of dupe or fool (as at *Rom.*, II. i. 16), and applies that in calling him an 'ass'.

200. *rides . . . grass*] i.e. rules, tyrannizes over me, and I long for freedom. Dromio is playing on the literal and

figurative senses of the words; for *ride*, cf. *Tw.N.*, III. iv. 276; going to grass (= pasture) was a phrase used metaphorically of a release from responsibilities (*O.E.D.*, sb.¹ 5b). N.C.S. compares Nashe, *Have with you to Saffron Walden* (1596; McKerrow, III. 97), 'hee is never wont to keepe anie man longer than the sute lasteth he brings with him, and then turne him to grasse and get one in new trappings'.

204. *put . . . weep*] used derisively of children or foolish behaviour; cf. *Shr.*, I. i. 79, and Tilley, F 229.

205. *laughs*] false concord; third person plural in -*s* is common, cf. I. i. 87 (Abbott, 322).

206. *gate*] i.e. one of the stage doors? cf. III. i. 33 below.

207. *above*] Can this be taken as an indication of the use of the upper stage or gallery in III. i? See III. i. 60, S.D. and note.

208. *shrive you*] i.e. hear your confession, and forgive you.

210. *forth*] out, cf. *Wiv.*, II. ii. 240.

Come, sister; Dromio, play the porter well.

Syr. Ant. [*Aside*] Am I in earth, in heaven, or in hell?
Sleeping or waking, mad or well advis'd?
Known unto these, and to myself disguis'd,
I'll say as they say, and persever so,　　　　　　　215
And in this mist at all adventures go.

Syr. Dro. Master, shall I be porter at the gate?

Adr. Ay, and let none enter, lest I break your pate.

Luc. Come, come, Antipholus, we dine too late.　　　[*Exeunt.*]

212–16. S.D. *Aside] Capell; not in F.*　　213–14. advis'd? . . . disguis'd,] *This ed.;*
aduisde: / . . . disguisde: *F;* advis'd: / . . . disguis'd? *F4;* advis'd? / . . . disguis'd?
Rowe 3+.　　219. S.D. *Exeunt.] Rowe 3; not in F.*

215. *persever*] with the accent on the second syllable, as is usual in Shakespeare's verse; *persevere* occurs only once, in a passage of prose in *Lear* (Onions).

216. *at . . . go*] carry on whatever the consequences.

219. S.D. Exeunt] not in F, where the scene ends at the foot of the second column on a crowded page (H3^r); the compositor simply dropped the stage-direction in order to squeeze in the catchword *Actus*, and began H3^v with the heading for Act III.

G

ACT III

SCENE I

Enter ANTIPHOLUS *of Ephesus, his man* DROMIO, ANGELO *the goldsmith, and* BALTHASAR *the merchant.*

Eph. Ant. Good signior Angelo, you must excuse us all,
My wife is shrewish when I keep not hours;
Say that I linger'd with you at your shop
To see the making of her carcanet,

ACT III
Scene I
ACT III SCENE I] *Actus Tertius. Scena Prima.* F.

SCENE I] Here Antipholus of Ephesus appears for the first time, giving a new interest and impetus to the action; whereas in *Menaechmi*, the corresponding twin only begins to get into difficulties with his wife in IV. ii, here Antipholus finds himself in trouble right away. He invites Balthasar to a feast to which they fail to achieve admittance, and this brings the first major discord of the action, in the slanging-match between those inside and those outside the gate (l. 31ff.); cf. v. i. 405, where the restoration of harmony is marked by a general feast. The scene moves from blank verse, the normal medium of serious action, into a stylized, rhymed discussion on whether a hearty welcome is more important than good food, thence into tumbling verse, which keeps the quarrel at the door within the bounds of farce, and finally returns to blank verse, and a more serious note, emphasizing the real anger of Antipholus, even though he is persuaded at last to speak of the business as a 'jest' (l. 123).

S.D.] An Antipholus appears here without the qualifying 'Errotis' or 'Surreptus'; from this point onwards they are identified in entries as of Ephesus or Syracuse.

1, 19. *signior*] The name Angelo seems to have made Shakespeare think of Italy, and use an Italian form of address, cf. IV. i. 36. Other early comedies, *Gent.* and *Shr.*, are set in Italy.

2. *My wife . . . hours*] So Antipholus identifies himself as of Ephesus, and reveals that he is still in the situation as it existed for Adriana when she first appeared in II. i, and had not encountered Antipholus of Syracuse.

keep not hours] another reference to bad timing, cf. I. ii. 43, II. ii. 29 and n.; if Adriana is overpossessive (see II. ii. 142 and n.), Antipholus is also to blame for his treatment of her; but this time he finds he has come 'too late' (l. 49).

4. *carcanet*] a necklace set with jewels; *O.E.D.* cites Nichols, *Progresses of Queen Elizabeth*, I. 323, where, among a list of gifts to the Queen in 1572, ap-

40

And that to-morrow you will bring it home.   5
But here's a villain that would face me down
He met me on the mart, and that I beat him,
And charg'd him with a thousand marks in gold,
And that I did deny my wife and house;
Thou drunkard, thou, what didst thou mean by this? 10

Eph. Dro. Say what you will, sir, but I know what I know;
That you beat me at the mart I have your hand to show.
If the skin were parchment and the blows you gave were
  ink,
Your own hand-writing would tell you what I think.

Eph. Ant. I think thou art an ass.

Eph. Dro.   Marry, so it doth appear 15
By the wrongs I suffer and the blows I bear;
I should kick, being kick'd, and being at that pass,
You would keep from my heels, and beware of an ass.

Eph. Ant. You're sad, signior Balthazar; pray God our cheer
May answer my good will, and your good welcome here.

Bal. I hold your dainties cheap, sir, and your welcome dear.

Eph. Ant. O signior Balthazar, either at flesh or fish   22

---

19. You're] F (Y'are).   22, 25. *Eph. Ant.*] *Anti.* | F.

---

pears 'One rich carkanet or collar of
gold, having in it two emeralds'. It is
the same as the 'chain' of II. i. 106 and
l. 115 below.

  6. *face me down*] impudently maintain.

  9. *deny*] disown.

  11–84.] This rhyming passage, in
mixed verses of five, six, and seven feet,
keeps the tone light, and prevents us
from taking at all earnestly what could
be a serious and bitter exchange; so
the transition to a serious tone at l. 85
comes only when Antipholus ceases to
think of violence, of breaking down the
door.

  11. *I know . . . know*] proverbial, cf.
Meas., III. ii. 142; Tilley, K 173.

  15–18. *ass . . . ass*] So both Dromios
are called asses in quick succession,
cf. II. ii. 199, and l. 47 below; these
images of transformation have a thematic importance in the play; see
Introduction, p. xliv.

  17. *I should*] i.e. I ought to (but do
not); cf. Abbott, 323.

  at . . . pass] in that predicament.

  19–29.] This debate on the relative
importance of good welcome and good
cheer is carried on in commonplaces
(see notes to ll. 20–1 and l. 23), and
cast in rhyme; it is, of course, not a
serious debate, but a trial of courtesy,
recalling, as H. F. Brooks points out,
the custom of discussing a set theme at
a supper or social gathering; cf. for
example, Castiglione, *The Courtier*, tr.
Sir T. Hoby (1561), Tudor Translations, 1900, pp. 33ff., and especially
Lyly, *Euphues and his England*, ed. Bond,
II. 161–2, where the same topic is canvassed.

  19. *sad*] serious (the usual meaning).
  cheer] fare.

  20–1. *good . . . dear*] an allusion to the
proverbial phrase 'Welcome (or, good
will and welcome) is the best cheer';
Tilley, W 258, G 338.

A table full of welcome makes scarce one dainty dish.
Bal. Good meat, sir, is common; that every churl affords.
Eph. Ant. And welcome more common, for that's nothing
    but words.   25
Bal. Small cheer and great welcome makes a merry feast.
Eph. Ant. Ay, to a niggardly host, and more sparing guest;
    But though my cates be mean, take them in good part;
    Better cheer may you have, but not with better heart.
    But soft, my door is lock'd; go bid them let us in.   30
Eph. Dro. Maud, Bridget, Marian, Cicely, Gillian, Ginn!
Syr. Dro. [*Within*] Mome, malthorse, capon, coxcomb,
    idiot, patch,
    Either get thee from the door or sit down at the hatch:

23. table full] *F;* table-full *F4.*   24. common; that] *Var. 1773;* common that
F.   32. S.D. *Within*] *Rowe; not in F.*

23. *A ... dish*] i.e. a hearty welcome is no substitute for rare and delicate food. Antipholus's deprecating attitude about the quality of his fare and Balthasar's equally polite reassurances are nicely comic in the light of our knowledge that their dinner is being eaten by someone else; here Antipholus rejects the proverb, 'A cheerful look makes a dish a feast' (Tilley, L 424), which Balthasar reaffirms in l. 26.

26. *Small . . . feast*] See l. 23 and n.

28. *cates*] provisions.

31. *Ginn*] probably=Jenny; *O.E.D., gin,* sb.⁴, cites an 18th-century use of 'Gin of all trades' as the female equivalent of 'Jack of all trades'.

32.] The reply nicely echoes the rhythm of Ephesian Dromio's catalogue of names; cf. the list of servants in *Shr.*, iv. i. 79–80, a scene in which Petruchio uses the term 'malt-horse' of Grumio.

32–60.] The slanging-match had a long history in English drama before Shakespeare, in the morality play especially; a notable example occurs in John Heywood's *The Four PP* (printed *c.* 1545).

32. *Mome*] blockhead; a word of obscure origin, used by Spenser (*F.Q.,*

vii. vi. 46), and in earlier plays, including N. Udall's Plautine *Ralph Roister-Doister* (iii. ii. 86).

malthorse] heavy brewer's horse, hence a drudge (cf. *Shr.*, iv. i. 113), or a stupid fellow, cf. Jonson, *Every Man in his Humour*, i. iii. 165, 'he has no more judgment than a malt-horse' (cited Cuningham).

patch] fool; perhaps from Italian *pazzo* = fool, but associated by Shakespeare with the pied colours of the professional fool, cf. *MND.*, iv. i. 209. The word occurs in Warner, Act V (Bullough, p. 37), but was well known long before the 1590s as the nickname oɪ Cardinal Wolsey's fool.

33. *sit . . . hatch*] perhaps = be silent, recalling the old proverb, 'It is good to have a hatch within the door' (Tilley, H 207, who cites Deloney, *Strange Histories*, 1607, 'A wise man, then sets hatch before the dore, / And, whilst he may doth square his speech with heed'). But the 'hatch' might refer to part of the stage structure; conceivably Dromio is speaking through a grating or half-door in the upper part of a stage door, and tells Dromio of Ephesus to sit at the hatch, or lower part of the door, i.e. out of his sight. Clearly Dromio of Syracuse is not visible to

Dost thou conjure for wenches, that thou call'st for
   such store
When one is too many? Go, get thee from the door.   35
Eph. Dro. What patch is made our porter? my master stays
   in the street.
Syr. Dro. Let him walk from whence he came, lest he catch
   cold on's feet.
Eph. Ant. Who talks within there? ho, open the door.
Syr. Dro. Right, sir, I'll tell you when, and you'll tell me
   wherefore.
Eph. Ant. Wherefore? for my dinner; I have not din'd to-day.
Syr. Dro. Nor to-day here you must not; come again when
   you may.   41
Eph. Ant. What art thou that keep'st me out from the house
   I owe?
Syr. Dro. The porter for this time, sir, and my name is
   Dromio.
Eph. Dro. O villain, thou hast stol'n both mine office and
   my name;
The one ne'er got me credit, the other mickle blame;   45
If thou hadst been Dromio to-day in my place,
Thou wouldst have chang'd thy office for an aim, or
   thy name for an ass.

40. *Eph. Ant.*] *Ant.* / *F (Ant., Anti. throughout scene).*   41. not; come] *As F4;* not
come *F.*   47. office] *This ed.;* face *F.*   an aim] *N.C.S.;* a name *F.*   an ass]
F; a face *Collier+.*

Dromio and Antipholus of Ephesus,
cf. l. 38. See l. 47 S.D. and n., and
Introduction, pp. xxxvii ff.
   37. *catch . . . feet*] See Tilley, F 579a.
   39. *when . . . wherefore*] See II. ii. 43–4
and n.; proverbial, Tilley, W 331.
   42. *owe*] own.
   43. *for this time*] for the time being,
cf. *Gent.*, II. iv. 28.
   45. *mickle*] much.
   47. *Thou . . . ass*] No one has made
sense of F here, and some emendation
seems necessary. The conjecture of
Collier, altering *ass* to *face*, is a sad
weakening of the line, and N.C.S. was
the first, with its brilliant suggestion of
'an aim' (= butt or mark) for 'a name',
to show what the point of the line prob-

ably is (cf. Kökeritz, p. 90). Dover
Wilson noted that Dromio is referring
to his recent experiences, to the changing of his name for that of 'an ass' at
ll. 15–18 above, and to the beatings he
received from Antipholus at I. ii. 82ff.,
and from Adriana at II. i. 78, which
have made him an 'aim' or target for
blows; he also drew attention to the
similar quibbling jests on *ell* and *nell*
(III. ii. 108), and *ears* and *years* (IV. iv.
28). He retained, however, in N.C.S.,
the Folio reading *face*, which is here
emended to *office*; face has no antecedent, whereas *name* recalls Dromio's
opening words in this speech, 'Thou
hast stolen both mine office and my
name . . .', and it is natural to assume

Enter LUCE [*concealed from Antipholus of Ephesus and his companions.*]

Luce. What a coil is there, Dromio? who are those at the
    gate?
Eph. Dro. Let my master in, Luce.
Luce.   Faith, no, he comes too late,
    And so tell your master.
Eph. Dro.   O Lord, I must laugh;   50
    Have at you with a proverb—shall I set in my staff?
Luce. Have at you with another, that's—when? can you tell?
Syr. Dro. If thy name be called Luce, Luce thou hast
    answer'd him well.

47. S.D. *Enter Luce*] F; *Luce within* | *Rowe*+ ; *Luce, the kitchen-maid, comes out upon
the balcony. N.C.S., conj. Dyce.   concealed . . . companions*] *This ed.; not in F.*   49–
51. late, . . . staff?*] *As Rowe 3;* late, . . . Master. | O . . . laugh, have . . . Proverbe, |
. . . staffe. F.

that he is still speaking about these
things three lines later. Palaeographically, this is not too difficult, especially
if the initial *o* was a mere dot; the
change of *an aime* to *a name* is easily
explicable as a minim misreading, and
there is no need to assert, as Wilson
does, that the text of F here is due to
dictation.

47. S.D. *Enter Luce*] Rowe omitted
this entry, and simply altered the
speech-heading to 'Luce within'; most
editors have followed suit. N.C.S.,
however, taking up Dyce's suggestion,
interprets this and Adriana's entry,
l. 60, also altered to 'within' by Rowe,
as being on to the balcony or gallery
above the stage. They point out that
no entry at all is provided for Dromio
of Syracuse, who is within the door on
the lower stage, and argue that Luce
and Adriana must come on elsewhere;
the arrangement is presumed to be for
a public stage, and they admit that
probably at Gray's Inn no balcony was
available. This interpretation derives
support from II. ii. 207, 'I'll dine *above*
with you to-day'. But Antipholus calls
on Luce to let him in (ll. 54, 57), as if
there is only a door between them; it
seems from their entries and dialogue

that Luce and Adriana advance to
where Dromio is, and perhaps some
structure or 'house' was arranged to
put them in view of the audience while
concealing, or appearing to conceal,
them from the characters outside the
'door'. F is not, however, explicit
enough to compel us to accept one
method of staging rather than another
here. See Introduction, p. xxxviii.

Luce] Luce appears only here (if
she is seen at all; see preceding note),
but Shakespeare was certainly thinking of her again in the references to
the wife of Dromio of Ephesus in III.
ii, where he changed her name to Nell,
at IV. iv. 72–3, and at V. i. 414. He may
have done this not for the sake of the
quibble at III. ii. 107–8, but in order
to avoid confusion between the names
Luciana and Luce. See Introduction,
p. xv.

48. *coil*] turmoil, disturbance.
51. *set . . . staff*] i.e. take up my
abode here, with a play on the action
itself, if Dromio here carries a staff, as
this line may indicate. The phrase is
proverbial (Tilley, S 804).
52. *when . . . tell?*] a phrase of
defiance, cf. *1H4*, II. i. 38 (Tilley,
T 88).

Eph. Ant. Do you hear, you minion, you'll let us in I trow?
Luce. I thought to have ask'd you.
Syr. Dro.   And you said, no.   55
Eph. Dro. So come, help, well struck, there was blow for
    blow.
Eph. Ant. Thou baggage, let me in.
Luce.   Can you tell for whose sake?
Eph. Dro. Master, knock the door hard.
Luce.   Let him knock till it ache.
Eph. Ant. You'll cry for this, minion, if I beat the door down.
Luce. What needs all that, and a pair of stocks in the town?

Enter ADRIANA [*to Luce*].

Adr. Who is that at the door that keeps all this noise?   61
Syr. Dro. By my troth, your town is troubled with unruly
    boys.
Eph. Ant. Are you there, wife? you might have come before.
Adr. Your wife, sir knave? go, get you from the door.
                        [*Exit with Luce.*]
Eph. Dro. If you went in pain, master, this knave would go
    sore.   65

54. trow] *Theobald;* hope *F.*   60. S.D. *Enter Adriana] F; Adr. Within | Rowe+ ;*
Adriana comes out upon the balcony | N.C.S., conj. Dyce.   *to Luce] This ed.; not in F.*
64. S.D. *Exit with Luce] Kittredge, after N.C.S.; not in F.*

54. *minion*] hussy, cf. *Gent.*, I. ii. 92.
54–6. *trow? . . . blow*] *hope* (F) is usually emended, as here, to *trow* for the
sake of the rhyme; the substitution of
a synonym in F is paralleled at II. i. 12
above; triple rhymes also occur at ll.
63–5, 75–7, etc. These lines, however,
remain obscure, and N.C.S., keeping
F, thinks Malone may have been right
in supposing that a line ending 'rope'
has dropped out. The point of Luce's
remark, 'I thought to have ask'd you',
is that she has just defied Dromio of
Ephesus with 'when? can you tell?',
and to the further question from his
master she replies with another mock-
ing retort (so Tilley, T 225, and see
Lyly, *Mother Bombie*, IV. ii. 36). Dromio
of Syracuse follows this up by remark-
ing that she has already said no to the

question Antipholus asks—see l. 49. I
take it that as he questions, Antipholus
beats on the door, and receives mental
blows in the form of saucy retorts as a
return for his physical blows; this
would explain 'blow for blow', l. 56.
But I am not sure that this interpretation could easily be made to emerge in
performance.

60. S.D. *Enter Adriana*] She is presumably visible to the audience, but
neither sees, nor is seen by, her husband. It is difficult to decide; see
S.D., l. 47 above, and note.

62. *boys*] fellows; 'lads' is still used
in this way, cf. *1H4*, II. iv. 268.

65. *in pain . . . sore*] Dromio's point
seems to be that if his master is 'sir
knave' to Adriana, then he, who is
properly a 'knave', i.e. servant, is

Angelo. Here is neither cheer, sir, nor welcome; we would
  fain have either.
Bal. In debating which was best, we shall part with neither.
Eph. Dro. They stand at the door, master; bid them welcome
  hither.
Eph. Ant. There is something in the wind that we cannot
  get in.
Eph. Dro. You would say so, master, if your garments were
  thin.   70
  Your cake here is warm within; you stand here in the
    cold;
  It would make a man mad as a buck to be so bought and
    sold.
Eph. Ant. Go fetch me something, I'll break ope the gate.
Syr. Dro. Break any breaking here and I'll break your
  knave's pate.
Eph. Dro. A man may break a word with you, sir, and words
  are but wind;   75
  Ay, and break it in your face, so he break it not behind.
Syr. Dro. It seems thou want'st breaking; out upon thee,
  hind.

71. cake here] *F;* cake *Dyce;* cake there *Cuningham.*   75. you, sir] *F2;* your sir *F.*

worse off still; if his master goes in pain, then he will suffer indeed. 'In pain' could mean 'under threat of punishment' (cf. the reference to the stocks, l. 60, and *2H6*, III. ii. 257), or simply 'punished' (cf. *Meas.*, II. iv. 86), and 'sore' suggests a worse punishment, another drubbing perhaps. J. C. Maxwell, *English Studies*, XXXII (1951), 30, sees the whole line as a roundabout way of saying, 'You are the knave she means'.

66. *cheer*] Cf. l. 19.
67. *part*] depart; a common usage.
68. *They . . . door*] i.e. Angelo and Balthasar; Dromio is, of course, jesting; they all stand at the door.
69. *in the wind*] i.e. some business going on (cf. Tilley, S 621), but Dromio takes up the remark as if a cold wind is indeed blowing.
71. *cake*] Probably a quibbling re-

ference to Adriana is intended; for the word's association with a woman (from its sense of 'dainty' or 'delicacy'?), cf. *Shr.*, I. i. 109ff., and *Troil.*, I. i. 15ff.
cake here] often emended to *cake there*, but the opposition is clear enough between inside and outside the door.
stand . . . cold] Cf. l. 37 above.
72. *mad . . . buck*] a proverbial phrase to describe anger (Tilley, B 697), perhaps related to 'horn-mad', cf. II. i. 57 and n.
bought and sold] tricked, betrayed (or, as N.C.S. notes, 'sold' in modern slang); cf. Tilley, B 787, and *R3*, v. iii. 305.
75. *break a word*] The phrase is usually *break a jest*, or *break news*, but it is altered here for the sake of the quibble.
words . . . wind] proverbial; Tilley, W 833–4.
77. *thou . . . breaking*] i.e. you deserve

Eph. Dro. Here's too much "out upon thee"; I pray thee let
    me in.
Syr. Dro. Ay, when fowls have no feathers, and fish have no
    fin.
Eph. Ant. Well, I'll break in; go, borrow me a crow.   80
Eph. Dro. A crow without feather; master, mean you so?
    For a fish without a fin, there's a fowl without a feather;
    If a crow help us in, sirrah, we'll pluck a crow together.
Eph. Ant. Go, get thee gone; fetch me an iron crow.
Bal. Have patience, sir, O, let it not be so;   85
    Herein you war against your reputation,
    And draw within the compass of suspect
    Th'unviolated honour of your wife.
    Once this,—your long experience of her wisdom,
    Her sober virtue, years and modesty,   90
    Plead on her part some cause to you unknown;
    And doubt not, sir, but she will well excuse
    Why at this time the doors are made against you.

---

78. "out upon thee"] *F* (out vpon thee), *Dyce.*   81. feather;...so?] *F4;* feather,
...so; *F.*   89. this,—] this *F;* this; *Rowe.*   89. her] *Pope;* your F.   91. her]
Rowe; your F.

a beating (cf. l. 74); and, you need
to be disciplined (broken in like a
horse).

   hind] in the pejorative sense 'boor',
usual in Shakespeare, as at *2H6*, III. ii.
271, 'rude, unpolish'd hinds'. N.C.S.
sees a reference to cutting up a deer
after the kill (*O.E.D., break,* v.2b),
which is quite inappropriate, though
hind was perhaps suggested by *buck,*
l. 72.

   79. *when . . . fin*] This looks proverbial, but Tilley does not record it.
There is a parallel in Warner, Act V
(Bullough, p. 33), where Menechmus
is bothered by the doctor asking him
what he drinks, and replies, 'Why
doest not as well aske mee whether I
eate bread, or cheese, or porredge, or
birdes that beare feathers, or fishes
that have finnes?'; see Introduction,
p. xxvi.

   83. *we'll . . . together*] proverbial =
settle our quarrel (Tilley, C 855); he
is addressing the other Dromio behind

the door, as his familiar 'sirrah' shows;
their enmity here contrasts with their
departure at the end of the play 'hand
in hand' (v. i. 426) in loving harmony;
see Introduction, p. xlix.

   85, 94. *patience . . . patience*] This
counsel of Balthasar's recalls Luciana's
advice to the jealous Adriana, cf. II. i.
9, 32, 41; Adriana and her husband
are alike in their impatience, their tendency to anger which, quickly aroused
by 'errors', drives them eventually to
outrage and violence; see IV. iv. 18–19
and Introduction, p. xliv.

   87. *suspect*] suspicion.

   89. *Once this*] = in short, to sum up,
from *once* meaning 'once for all', as at
Ado, I. i. 280, ''Tis once, thou lovest';
see Abbott, 57.

   89, 91. *her . . . her*] *your . . . your* F, an
obvious error, probably a slip of the
eye carrying over from the three uses
of *your* in ll. 86, 88, and 89.

   90. *years*] maturity.

   93. *made*] shut; cf. *AYL.,* IV. i. 144.

Be rul'd by me, depart in patience,
And let us to the Tiger all to dinner,   95
And about evening, come yourself alone
To know the reason of this strange restraint.
If by strong hand you offer to break in
Now in the stirring passage of the day,
A vulgar comment will be made of it;   100
And that supposed by the common rout
Against your yet ungalled estimation,
That may with foul intrusion enter in,
And dwell upon your grave when you are dead;
For slander lives upon succession,   105
For e'er hous'd where it gets possession.
Eph. Ant. You have prevail'd, I will depart in quiet,
And in despite of mirth mean to be merry.
I know a wench of excellent discourse,
Pretty and witty; wild and yet, too, gentle;   110
There will we dine. This woman that I mean,
My wife (but I protest, without desert)
Hath oftentimes upbraided me withal;
To her will we to dinner; [*to Angelo*] get you home

---

105. slander] *F;* lasting slander *conj. Johnson.*   106. hous'd . . . gets] *As F;*
hous'd . . . once gets *F2;* housed . . . gets *Singer.*   108. mirth] *F;* wrath *Theobald.*
110. yet, too, gentle] *Theobald, after Rowe 3;* yet too gentle *F.*   114. S.D. *to
Angelo] Clark and Glover; not in F.*

---

95. *Tiger*] Perhaps a London inn or
brothel bore this sign, but I have not
found a reference to one.

99. *stirring passage*] busy traffic (Cuningham). This use of passage = the
passing of people seems to have been
Shakespeare's innovation; cf. *Oth.*, v.
i. 37.

100. *vulgar*] public.

of] = on; Abbott, 175.

102. *ungalled*] uninjured; perhaps
Shakespeare's coinage, used only here
and at *Ham.*, III. ii. 266.

estimation] reputation.

103. *intrusion*] Cf. II. ii. 179 and n.

105. *lives upon succession*] 'i.e. by be-
getting other slanders to succeed it, so
that the line of its heirs is never extinct'
(N.C.S.); an expansion of the pro-

verb 'Envy never dies', Tilley, E 172.

106. *e'er*] necessary metrically (*euer*
F), making *possession* a four-syllable
word, like *succession* in the preceding
line.

108. *in . . . mirth*] i.e. in defiance of
mirth which runs counter to my present feelings; this extends the normal
sense of (*in*) *despite of*, meaning 'in
defiance of another's wish'; cf. *Meas.*,
I. ii. 23, 'Grace is grace, despite of all
controversy'. The phrase suggests his
difficulty in overcoming his anger, and
the extremity of his action in going to
the courtesan. Theobald's emendation of *mirth* to *wrath*, which has
attracted many editors, including
Cuningham and N.C.S., reduces the
line to commonplace.

And fetch the chain, by this I know 'tis made;   115
Bring it, I pray you, to the Porpentine,
For there's the house—that chain will I bestow
(Be it for nothing but to spite my wife)
Upon mine hostess there—good sir, make haste.
Since mine own doors refuse to entertain me,   120
I'll knock elsewhere, to see if they'll disdain me.
Angelo. I'll meet you at that place some hour hence.
Eph. Ant. Do so; this jest shall cost me some expense.   *Exeunt.*

SCENE II

Enter LUCIANA, *with* ANTIPHOLUS *of Syracuse.*

Luc. And may it be that you have quite forgot

116. Porpentine] Porcupine *Rowe*+.

Scene II

SCENE II] *Pope; not in F.*   S.D. *Luciana*] As *F2; Iuliana F.*   *Syracuse*] *Rowe;*
Siracusia F.   1. *Luc.*] *Rowe; Iulia F.*

115. *chain*] the 'carcanet' of l. 4, and cf. II. i. 106.

116. *Porpentine*] Shakespeare always uses this form for the modern 'porcupine'. Sisson, *New Readings*, I. 93, states that there was an inn called the Porpentine 'on Bankside... Shakespeare's audience probably knew it well.' N.C.S. (1962) notes that a London brothel also bore this name.

Scene II

SCENE II] No break in the action is indicated here—as one group of characters leaves, the other group enters from the house—through the door that Dromio of Syracuse has been guarding. Ll. 1–52 are in quatrains, and 53–70 in rhyming couplets; so Shakespeare modulates from the doggerel of the comic business attending the locking-out of Antipholus of Ephesus, through the blank verse of his and Balthasar's consideration of what to do, to a lyrical patterning in this attempt by Antipholus of Syracuse to make love to Luciana; this in turn is broken at the entry of Dromio at l. 70, with a return to the prose of a burlesque catechism, which is followed by a return to the blank verse of normal intercourse for the dealing between Antipholus and Angelo, though both Dromio and Antipholus go off on a rhyme.

S.D. and S.H. Luciana, Luc.] It is difficult to account for *Iuliana, Iulia.* (F) except as a slip of the author (perhaps momentarily thinking of Julia in *Two Gentlemen of Verona*?), but see Introduction, p. xv.

1–70.] These lines recall, in manner, in their patterning in rhyme, in the stychomythic exchange at ll. 53–60, the debate between Adriana and Luciana in II. i; see headnote to that scene. Luciana is, in effect, continuing that discussion on the proper relationship of husband and wife, but is hardly prepared for the response she gets.

A husband's office? shall, Antipholus,
Even in the spring of love, thy love-springs rot?
Shall love in building grow so ruinous?
If you did wed my sister for her wealth,   5
Then for her wealth's sake use her with more kindness;
Or if you like elsewhere, do it by stealth,
Muffle your false love with some show of blindness.
Let not my sister read it in your eye;
Be not thy tongue thy own shame's orator;   10
Look sweet, speak fair, become disloyalty;
Apparel vice like virtue's harbinger;
Bear a fair presence, though your heart be tainted;
Teach sin the carriage of a holy saint,
Be secret false; what need she be acquainted?   15
What simple thief brags of his own attaint?
'Tis double wrong to truant with your bed,
And let her read it in thy looks at board;
Shame hath a bastard fame, well managed;
Ill deeds is doubled with an evil word.   20

2. Antipholus,] *F* (*Antipholus*); Antipholis, hate *Hanmer*.   4. building] *Theo-*
bald; buildings *F*.   ruinous] *Capell, conj. Theobald;* ruinate *F*.   16. attaint]
Rowe; attaine *F*.   20. is] *F;* are *F2*+.

3. *love-springs*] The image is of shoots
of a tree (*O.E.D.*, sb.[1] 9; and cf. *Lucr.*,
950, 'To dry the old oak's sap and
cherish springs') which accounts for
'rot', and the leap to 'building' in the
next line.
    4. *building*] an image used several
times of love by Shakespeare; cf. *Sonn.*
cxxiv. 5, *Ant.*, iii. ii. 30, and *Gent.*, v.
iv. 7–10, where Valentine wishes for
the absent Silvia to return to the 'mansion' of his breast, 'Lest, growing ruinous, the building fall'.
    ruinous] F's *ruinate* is usually emend-
ed, as here, for the sake of the rhyme.
Theobald's suggestion 'Antipholus
hate?' as an alternative emendation
(l. 2) is preferred by N.C.S. as *ruinate*
has 'the true Shakespearian ring'; in
fact, the word is used only as a verb by
Shakespeare, who always employs the
adjective *ruinous*, as in the similar

image from *Gent.*, cited in the previous
note.
    8–9. *Muffle* . . . *eye*] The sense jumps
from muffle = conceal to its special
meaning, to blindfold (cf. *Rom.*, i. i.
169), and so to the rest of the image.
    9–10. *Let* . . . *orator*] quasi-prover-
bial, cf. Tilley, T 140, 392.
    11. *become disloyalty*] i.e. be disloyal
with grace.
    12. *Apparel* . . . *harbinger*] quasi-pro-
verbial, cf. Tilley, V 44, 'Vice is often
clothed in virtue's habit' (first citation
1616).
    13. *Bear* . . . *tainted*] cf. Tilley, F 3,
'Fair face, foul heart'.
    14. *carriage*] demeanour.
    16. *attaint*] corruption, or disgrace.
    17. *truant with*] be unfaithful to; an
odd usage, not elsewhere found in
Shakespeare.
    20. *Ill* . . . *word*] quasi-proverbial, cf.

Alas, poor women, make us but believe
(Being compact of credit) that you love us;
Though others have the arm, show us the sleeve;
We in your motion turn, and you may move us.
Then, gentle brother, get you in again;   25
Comfort my sister, cheer her, call her wife;
'Tis holy sport to be a little vain
When the sweet breath of flattery conquers strife.

Syr. Ant. Sweet mistress, what your name is else I know not,
Nor by what wonder you do hit of mine;   30
Less in your knowledge and your grace you show not
Than our earth's wonder, more than earth divine.
Teach me, dear creature, how to think and speak;
Lay open to my earthy gross conceit,
Smother'd in errors, feeble, shallow, weak,   35

21. but] *Pope 2;* not *F.*   26. wife] *F2;* wise *F.*   29. *Syr. Ant.*] *S. Anti.* | *F.*

Tilley, W 800, 'Fine words dress ill deeds', 811, 822.

Ill deeds is] See I. i. 87 (Abbott, 333).

22. *compact of credit*] made of trust, and so eager to believe. For *compact* in this sense, cf. *MND.*, v. i. 8.

23. *Though . . . sleeve*] Cf. II. ii. 173, where Adriana fastens on her husband's sleeve as a vine on an elm, as if that were to possess him; Luciana, present then, recalls the image now, and develops it further.

24. *motion*] commonly used of the movements of heavenly bodies, and perhaps here carries the sense 'orbit'.

27. *be . . . vain*] to use empty words, the 'flattery' of the next line.

29–52.] T. W. Baldwin traces the pattern of Antipholus's argument to the advice of Erasmus on writing love-letters; see *Shakspere's Small Latine*, II. 282–4.

30. *hit of*] hit on, guess; for the common confusion of *of* and *on*, see Abbott, 175.

32. *our . . . divine*] Douce suggested that this might be a compliment to Queen Elizabeth. The play may have been performed before her; it is inter-esting that the Chamber Accounts list a payment to Shakespeare, William Kemp, and Richard Burbage on be-half of their company of players for a performance at Court on Innocents' Day, 1594 (28 December), the same day on which the play was performed at Gray's Inn (Chambers, *E.S.*, IV. 56, 164, regards the Court entry as a mistake for 27 December). The play was performed at Court on Innocents' Day, 1604. See Appendix II, pp. 115–16.

34–7. *gross conceit . . . pure truth*] 'gross conceit' is the dull apprehension which is all that mortals have in relation to the gods, in Plato's allegory of the cave, *Republic*, Book 7, or to the soul liberated from 'this muddy vesture of decay' (*Mer.V.*, v. i. 64) in Christian terms; but this is opposed to Antipholus's 'pure truth' of soul, his absolute knowledge that it is Luciana he loves.

35. *errors*] catching up the title of the play, as at II. ii. 184, and extending the meaning of *errors* beyond merely accidental mistakes to include failures of judgement, the 'errors' that result from the limitations of man; see preceding note.

The folded meaning of your words' deceit.
Against my soul's pure truth, why labour you
To make it wander in an unknown field?
Are you a god? would you create me new?
Transform me then, and to your power I'll yield.   40
But if that I am I, then well I know
Your weeping sister is no wife of mine,
Nor to her bed no homage do I owe;
Far more, far more to you do I decline;
O, train me not, sweet mermaid, with thy note   45
To drown me in thy sister's flood of tears;
Sing, siren, for thyself, and I will dote;
Spread o'er the silver waves thy golden hairs,
And as a bed I'll take thee, and there lie,
And in that glorious supposition think   50
He gains by death that hath such means to die;

46. sister's] *F2;* sister *F.*   49. bed] *F2;* bud *F.*   thee] *F;* them *Capell, conj. Edwards.*

36. *folded*] hidden, cf. *Tit.,* II. iii. 266.

39–40. *create . . . Transform*] This is metamorphosis of a different kind from the Dromios' sense of being changed to asses, see ll. 72–80 below, II. ii. 199, III. i. 18; Antipholus would willingly change his identity to serve her. For its relevance in the play's structure, see Introduction, p. xliii.

44. *decline*] incline; an obsolete usage (*O.E.D.,* v.4); here it seems to carry the sense of turning away from Adriana.

45–66.] a complex passage; see I. ii. 35–8, II. ii. 123–9, II. ii. 142 and notes. Antipholus had been discontented because he felt lost, like a drop of water in an ocean; now he rejects a union with Adriana in a similar image of drowning in her tears. At the same time he desires another kind of dissolution—is lost ('mated', l. 54) in a different sense, as he would become one with Luciana ('I am thee', l. 66); and finds a new identity, too, in his love, is in a fine sense transformed and made 'new' (l. 39). His claims are here, of course, exaggerated, and recall Adriana's too

possessive feeling for her husband (cf. l. 62 with II. ii. 123), but he has the excuse of not knowing whether she is goddess, siren, or woman.

45. *train*] entice.

mermaid] siren, as commonly, cf. *Lucr.,* 1411. Notice how Antipholus first thinks of Luciana as a goddess belonging to a higher sphere of existence than his own (l. 39), then wonders if she is deliberately trying to lead him astray, like a siren, drawing him to confusion by claiming him for her sister.

49. *bed*] This generally accepted emendation of *bud* (F) is not wholly satisfactory, since it makes almost ludicrously concrete what is already suggested in the full image; on the other hand, it provides a proper antecedent for 'there'. Antipholus wants to 'take' Luciana herself, and *bud* fits this meaning in its common use as an image for a maid, cf. *Rom.,* I. ii. 29, and *Lucr.,* 848. It is tempting to restore *bud,* and to take 'hairs' as the antecedent of 'there'.

51. *death . . . die*] playing on the com-

Let love, being light, be drowned if she sink.
Luc. What, are you mad that you do reason so?
Syr. Ant. Not mad, but mated, how I do not know.
Luc. It is a fault that springeth from your eye.　　55
Syr. Ant. For gazing on your beams, fair sun, being by.
Luc. Gaze where you should, and that will clear your sight.
Syr. Ant. As good to wink, sweet love, as look on night.
Luc. Why call you me love? Call my sister so.
Syr. Ant. Thy sister's sister.
Luc.　　　　　　　　That's my sister.
Syr. Ant.　　　　　　　　　　　　No,　　60
　　It is thyself, mine own self's better part,
　　Mine eye's clear eye, my dear heart's dearer heart,
　　My food, my fortune, and my sweet hope's aim,

52. she] *F; he Rowe.*　　54. *Syr. Ant.*] *Ant. | F (Ant. or Anti. to end of scene).*
57. where] *Rowe 2+ ; when F.*　　60–1. sister. No, | It] *Pope; sister. | No: it F.*

mon use of *die* in reference to the consummation of love, cf. *Sonn.* XCII. 12, 'Happy to have thy love, happy to die.'

52. *love . . . sink*] Malone compared *Ven.*, 149–50: 'Love is a spirit all compact of fire, / Not gross to sink, but light, and will aspire.' This illustrates something of the play on senses of *light*, which is opposed to heaviness, to darkness (as *drowned* may mean extinguished), and carries overtones of wantonness (as in 'light of love'). The line thus combines Antipholus's passion for Luciana with his suspicion of her as a siren luring him on by her deceit.

53.] After the quatrains of the two long speeches, the verse changes to couplets with this transition to the quick interchange of stichomythia.

reason] talk, as at *R3*, IV. iv. 537, 'while we reason here / A royal battle might be won and lost'.

54. *mated*] quibbling on the senses 'confounded, overcome' (cf. V. i. 282 below) and 'partnered' (wedded).

55–7. *It . . . sight*] The sight was regarded as the chief of the senses, and it was a commonplace of poetic convention, inherited from the literature

of courtly love, that beauty, impinging on a man's eye, might cause him at once to fall in love; it was also respectable psychology, and Burton, *Anatomy of Melancholy*, ed. A. R. Shilleto (1896), III. 76, says 'what prerogative this beauty hath, of what power and sovereignty it is . . . no man doubts of these matters; the question is, how and by what means beauty produceth this effect? By sight: the eye betrays the soul, and is both active and passive in this business; it wounds and is wounded, is an especial cause and instrument, both in the subject and the object'. Of course, Luciana regards the sudden passion of Antipholus not as a rational love, but as mere lust; a common Shakespearian meaning of her word *fault* is 'offence', 'sin'.

58. *wink*] close one's eyes; N.C.S. compares *Gent.*, V. ii. 13–14.

61. *better part*] Cf. II. ii. 120–3 and n.; Antipholus echoes here what Adriana earlier said to him, but applies the phrase to Luciana.

62. *Mine . . . heart*] a line reminiscent of the conceits of *Sonn.* XLVI, which decides 'The clear eye's moiety and the dear heart's part' in a mistress.

My sole earth's heaven, and my heaven's claim.
Luc. All this my sister is, or else should be.   65
Syr. Ant. Call thyself sister, sweet, for I am thee;
    Thee will I love, and with thee lead my life;
    Thou hast no husband yet, nor I no wife—
    Give me thy hand.
Luc.   O, soft, sir, hold you still;
    I'll fetch my sister to get her good will.   *Exit.*   70

Enter DROMIO *of Syracuse.*

Syr. Ant. Why, how now Dromio, where run'st thou so fast?
Syr. Dro. Do you know me sir? Am I Dromio? Am I your
    man? Am I myself?
Syr. Ant. Thou art Dromio, thou art my man, thou art
    thyself.   75
Syr. Dro. I am an ass, I am a woman's man, and besides
    myself.
Syr. Ant. What woman's man? and how besides thyself?
Syr. Dro. Marry, sir, besides myself, I am due to a
    woman, one that claims me, one that haunts me, one   80
    that will have me.
Syr. Ant. What claim lays she to thee?

66. am] *F; mean Pope; aim Capell; claim conj. Cuningham.*   70. S.D. *Dromio of Syracuse] As Rowe; Dromio, Siracusia | F.*   71–7.] *As Rowe 2; verse in F.*   72. *Syr. Dro.] S. Dro. | F.*   76. *Syr. Dro.] Dro. | F (so to end of scene).*

64. *My . . . claim*] my only heaven on earth, and my claim on heaven hereafter (Cuningham).

66. *I am thee*] often emended, but, as N.C.S. notes, Antipholus has just identified himself with Luciana as his 'better part', and counters her 'All this my sister is' with a further conceit; let Luciana call herself the woman she says he is married to, 'Call yourself "sister" if you will, for it is in you that I have lost my identity'; cf. Introduction, p. xliii, and ll. 39–40 above and n.

76ff.] Dromio's situation parallels and parodies that of his master; Antipholus is claimed by Adriana, and by Luciana for her sister, while Dromio

is claimed by a kitchen-wench; as Antipholus speaks of being transformed through love, created new (l. 39), so Dromio too talks of being metamorphosed—but into an ass, or beast (l. 84), or dog (l. 145). It is another link in the chain of images of transformation or loss of identity, cf. II. i. 14 and n., and Introduction, p. xliv.

76–7. *besides myself*] The modern form is 'beside'; Dromio is quibbling on the senses 'in addition to myself,' and 'out of my wits'.

80–3. *claims . . . claim*] contrasting with Antipholus's 'claim' to Luciana above, and comically underscoring both this and Adriana's earlier claims upon her husband (II. ii).

Syr. Dro. Marry sir, such claim as you would lay to your
horse; and she would have me as a beast, not that I
being a beast she would have me, but that she being a   85
very beastly creature lays claim to me.

Syr. Ant. What is she?

Syr. Dro. A very reverend body; ay, such a one as a man
may not speak of, without he say "sir-reverence";
I have but lean luck in the match, and yet is she a   90
wondrous fat marriage.

Syr. Ant. How dost thou mean, a fat marriage?

Syr. Dro. Marry, sir, she's the kitchen wench, and all
grease, and I know not what use to put her to but to
make a lamp of her, and run from her by her own   95
light. I warrant her rags and the tallow in them will
burn a Poland winter; if she lives till doomsday she'll
burn a week longer than the whole world.

Syr. Ant. What complexion is she of?

Syr. Dro. Swart like my shoe, but her face nothing like   100
so clean kept; for why? she sweats, a man may
go over-shoes in the grime of it.

Syr. Ant. That's a fault that water will mend.

Syr. Dro. No sir, 'tis in grain; Noah's flood could not do
it.   105

85-6. *a beast . . . beastly*] Kökeritz, p. 88, notes a quibble here on *abased* (cf. *Tim.*, IV. iii. 322), and on *baste* (the sounds were similar, cf. *grease*, l. 94 and n.); as *a beast* refers back to *ass* (= beast of burden), l. 76; the phrase could apply to her or to him, and Dromio takes care to expand it, cf. *Mother Bombie*, IV. ii. 168ff.

88. *reverend*] *reverent* (F) was the earlier form of the word; F is not consistent, cf. v. i. 134, and the modern spelling has been adopted throughout.

89. *sir-reverence*] a corruption of 'save (your) reverence', a phrase of apology or respect introducing an offensive remark; also a euphemism for dung, as at *Rom.*, I. iv. 42, 'the mire of this sir-reverence love'. See Tilley, R 93.

94. *grease*] quibbling, as N.C.S.

notes, on *grace* (cf. Kökeritz, p. 110).

98. *week*] Cuningham sees a quibble here on *wick* (so Kökeritz, p. 153).

99-143.] This catechism is probably indebted, like the similar catalogue of the qualities of Launce's mistress in *Gent.*, III. i. 293ff., to Lyly's *Midas*, I. ii. 19ff., where Licio unfolds 'every wrinkle of my mistres disposition' in comic vein, and possibly also to Friar John's geographical account of the head and body of Panurge in Rabelais, *Gargantua and Pantagruel*, Book III, Chapter 28.

100. *Swart*] swarthy, dark.

102. *over-shoes*] shoe-deep, cf. *Gent.*, I. i. 24; proverbially = to be deeply immersed in something (Tilley, S 380).

104. *in grain*] literally, fast dyed (dyed in grain); hence, ingrained, inherent, cf. *Tw.N.*, I. v. 222.

H

Syr. Ant. What's her name?

Syr. Dro. Nell, sir; but her name and three quarters, that's an ell and threequarters, will not measure her from hip to hip.

Syr. Ant. Then she bears some breadth?   110

Syr. Dro. No longer from head to foot than from hip to hip; she is spherical, like a globe; I could find out countries in her.

Syr. Ant. In what part of her body stands Ireland?

Syr. Dro. Marry, sir, in her buttocks; I found it out by   115
the bogs.

Syr. Ant. Where Scotland?

Syr. Dro. I found it by the barrenness, hard in the palm of the hand.

Syr. Ant. Where France?   •   120

---

107. and] *Theobald, conj. Thirlby;* is F.

107. *Nell*] Shakespeare clearly intended her to be the same as Luce (see IV. iv. 72 and note); he altered her name for the sake of the quibble on *ell*, and perhaps to avoid possible confusion with Luciana, but see also Introduction, p. xv. Nell never appears on stage, but is referred to again at the end of the play, v. i. 414–16.

108. *ell*] 1¼ yards.

118. *barrenness, hard*] N.C.S. unnecessarily emends to 'barren-nesses', arguing that the idea of headlands gives point to 'hard' as suggesting callosities in the hand, and describes Scotland. This makes clear the point, at any rate. Compare the proverb, 'A moist hand argues fruitfulness' (Tilley, H 86).

120-2. *France? . . . heir*] It is usually argued that this must have been written between 1589 and 1593, when there was civil war in France between Henry of Navarre and the Catholic league led by the Duke of Guise. Henry III of France named Henry of Navarre as his heir in 1589, and he succeeded to the throne in 1593. In fact, contemporary publications on the war make it clear that a civil war was regarded

as taking place in France for at least three years before 1589, and some years after 1593. As Baldwin noted, an interest in French affairs is shown in *Love's Labour's Lost*, which seems to reflect in its court of Navarre the persons of Henry and some of his followers; Richard David, the editor of the Arden edition (1951, pp. xxviiiff.) points out that the interest in Henry was at its height in England in 1591, that the English troops sent to France in support of Henry were finally withdrawn in November 1593, and that in consequence 'A playwright would be most tempted to write a play about Navarre in 1591–3'; on other evidence, however, he dates the composition of this play in 1593–4. So here the reference to France cannot be taken as rigid evidence for dating the play; but see Introduction, p. xx. Dr Johnson was no doubt right in seeing an allusion here to venereal disease (the 'French disease'), or rather to the effects of it, suggesting that *armed* = with eruptions, and *reverted* = turned back on itself, implying a receding forehead (and loss of hair); cf. *MND.*, I. ii. 86. A further complication might be a possible

Syr. Dro. In her forehead, armed and reverted, making
   war against her heir.
Syr. Ant. Where England?
Syr. Dro. I looked for the chalky cliffs, but I could find
   no whiteness in them. But I guess it stood in her   125
   chin, by the salt rheum that ran between France
   and it.
Syr. Ant. Where Spain?
Syr. Dro. Faith, I saw it not; but I felt it hot in her
   breath.   130
Syr. Ant. Where America, the Indies?
Syr. Dro. O, sir, upon her nose, all o'er-embellished
   with rubies, carbuncles, sapphires, declining their
   rich aspect to the hot breath of Spain, who sent
   whole armadoes of carracks to be ballast at her   135
   nose.
Syr. Ant. Where stood Belgia, the Netherlands?
Syr. Dro. O, sir, I did not look so low. To conclude, this

122. heir] *F* (heire); haire *F2*.   124. chalky] *F2*; chalkle *F*.   135. carracks]
F (Carrects), *Hanmer.*   ballast] *F*; ballasted *Capell.*

allusion to a strange event of 1588, recorded in *A myraculous . . . discourse of a
Woman . . . in the midst of whose fore-head
. . . there groweth out a crooked Horne*
(1588); the horn 'crooketh towards
her right eye, and groweth so fast, that
she is fayne to have it cut' (A2ʳ–A2ᵛ).
I do not believe that Shakespeare is referring to this occurrence.

   124. *chalky cliffs*] i.e. teeth.
   126. *rheum*] watery matter discharg-
ed from the eyes or nose; perhaps
quibbling on *rhumb*, a line 'drawn
through a point on a map or chart and
indicating the course of an object
moving always in the same direction'
(*O.E.D.*); see *Shakespeare's England*, I.
174, and Introduction, p. xx n. 1.
   131. *America*] the only specific reference to America in Shakespeare's writ-
ings; here, like the 'Indies', named in
reference to its proverbial wealth.
   133–4. *declining . . . aspect*] implying
a hook nose?
   135. *armadoes of carracks*] fleets of

galleons; *armado* was the usual early
form of the word, which properly refers to ships of war; a *carrack* (F's *Carrects* was an alternative form of a word
that was spelt in numerous ways in
English) was a large merchant-ship, a
galleon, fitted also as a warship. Shakespeare may have had the great Armada of 1588 in mind in using this
phrase, or possibly the Great Carrack,
the *Madre de Dios*, a huge Portuguese
galleon captured and brought to England in September 1592 (G. B. Harrison, *Elizabethan Journal* (1955), pp.
160–5).
   135. *ballast*] = ballasted, i.e. loaded;
the *-ed* of the past participle was often
omitted from words ending in *-t* or *-d*;
see Abbott, 342.
   137. *Belgia*] loosely used for an area
which included Holland and the present Belgium (established in 1830),
and known as Low Germany; cf. *3H6*,
IV. viii. 1–2. Properly, the territory in-
habited by the Belgae.

drudge or diviner laid claim to me, called me
Dromio, swore I was assured to her, told me what   140
privy marks I had about me, as the mark of my
shoulder, the mole in my neck, the great wart on my
left arm, that I, amazed, ran from her as a witch.
And I think if my breast had not been made of faith,
   and my heart of steel,
She had transform'd me to a curtal dog, and made me
   turn i'th'wheel.   145
Syr. Ant. Go, hie thee presently, post to the road;
And if the wind blow any way from shore
I will not harbour in this town to-night.
If any bark put forth, come to the mart,
Where I will walk till thou return to me;   150
If everyone knows us and we know none,
'Tis time I think to trudge, pack and be gone.

144–5.] *As Knight+ ; prose in F.*   144. faith] *F; flint Hanmer.*   145. curtal] *F* (Curtull).

139. *diviner*] magician; not used elsewhere by Shakespeare. See l. 155 below and n. As Antipholus thought Luciana might be a goddess or siren, so Dromio thinks of 'Nell' as diviner or witch (l. 143); see note to l. 76 above.

140. *assured*] betrothed.

141. *of*] = on, as commonly (Abbott, 175).

143. *witch*] As Antipholus is drawn to Luciana as goddess or siren, disclaiming Adriana, so Dromio runs from the kitchen-wench as a witch in a comic reversal and parody of his master's situation. Thus for both of them Antipholus's prejudice about the city as a place of witchcraft (I. ii. 97ff.) is steadily confirmed; see l. 155 below, and Introduction, pp. xlivff.

144–5. *breast ... wheel*] Probably another echo (cf. II. i. 7–25 and n.) of *Ephesians*, vi. 11ff., 'Put on the whole armour of God that ye may be able to stand against the assaults of the devil . . . and your loins girde about with verity, and having on the brest plate of righteousness... Above all take the

shield of faith, wherewith yee may quench all the fyrie darts of the wicked'. See Appendix I, p. 115.

145. *curtal dog*] a dog with its tail docked, a common dog. With this talk of transformation, cf. above, ll. 76ff., and note; see also Introduction, p. xlv.

turn i'th'wheel] i.e. tread a wheel turning a spit; cf. the proverb, 'A covetous man is like a dog in a wheel, that roasts meat for others', Tilley, M 87.

146. *presently*] instantly.

road] harbour, roadstead.

147. *And if*] = if; a common usage, cf. Abbott, 101–3.

148. *harbour*] lodge.

151–2.] Antipholus had said, I. ii. 30, 'I will go lose myself', believing himself to be unknown in Ephesus, only to discover that everyone claims acquaintance with him. He can explain this foisting of an unwanted identity on him only in terms of witchcraft (l. 155).

152. *trudge, pack ... be gone*] These are synonymous.

Syr. Dro. As from a bear a man would run for life,
   So fly I from her that would be my wife.   *Exit.*
Syr. Ant. There's none but witches do inhabit here,   155
   And therefore 'tis high time that I were hence;
   She that doth call me husband, even my soul
   Doth for a wife abhor. But her fair sister,
   Possess'd with such a gentle sovereign grace,
   Of such enchanting presence and discourse,   160
   Hath almost made me traitor to myself;
   But lest myself be guilty to self-wrong,
   I'll stop mine ears against the mermaid's song.

      Enter ANGELO *with the chain.*

Angelo. Master Antipholus.
Syr. Ant.   Ay, that's my name.
Angelo. I know it well, sir; lo, here's the chain;   165
   I thought to have ta'en you at the Porpentine,
   The chain unfinish'd made me stay thus long.
Syr. Ant. What is your will that I shall do with this?
Angelo. What please yourself, sir; I have made it for you.
Syr. Ant. Made it for me, sir? I bespoke it not.   170
Angelo. Not once, nor twice, but twenty times you have.
   Go home with it, and please your wife withal,

156. high] hie *F.*   162. to] *F; of Pope.*   164. Master] *F* (M^r).   165. here's]
F; here is *Pope.*

154, 157–8.] The parallel between the situations of Dromio and Antipholus, each fleeing from a wife he abhors, is emphasized here; see above, l. 76 and note.

155. *witches*] applied to both sexes; cf. IV. iv. 145 and I. ii. 95ff. The sense of Ephesus as a place of sorcery is carefully maintained in the speeches of Antipholus and Dromio of Syracuse; see ll. 139 and 145 above.

158–63.] Cf. ll. 34–7 and n. If Antipholus loses himself in confusion of identities in Ephesus (see note to ll. 151–2), he also finds a new identity in his love for Luciana (cf. 'I am thee', l. 66), who yet tempts him to 'self-wrong' if she is a witch; hence the

double image of her here, full of 'sovereign grace', like a goddess, and at the same time a mermaid; the word 'enchanting' nicely links the two ways in which he sees her. See Introduction, p. xliii.

162. *guilty to*] = guilty to the extent of, or perhaps simply guilty of; the phrase occurs again at *Wint.*, IV. iv. 530.

163. *stop . . . song*] As Ulysses stopped the ears of his crew with wax, so that they could pass the sirens safely (*Odyssey*, Book XII).

mermaid's song] Cf. ll. 45–7 above.
166. *Porpentine*] See III. i. 116 and n.
169. *What . . . yourself*] = what (it may) please you; cf. Abbott, 254.

And soon at supper-time I'll visit you,
And then receive my money for the chain.
Syr. Ant. I pray you, sir, receive the money now,   175
     For fear you ne'er see chain nor money more.
Angelo. You are a merry man, sir; fare you well.   *Exit.*
Syr. Ant. What I should think of this I cannot tell;
     But this I think, there's no man is so vain
     That would refuse so fair an offer'd chain.   180
     I see a man here needs not live by shifts
     When in the streets he meets such golden gifts.
     I'll to the mart, and there for Dromio stay;
     If any ship put out, then straight, away.   *Exit.*

---

173. *soon*] See I. ii. 26 and n.

176. *ne'er . . . more*] Angelo's discomfiture begins in the next scene, for which these lines serve as ironic preparation.

179. *there's . . . vain*] Such elliptical expressions are common, cf. *R3*, I. i. 71, 'I think there is no man is secure', and

Abbott, 382, 400.

vain] silly; cf. 'vain fool', *Lr.*, IV. ii. 61.

180. *so . . . offer'd*] The modern construction would be 'a chain so fairly offered'; see Abbott, 422.

184. *straight*] at once.

ACT IV

SCENE I

Enter [Second] Merchant, [the] Goldsmith [ANGELO], and an Officer.

Sec. Mer. You know since Pentecost the sum is due,
And since I have not much importun'd you,
Nor now I had not, but that I am bound
To Persia, and want guilders for my voyage;
Therefore make present satisfaction,   5
Or I'll attach you by this officer.
Angelo. Even just the sum that I do owe to you
Is growing to me by Antipholus,
And in the instant that I met with you
He had of me a chain; at five o'clock   10

ACT IV

Scene 1

ACT IV SCENE I] *Pope; Actus Quartus. Scœna Prima. F.*   S.D. *Second*] *Dyce; not in F.   the*] *not in F.   Angelo*] *not in F.*   1. *Sec. Mer.*] *Mar. | F.*   7. *Angelo*] *Gold. | F* (*so throughout scene*).

SCENE I] A blank-verse scene, which forwards the action, and extends confusion and disorder out beyond the relationships of husband and wife, master and servant, into a wider sphere, see note to ll. 41–80. There is less rhyme, and less good humour, in this act than in Acts II and III, as the sense of disorder, frustration, and witchcraft grows, leading to outbreaks of violence and serious enmity in IV. iv especially.

Entry. [Second] Merchant] This is evidently not the same merchant as the one who befriended Antipholus of Syracuse in I. ii, for the latter knew all about the city of Ephesus, while this one has to ask, v. i. 4, how Antipholus (of Ephesus, but they are twins) is 'esteem'd here in the city'. However, they may have been played by the same actor, and could still be so played.

1. *Pentecost*] Whitsuntide; another hint of a Christian colouring.

4. *guilders*] See I. i. 8 and n.

5. *present*] instant.

6. *attach*] arrest.

8. *growing*] i.e. growing due; cf. IV. iv. 119.

10. *five o'clock*] Shakespeare takes care to point to this hour as the resolution of action, cf. I. ii. 26, III. ii. 173, and v. i. 118. It was a usual supper

I shall receive the money for the same.
Pleaseth you walk with me down to his house,
I will discharge my bond, and thank you too.

Enter ANTIPHOLUS *of Ephesus* [*and*] DROMIO *from the*
Courtesan's.

Offic. That labour may you save; see where he comes.
Eph. Ant. While I go to the goldsmith's house, go thou   15
And buy a rope's end; that will I bestow
Among my wife and her confederates
For locking me out of my doors by day—
But soft, I see the goldsmith; get thee gone,
Buy thou a rope and bring it home to me.   20
Eph. Dro. I buy a thousand pound a year, I buy a rope! *Exit.*
Eph. Ant. A man is well holp up that trusts to you;
I promised your presence and the chain,
But neither chain nor goldsmith came to me.
Belike you thought our love would last too long   25
If it were chain'd together, and therefore came not.
Angelo. Saving your merry humour, here's the note

13. S.D. *of Ephesus*] *Ephes. F.*   *and*] not in F.   15. *Eph. Ant.*] *Ant. | F.*   17. her]
Rowe; their *F.*   21. *Eph. Dro.*] *Dro. | F.*   23. I] *F;* You *Dyce.*

hour, as testified by W. Harrison, *De-*
scription of England (1587), cited J. D.
Wilson, *Life in Shakespeare's England*
(Penguin Edition, 1944, p. 282), 'the
nobility, gentry and students do ordi-
narily go to dinner at eleven before
noon, and to supper at five . . .'; cf.
Mer.V., II. ii. 102. F has *a clocke*, the
common spelling, and still a common
pronunciation. Cf. Abbott, 140.
    12. *Pleaseth*] = if it please, the
indicative used for the subjunctive; see
Abbott, 361.
    13. S.D. from the Courtesan's] That
is, probably, from the door marked by
the sign of the Porcupine (cf. III. i. 116).
The direction may be an author's literary S.D., but the staging of the play,
as suggested by the text, seems to indicate the use of three doors or areas
marked by signs representing the courtesan's house, Antipholus's house (the
Phoenix), and the Priory; see Intro-

duction, p. xxxiv.
    21. *I . . . rope*] unexplained. The
point of the jest may simply lie in its
reference to 'bestow', l. 16; in buying
a rope, Dromio buys the equivalent of
a large sum of money, and provides for
'paying' Adriana and her associates;
cf. Dromio's opening line on re-enter-
ing at IV. iv. 10, 'Here's that, I warrant
you, will pay them all'. N.C.S. suggests that in buying a rope, Dromio
will buy 'a thousand pounds (i.e.
blows) a year', but *pound* was not used
in this sense before the 19th century.
It is conceivable that *pound* was somehow substituted for *marks*, which would
make a quibble of this kind, echoing
I. ii. 81.
    22. *holp*] = holpen, the strong past
participle of *help*; see Abbott, 343, and
V. i. 388 below.
    26. *together*] See note on *whe'er*, l. 60
below.

How much your chain weighs to the utmost carrat,
The fineness of the gold, and chargeful fashion,
Which doth amount to three odd ducats more   30
Than I stand debted to this gentleman;
I pray you see him presently discharg'd,
For he is bound to sea and stays but for it.

Eph. Ant. I am not furnish'd with the present money;
Besides, I have some business in the town;   35
Good signior, take the stranger to my house,
And with you take the chain, and bid my wife
Disburse the sum on the receipt thereof;
Perchance I will be there as soon as you.

Angelo. Then you will bring the chain to her yourself.   40

Eph. Ant. No, bear it with you, lest I come not time enough.

Angelo. Well sir, I will. Have you the chain about you?

Eph. Ant. And if I have not, sir, I hope you have,
Or else you may return without your money.

Angelo. Nay, come, I pray you, sir, give me the chain;   45
Both wind and tide stays for this gentleman,
And I, to blame, have held him here too long.

28. carrat] *F* (charect).   34. *Eph. Ant.*] *Anti. F (Anti., Ant., or An. to end of scene).*
46. stays] *F;* stay *Rowe 2.*   47. to blame] *F3;* too blame *F.*

29. *chargeful*] costly.
30. *ducats*] Gold coins of several European countries were so called, though the original ducats were Italian, the first gold ones Venetian. It is interesting that Shakespeare uses guilders in a general sense for money (I. i. 8, and l. 4 above), and now switches to ducats for a precise figure. Ducats remain the coinage for the rest of the play, except for a passage of jesting on the word *angel* at IV. iii. 19ff.
31. *debted*] i.e. indebted.
32. *presently*] instantly.
36. *signior*] Perhaps the Italian name Angelo made Shakespeare think of Italy, change the play's currency into ducats (l. 30), and use this form of address; cf. III. i. I, where Angelo is called 'signior' on his first appearance in the play.
39. *Perchance I will*] See Abbott, 319.

41-80.] The strong emphasis on mistiming here continues an element in the play's action that began in I. ii. 41ff., and was given prominence in the mock-dialectic on time at II. ii. 54ff. Now the serious and public effects of mistiming in disorder begin to emerge, as the Second Merchant and Angelo become involved with Antipholus, and the last two are put under arrest; see Introduction, pp. xlv ff.
41. *time enough*] in time.
46. *wind . . . gentleman*] alluding to the proverb, 'Time and tide stay for no man', Tilley, T 323; cf. the play on this in *Gent.*, II. iii. 30ff.
stays] Cf. I. i. 87 (Abbott, 333).
47. *to blame*] *too* (F) may be correct, for 'In the 16th-17th c. the *to* was misunderstood as *too*, and *blame* taken as an adj. = blameworthy, culpable' (*O.E.D.*); cf. *1H4*, III. i. 177, 'you are too wilful blame'.

Eph. Ant. Good Lord! You use this dalliance to excuse
Your breach of promise to the Porpentine;
I should have chid you for not bringing it,   50
But like a shrew you first begin to brawl.
Sec. Mer. The hour steals on; I pray you, sir, dispatch.
Angelo. You hear how he importunes me; the chain!
Eph. Ant. Why, give it to my wife and fetch your money.
Angelo. Come, come, you know I gave it you even now.   55
Either send the chain or send me by some token.
Eph. Ant. Fie, now you run this humour out of breath;
Come, where's the chain? I pray you let me see it.
Sec. Mer. My business cannot brook this dalliance;
Good sir, say whe'er you'll answer me or no;   60
If not, I'll leave him to the officer.
Eph. Ant. I answer you? What should I answer you?
Angelo. The money that you owe me for the chain.
Eph. Ant. I owe you none, till I receive the chain.
Angelo. You know I gave it you half an hour since.   65
Eph. Ant. You gave me none; you wrong me much to say so.
Angelo. You wrong me more, sir, in denying it.
Consider how it stands upon my credit.

48. Lord!] *Rowe;* Lord, F.   52, 59, 69. *Sec. Mer.*] *Mar.* | *F.*   53. me; the chain!] *Dyce, after Pope;* me, the Chaine. *F.*   56. me by] *F;* by me *Alexander, after Singer.*

48. *Good Lord!*] F has merely a comma after *Lord*, but this would be an odd form of address to Angelo; the phrase is used elsewhere as an interjection by Shakespeare, cf. *Shr.*, IV. v. 2.
49. *Porpentine*] See l. 13, S.D. and n.
50-1. *I . . . brawl*] Cf. the proverb, 'Some complain to prevent complaint' (Tilley, C 579). The same phrase occurs at *R3*, I. iii. 324, 'I do the wrong, and first begin to brawl'.
51. *shrew*] formerly applied to either sex.
56. *Either*] See note on *whe'er*, l. 60 below.
send . . . token] i.e. send me with some evidence that will show my right to receive payment for the chain; for the construction, cf. *R3*, IV. ii. 81, 'Go, by this token', where *by* = 'by means of', or 'with'.

57. *run . . . breath*] i.e. jest too far; cf. Tilley, B 641.
59. *dalliance*] idle delay (perhaps the sense intended at l. 48 above, where the more usual 'trifling' also fits); cf. *1H6*, v. ii. 5, 'keep not back your powers in dalliance'.
60. *whe'er*] so F (*whe'r*); N.C.S. notes an example of the same contraction at *Tp.*, v. i. 111. Abbott, 466, says that it is common in Shakespeare, and adds 'It is impossible to tell in many of these cases what degree of "softening" takes place;' this remark applies to *Either*, l. 56, and *together*, l. 26, where the metre demands a slurring. The modern *or*, as in *either . . . or*, is a reduced form of *other*.
answer] pay.
68. *stands upon*] is of importance to; cf. *R3*, IV. ii. 60.

Sec. Mer. Well, officer, arrest him at my suit.
Offic. I do,   70
    And charge you in the duke's name to obey me.
Angelo. This touches me in reputation;
    Either consent to pay this sum for me,
    Or I attach you by this officer.
Eph. Ant. Consent to pay thee that I never had?   75
    Arrest me, foolish fellow, if thou dar'st.
Angelo. Here is thy fee, arrest him officer.
    I would not spare my brother in this case
    If he should scorn me so apparently.
Offic. I do arrest you, sir; you hear the suit.   80
Eph. Ant. I do obey thee, till I give thee bail.
    But sirrah, you shall buy this sport as dear
    As all the metal in your shop will answer.
Angelo. Sir, sir, I shall have law in Ephesus,
    To your notorious shame, I doubt it not.   85

Enter DROMIO *of Syracuse from the bay.*

Syr. Dro. Master, there's a bark of Epidamnum
    That stays but till her owner comes aboard,
    And then she bears away. Our fraughtage, sir,
    I have convey'd aboard, and I have bought
    The oil, the balsamum and aqua-vitae.   90
    The ship is in her trim, the merry wind
    Blows fair from land; they stay for nought at all

70–1.] *As Capell; prose in F.*   85. S.D. *of Syracuse*] *Sira. | F.*   86. *Syr. Dro.*]
Dro. | F.   there's] *F; there is Pope.*   86, 95. Epidamnum] *Pope; Epidamium F.*
88. then she] *Capell;* then sir she *F.*

70. *I do*] Cf. i. i. 61 (Abbott, 511–12);
short lines of emphatic statement or
interjection are common in Shakespeare.
   79. *apparently*] openly.
   82. *sirrah*] There is a nice declension
in Antipholus's mode of addressing
Angelo, from 'good signior' (l. 36),
through 'sir' (l. 43) and 'fellow' (l. 76),
to the contemptuous 'sirrah' of this
line.
   85. S.D. *from the bay*] an author's
direction, suggested to Shakespeare by
his reading of Plautus; in *Menaechmi*

and *Amphitruo* one side of the stage
clearly leads to the bay or harbour,
the other to the city or forum. See
Introduction, p. xxxvi.
   88. *then she*] then sir she, F; as N.C.S.
suggests, the compositor may have
caught *sir* from the end of the line;
but see l. 99 and note.
   fraughtage] cargo (freightage).
   90. *balsamum*] balm, an aromatic
resin.
   aqua-vitae] alcohol, spirits.
   91. *in her trim*] fully-rigged and ready
to sail (Onions).

But for their owner, master, and yourself.

Eph. Ant. How now? a madman? Why, thou peevish sheep,
   What ship of Epidamnum stays for me?   95

Syr. Dro. A ship you sent me to, to hire waftage.

Eph. Ant. Thou drunken slave, I sent thee for a rope,
   And told thee to what purpose and what end.

Syr. Dro. You sent me for a rope's end, sir, as soon;
   You sent me to the bay, sir, for a bark.   100

Eph. Ant. I will debate this matter at more leisure,
   And teach your ears to list me with more heed.
   To Adriana, villain, hie thee straight:
   Give her this key, and tell her in the desk
   That's cover'd o'er with Turkish tapestry,   105
   There is a purse of ducats; let her send it.
   Tell her I am arrested in the street,
   And that shall bail me; hie thee slave, be gone;
   On, officer, to prison, till it come. *Exeunt [all but Dromio].*

Syr. Dro. To Adriana,—that is where we din'd,   110
   Where Dowsabel did claim me for her husband;
   She is too big I hope for me to compass.
   Thither I must, although against my will;
   For servants must their masters' minds fulfil.   *Exit.*

99. You] *F;* A rope! you *Capell.*   me for] *F;* me, Sir, for *Steevens.*   end, sir, as]
Cuningham; end as *F.*   109. S.D. all but Dromio] *Kittredge, after Dyce; not in F.*

93. *master*] ambiguous; probably
direct address to Antipholus (so Baldwin), though this word could refer to
the master, the captain of the ship.

94. *madman*] Each character in his
private world of experience tends to
see the others as mad, or to feel he is
himself mad, like Dromio at III. ii. 76,
or Antipholus at III. ii. 53–4. See Introduction, p. xlvii.

peevish] senseless.

94–5. *sheep . . . ship*] There is a similar
quibble in *Gent.*, I. i. 72–3, 'he is
shipp'd already, / And I have play'd
the sheep in losing him.' Kökeritz, p.
145, lists other examples.

96. *hire*] a disyllable, as not uncom-
monly in Shakespeare; see Abbott,
480.

waftage] conveyance by water.

99. *rope's end*] i.e. a whipping, cf. l. 16
above; the jest is that Dromio of Ephesus was sent to buy a rope's end.

sir] not in F; the word seems necessary both to justify the metre and to
balance the next line. Compare IV. iv.
16–17.

105. *Turkish tapestry*] Turkey-work,
or needlework imitating an eastern
carpet, here perhaps adding some local
colour; see *Shakespeare's England*, II.
128.

106. *ducats*] See l. 30 and n.

111. *Dowsabel*] an English form of
Dulcibella or *Douce et belle*, a generic
name for a sweetheart or pretty maid,
here applied ironically to the Nell of
III. ii. 110–15.

112. *compass*] embrace, and win,
playing on both senses.

SCENE II

Enter ADRIANA *and* LUCIANA.

Adr. Ah, Luciana, did he tempt thee so?
 Might'st thou perceive austerely in his eye
 That he did plead in earnest, yea or no?
 Look'd he or red or pale, or sad or merrily?
 What observation mad'st thou in this case,   5
 Of his heart's meteors tilting in his face?
Luc. First he denied you had in him no right.
Adr. He meant he did me none; the more my spite.
Luc. Then swore he that he was a stranger here.
Adr. And true he swore, though yet forsworn he were.   10
Luc. Then pleaded I for you.
Adr.   And what said he?
Luc. That love I begg'd for you, he begg'd of me.
Adr. With what persuasion did he tempt thy love?

Scene II

SCENE II] *Warburton, after Pope; not in F.*   4. merrily] *F;* merry *Dyce, conj.*
Walker.   5–6. case, / Of] *F4, after F2;* case? / Oh, *F.*

SCENE II] The dialogue here takes up directly from Luciana's exit at III. ii. 70, with a return to rhyme and patches of stichomythia, which mark off with a poetic elevation the discussions of marital relations between Adriana and Luciana, and Syr. Antipholus's wooing of Luciana. The tone changes on Dromio's entry, but he speaks at first in regular verse before modulating to tumbling verse and prose.

Entry.] Adriana and Luciana enter presumably from their house, the Phoenix, i.e. from the centre door or 'mansion'; Dromio went off at the end of the last scene as if he had some way to go to reach their house, and returns at l. 28.

2. *austerely*] Its suggestions of self-discipline and abstinence tie this word to Luciana rather than to Antipholus, as N.C.S. notes; but it may be simply equivalent to '*in earnest*' in the next

line, and so apply to him as well.

4. *or sad or merrily*] The same phrase occurs at *1H4*, v. ii. 12; cf. Abbott, 136.

6. *Of*] the generally accepted emendation of F 'Oh'. *Of* not only makes readier sense, but gives the final couplet of Adriana's speech a flow which the verse pattern seems to demand.

heart's . . . face] the conflict of his emotions as reflected in his change of expression. Any kind of luminous appearance in the sky might be called a meteor. N.C.S. aptly compares *Rom.*, III. v. 12–13, 'Yond light is not daylight. . . It is some meteor that the sun exhales'; so Antipholus's heart, 'like the unseen sun below the horizon, reveals its influence by swift changes of colour and expression in the face'.

7. *denied . . . no*] strengthening the negative; cf. Abbott, 406.

8. *spite*] vexation.

Luc. With words that in an honest suit might move:
　　First he did praise my beauty, then my speech.   15
Adr. Did'st speak him fair?
Luc.   Have patience, I beseech.
Adr. I cannot, nor I will not hold me still.
　　My tongue, though not my heart, shall have his will.
　　He is deformed, crooked, old and sere,
　　Ill-fac'd, worse bodied, shapeless everywhere;   20
　　Vicious, ungentle, foolish, blunt, unkind,
　　Stigmatical in making, worse in mind.
Luc. Who would be jealous then of such a one?
　　No evil lost is wail'd when it is gone.
Adr. Ah, but I think him better than I say,   25
　　And yet would herein others' eyes were worse:
　　Far from her nest the lapwing cries away;
　　My heart prays for him, though my tongue do curse.

Enter DROMIO *of Syracuse.*

Syr. Dro. Here, go: the desk; the purse; sweat now, make
　　haste.
Luc. How hast thou lost thy breath?

28. S.D. *Dromio of Syracuse*] S. *Dromio F.*   29. *Syr. Dro.*] *Dro.* / *F.*   29. sweat]
N.C.S.; sweet F.

14. *honest suit . . . move*] pointing forward to the prospective union of Luciana and Antipholus of Syracuse at
the end; cf. v. i. 374–6.
　16. *him fair*] kindly to him.
　patience] Here, as in II. i (see ll. 32,
41, 86), Luciana preaches patience to
Adriana, whose impatience gets the
better of her on each occasion. See also
IV. iv. 18–19 and n.
　18. *tongue . . . heart*] Adriana is careful not to commit herself, and rejects
the proverb, 'What the heart thinks
the tongue speaks' (Tilley, H 334, and
cf. H 312 and M 602).
　his] the usual genitive of *it* in Shakespeare, as also in the Authorized Version of the Bible; see Abbott, 228.
　20. *shapeless*] ugly, unshapely, cf.
LLL., v. ii. 303.
　22. *Stigmatical*] marked by nature

with deformity.
　26. *worse*] so that they should not see
his deformity.
　27. *lapwing*] peewit; the allusion is to
the bird's method of drawing intru-
ders away from the nest; so Adriana
speaks 'Tongue far from heart', as
Lucio glosses a similar image at *Meas.*,
I. iv. 33. See Tilley, L 68; though the
idea was common, Shakespeare may
have drawn this image from Lyly, who
was fond of it, cf. *Campaspe*, II. ii. 9, and
Euphues and his England, II. 4, 'the Lapp-
wing, . . . flyeth with a false cry farre
from their nestes'.
　29. *sweat*] *sweet* (F) is not appropriate in Dromio's mouth here, and
might well represent the compositor's
interpretation of MS. *swet(e)*, or arise
as a simple misreading. Dromio seems
to be talking half to himself.

Syr. Dro.   By running fast.   30
Adr. Where is thy master, Dromio? is he well?
Syr. Dro. No, he's in Tartar limbo, worse than hell.
   A devil in an everlasting garment hath him,
   One whose hard heart is button'd up with steel;
   A fiend, a fury, pitiless and rough,   35
   A wolf, nay worse, a fellow all in buff;
   A back-friend, a shoulder-clapper, one that
      countermands

30. *Syr. Dro.*] *S. Dro.* | *F* (*so to end of scene*).   34. One] *F* (On), *F2*.   35. fury]
Pope 2, after Theobald; Fairie *F.*   rough] *F* (ruffe).

31–47.] As earlier (see II. ii. 54–109 and n.), Dromio in his foolery here and in the next scene uses, or misuses, figures of rhetoric, combining what Sir Thomas Wilson called 'Transmutation of a word', or metonymy, with 'Transumption', which is 'when by degrees wee goe to that, which is to be shewed' (*Arte of Rhetorique*, ed. Mair, p. 175). It has relevance to the action, for Dromio's image of the Officer as a devil ironically matches his real master's growing sense of Ephesus as a place of evil, and points forward to his treatment of the Courtesan as a fiend (see IV. iii. 46–8, 63); at the same time, his words relate to Antipholus of Ephesus, who is soon to be regarded by Adriana herself as being possessed by a fiend, see IV. iv. 105–6, and to be thrust into a real 'limbo' by Doctor Pinch.

32. *Tartar limbo*] *limbo* means prison, as commonly, cf. Sugden, *Dictionary*, p. 308, and also hell, as at *All's W.*, v. iii. 258. *Tartar* is an abbreviated form of 'Tartarus', as at *Tw. N.*, II. v. 184, 'To the gates of Tartar', but it also suggests the Tartars, notorious as savages, as the reference to the 'flinty Tartar's bosom', *All's W.*, IV. iv. 7, indicates. N.C.S. comments, 'The jest is that the clown Dromio takes "Tartar limbo" to mean the hell of the Tartars or Mohammedans, and so worse than the Christian hell', but an audience would have to be quick-witted to catch this.

33. *everlasting garment*] 'everlasting' was the name of a material used in '16–17th c. for the dress of sergeants and catchpoles' (*O.E.D.*, B 3a); the word as adjective is, of course, appropriate to the devil, and also to the lasting qualities of 'buff', l. 36; cf. the quibble at IV. iii. 26.

hath him] The verse is regular, and perhaps there is no need to suppose with Spedding that a rhyme-word has dropped out; cf. III. ii. 4 and n. and II. ii. 195–6, where two lines in a series of couplets do not rhyme.

35. *fury*] Theobald's emendation seems appropriate, cf. *3H6*, I. iii. 31, 'a fury to torment my soul', and a compositor might misread *u* as *ai* in English secretary hand. But *fairy* can be defended, as signifying a malevolent power, cf. II. ii. 189–92 above, and Lyly, *Endimion*, IV. iii. 112, 'so by Fayries or fiendes have been thus handled' (cited Cuningham—the fairies in this play are in fact mischievous and malicious rather than evil, but Shakespeare evidently knew Lyly's work well when he wrote this play, see Introduction, p. xxxiii).

36. *wolf*] Probably the phrase 'wolf of hell' (=fiend) is recalled here.

buff] buff-leather, hard-wearing and used for the dress of sergeants.

37. *back-friend*] properly an enemy who pretends friendship, a false friend, but alluding here to the sergeant's method of arresting people.

shoulder-clapper] a common name

The passages of alleys, creeks and narrow lands;
A hound that runs counter, and yet draws dry-foot well,
One that, before the judgment, carries poor souls to hell.
Adr. Why, man, what is the matter?   41
Syr. Dro. I do not know the matter; he is 'rested on the case.
Adr. What, is he arrested? tell me at whose suit?
Syr. Dro. I know not at whose suit he is arrested well;
But is in a suit of buff which 'rested him, that can I tell: 45

38. alleys] F (allies), *Capell.*   lands] F; lanes *conj. Grey.*   44–5.] *As Capell;*
prose in F.   45. is] F; he's F3+.

for a bailiff or officer whose duty was
to arrest offenders, but this is the first
use of the word known to *O.E.D.*
    countermands] prohibits; quibbling
perhaps on the Counter, the name
of various prisons for debtors, one of
which was in Southwark, the others
in the Poultry and in Wood Street
in the City of London; see l. 39 below.
    38. *passages*] i.e. of people; cf. III. i.
99.
    creeks] winding alleys; *O.E.D.* sb.²
5 cites T. Watson, *Century of Love*
(1582), xcv, 'A Labyrinth is a place
made full of turnings and creeks'; but
see next note.
    narrow lands] unexplained. It would
be tempting to read *lanes* were it not
for the rhyme. Probably *lands* =
launds, glades or clearings in woods;
Onions notes two instances in Shakespeare, at *LLL.*, v. ii. 309, 'as roes run
o'er land', and *Tp.*, IV. i. 130, where
land, rhyming respectively with *hand*
and *command*, is almost certainly a
form of *laund.* If this interpretation is
correct, Shakespeare may have been
thinking of possible escape routes from
London, of town lanes, creeks of
water, and passages through fields and
woods; and this word may have suggested the image of the next line.
    39. *runs counter*] in hunting, follows
the scent in the opposite direction to
that taken by the game; also a quibble
on the common name for a debtor's
prison, cf. 'countermands', l. 37.
    draws dry-foot] in hunting, tracks

game 'by the mere scent of the foot'
(*O.E.D.*); cf. *Shakespeare's England*, II.
335–6. The phrase does not occur elsewhere in Shakespeare.
    40. *hell*] another reference to prison:
O.E.D., sb. 5, cites Fuller, *Worthies*
(1662), II. 236, 'There is no redemption from Hell. There is a place partly
under, partly by the Exchequer
Chamber, commonly called Hell . . .
formerly . . . a prison for the King's
debtors', and cf. Sugden, *Dictionary*,
p. 246.
    42. *'rested on the case*] alluding to an
obsolete form of procedure in common
law designed to provide a remedy for
personal wrongs not specifically covered by prescribed causes: 'a new writ
was ordered to be issued in any case
which could not be met by the old
fixed forms. Actions commenced by
these new writs became known as
actions of 'trespass on the case' (or,
shortly, 'actions on the case') because
the special facts of each case were
stated in a writ framed as near as possible by analogy to the old writ of
trespass' (see *Shakespeare's England*, I.
390–1). There is probably, as Malone
noted, a quibble on *case* = suit of
clothes, cf. IV. iii. 22–3, and the
phrase suggests the hand of the
'shoulder-clapper' falling on Antipholus.
    45. *is*] The nominative, especially
the pronoun *he*, is frequently omitted,
commonly before *is, has*, and *was*
(Abbott, 400).

Will you send him, mistress, redemption, the money in
his desk?
Adr. Go, fetch it, sister; this I wonder at,   *Exit Luciana.*
That he unknown to me should be in debt.
Tell me, was he arrested on a band?   50
Syr. Dro. Not on a band, but on a stronger thing;
A chain, a chain, do you not hear it ring?
Adr. What, the chain?
Syr. Dro.   No, no, the bell, 'tis time that I were gone,
It was two ere I left him, and now the clock strikes one.
Adr. The hours come back; that did I never hear.   55
Syr. Dro. O yes, if any hour meet a sergeant, 'a turns back
    for very fear.
Adr. As if time were in debt; how fondly dost thou reason.
Syr. Dro. Time is a very bankrupt, and owes more than he's
    worth to season.

46. mistress, redemption] *Hanmer* (Mistris redemption *F*); Mistris Redemption
F4.   49. That] *F2;* Thus *F.*   52, 55. hear] *F* (here).   55. hours] *F;* hours'
F4.   58. bankrupt] *F* (bankerout).

46. *mistress, redemption*] a quibble,
see the passage cited in the note to
'hell', l. 40. The primary sense here is
ransom, the release of a prisoner by
payment (*O.E.D.*, sb. 2), as at *Oth.*,
I. iii. 138. N.C.S. reads 'Mistress
Redemption' after F4, 'since the
reading throws us back into the atmosphere of the morality plays', which, it
is claimed, provide many of Dromio's
images 'in this and the following
scene'. With this jest, cf. Costard's
play on 'remuneration' and 'guerdon',
LLL., III. i. 129, 160.
    49. *That*] *Thus* (F) may be due to the
compositor's eye catching together
and confusing 'this . . . at, That'.
    50, 51. *band*] quibbling on the com-
mon meanings, bond (it is the same
word), and ruff or neck-band (see
Shakespeare's England, I. 25–7), so con-
necting with the 'chain', l. 53, which
would have been worn round the neck.
I see no reason to interpret this with
N.C.S. as 'a leash to tie up a dog'
(*O.E.D.*, sb.¹ 5).
    53–62.] This jesting on time recalls

the same Dromio's mock-reasoning on
the theme of Time and hair in II. ii.
54ff., and relates to the mistiming
which is such a prominent element in
the play; cf. IV. i. 41 and n.
    54. *one*] Dromio says *on*, but Adriana
understands *one*, the quibble arising
from the fact that these were pronounced alike (so Baldwin); Kökeritz,
p. 132, cites the rhyme *on–one* at *Gent.*,
III. i. 1–2. The jest is lost in modern
pronunciation, and it seems best to
print *one*, like F; cf. l. 34 above, where
F has *On* = One.
    55–62. *hours . . . hour*] Kökeritz, p.
117, sees here a quibble on *hour-whore*,
comparing *AYL*, II. vii. 26.
    56. *sergeant*] formerly the proper
title of officers charged 'with the
arrest of offenders or the summoning
of persons to appear before the court'
(*O.E.D.*, sb. 4).
    57. *fondly*] foolishly.
    58. *owes . . . season*] not satisfactorily
explained. Season is usually taken to
mean 'opportunity' here, and the
phrase may be interpreted as 'there is

I

Nay, he's a thief too; have you not heard men say
That time comes stealing on by night and day?   60
If 'a be in debt and theft, and a sergeant in the way,
Hath he not reason to turn back an hour in a day?

Enter LUCIANA [*with the money*].

Adr. Go, Dromio, there's the money, bear it straight,
And bring thy master home immediately.
Come, sister, I am press'd down with conceit;   65
Conceit, my comfort and my injury.   *Exeunt.*

SCENE III

Enter ANTIPHOLUS *of Syracuse.*

Syr. Ant. There's not a man I meet but doth salute me
As if I were their well-acquainted friend,
And every one doth call me by my name:

61. 'a] *Staunton; I F;* Time *Rowe;* he *Malone.*   62. S.D. *with the money*] *Dyce* (*with the purse*) *; not in F.*   66. S.D. *Exeunt*] *Rowe; Exit F.*

SCENE III] *Capell, after Pope; not in F.*   S.D. *of Syracuse*] Siracusia *F.*   1. *Syr. Ant.*] *Rowe; not in F.*

never time to do all that occasion offers' (N.C.S.). It is possible, in view of the context, that Shakespeare had the meaning 'A term or session of court . . .' (*O.E.D.*, sb. 7) in mind. Kökeritz, p. 114, suggests a play on *seisin*, i.e. in law, possession as of freehold; but *seizing*, cf. 'stealing', l. 60, seems a better possibility.

60. *time . . . day*] proverbial, cf. Tilley, Y 313, 327.

65, 66. *conceit*] what is conceived by the mind; both 'understanding' of past injury, cf. III. ii. 34 above, and 'imagination' (of comfort to come), as at *R2*, II. ii. 33. This passage (ll. 63–6) probably forms a quatrain, for *conceit* could rhyme with *straight*; see Kökeritz, p. 198.

66. S.D. Exeunt] The women go back into the house, while Dromio hurries off a different way, as if to return to the mart; cf. the note at the head of this scene.

Scene III

SCENE III] The mood of the previous scene is continued, as Dromio enlarges his quibbling description of the Officer (IV. ii. 32ff.) in speaking now to Antipholus. But the theme of his foolery, the devil, points up an increasing sense of confusion, witchcraft, and evil in the main action, as by the end of this scene his master believes in earnest what Dromio had said in jest.

1. *Syr. Ant.*] The speech-heading is omitted from F, as at V. i. 168; see Introduction, p. xiv n.

Some tender money to me, some invite me,
Some other give me thanks for kindnesses,   5
Some offer me commodities to buy.
Even now a tailor call'd me in his shop,
And show'd me silks that he had bought for me,
And therewithal took measure of my body.
Sure these are but imaginary wiles,   10
And Lapland sorcerers inhabit here.

Enter DROMIO *of Syracuse.*

Syr. Dro. Master, here's the gold you sent me for: what,
  have you got the picture of old Adam new-apparelled?
Syr. Ant. What gold is this? What Adam dost thou mean?   15
Syr. Dro. Not that Adam that kept the paradise, but that
  Adam that keeps the prison; he that goes in the
  calf's-skin that was killed for the prodigal; he that

11. S.D. *of Syracuse*] *Sir.* / *F.*   12–13. what, have] *Rowe 2* (what haue *F*) ; Where
have *N.C.S.*   13. got] *F;* got rid of *Theobald+*.   15. *Syr. Ant.*] *Ant.* / *F* (so to
end of scene).   18. calf's-skin] *F* (calues-skin).

5. *other*] a proper plural, cf. Abbott, 12 (p. 25), 'Our modern "others said" is only justified by a custom which might have compelled us to say "manys" or "alls said" '.

10. *imaginary wiles*] tricks of the imagination, having no real existence.

11. *Lapland*] proverbially a home of 'witches and magicians' (*O.E.D.*). N.C.S. cites Giles Fletcher, *Of the Russe Common Wealth* (1591), 'For practice of witchcraft and sorcery they [the Lapps] pass all nations in the world' (ed. E. A. Bond, *Hakluyt Society*, Series I, Vol. xx, 1856, p. 100).

12–14. *what . . . new-apparelled*] i.e. is the sergeant still with you?; or, possibly, as Singer notes, 'new-apparelled' = new-suited, and Shakespeare, ever alert to quibbles, had in mind *suit* = law-suit, giving the sense 'have you got the sergeant a new suit, other business, and so shaken him off?' The 'old Adam' is the 'offending Adam' (*H5*, I. i. 29), man in his fallen state; see

Tilley, A 29, and *Ephesians*, iv. 22–4, 'that ye cast off . . . the olde man, which is corrupt . . . And put on that new man, which after God is created in righteousnes and true holines' (Geneva). There is also a quibbling allusion to *Genesis*, iii. 21, 'Unto Adam also and to his wife did the Lord God make coats of skins, and clothed them'. The sergeant was clothed in buff or 'calves-skin' (l. 18), cf. IV. ii. 36. Commentators have suspected corruption in this passage, but the widely-accepted emendation 'got rid of' is first recorded by *O.E.D.* in 1665, and N.C.S., reading 'Where have' for 'what, have', hardly improves the construction or the sense.

18. *calf's-skin . . . prodigal*] a quibbling allusion to the parable of the prodigal son (*Luke*, xv. 11–32), in which the father kills the fatted calf to celebrate the return of his son, who has 'wasted his substance with riotous living'. Dromio looks beyond this, so to speak, to the sergeant dressed in his

came behind you, sir, like an evil angel, and bid you
forsake your liberty.   20

Syr. Ant. I understand thee not.

Syr. Dro. No? why, 'tis a plain case; he that went like a
bass-viol in a case of leather; the man, sir, that when
gentlemen are tired gives them a sob, and rests them;
he, sir, that takes pity on decayed men and gives   25
them suits of durance; he that sets up his rest to do
more exploits with his mace than a morris-pike.

Syr. Ant. What, thou mean'st an officer?

Syr. Dro. Ay, sir, the sergeant of the band; he that brings
any man to answer it that breaks his band; one that   30
thinks a man always going to bed, and says, "God
give you good rest".

Syr. Ant. Well, sir, there rest in your foolery. Is there any
ship puts forth to-night? may we be gone?

24. sob] *F;* fob *Rowe;* bob *Hanmer;* sop *conj. Dyce.*   rests] *F;* 'rests *Warburton+.*
34. ship] *F2;* ships *F.*

leather coat, who lies in wait for the
spendthrift, to arrest him. The jest
depends on the contrast between the
father and the sergeant.

19. *evil angel*] another quibbling
allusion to the Bible, this time to the
good angel who came down to Peter as
he lay chained in Herod's jail, struck
him on the side, and 'delivered' him
from prison (*Acts,* xii. 8–12). The sergeant, by contrast, is an evil angel; cf.
the similar wordplay at *2H4,* I. ii.
155ff. See also l. 38 and n. below.

20. *liberty*] probably echoing the
biblical use of the word, cf. *2 Corinthians,* iii. 17, 'where the spirit of the
Lord is, there is liberty'.

22–3. *case . . . case of leather*] playing
again on the meanings of 'case', cf.
IV. ii. 42 and n.

23. *bass-viol*] a stringed instrument
like a violoncello, used to play the bass
part in concerted music; the word *bass*
carries also the meaning 'base', and is
so spelled in F.

24. *sob*] a rest given to a horse to
recover its wind (*O.E.D.,* sb. 1c.); the
quibble on the usual sense of the word

is continued in 'rests' (arrests) and
'takes pity'.

26. *durance*] quibbling on the meanings 'a stout durable cloth' (*O.E.D.,* 3),
and 'imprisonment', and suggesting a
long spell in jail. As N.C.S. notes,
Shakespeare seems to confuse the cloth
'durance' with buff, cf. *1H4,* I. ii. 42.

sets up his rest] is absolutely determined, as at *Mer. V.,* II. ii. 97. Originally a metaphor derived from the
game of primero, in which the 'rest'
was the stake kept in reserve, the
phrase 'to set up one's rest' came to
mean 'to venture all'. The play on
rest and *arrest* continues.

27. *morris-pike*] a form of pike supposed to be of Moorish origin; the
'buff' worn by the sergeant was also
the dress of soldiers, cf. next note.

29–30. *sergeant of the band . . . band*]
literally an officer in charge of a number of soldiers, but quibbling on *band*
= *bond,* cf. IV. ii. 50–1 and n.

32. *rest*] continuing the play on the
senses 'repose' and 'arrest', cf. ll. 24, 26
above.

34. *ship*] *ships* (F) is possible, since a

Syr. Dro. Why, sir, I brought you word an hour since,   35
    that the bark *Expedition* put forth to-night, and then
    were you hindered by the sergeant to tarry for the
    hoy *Delay*. Here are the angels that you sent for to
    deliver you.
Syr. Ant. The fellow is distract, and so am I,   40
    And here we wander in illusions—
    Some blessed power deliver us from hence!

Enter a Courtesan.

Cour. Well met, well met, master Antipholus;
    I see, sir, you have found the goldsmith now;
    Is that the chain you promis'd me to-day?   45
Syr. Ant. Satan avoid, I charge thee tempt me not.
Syr. Dro. Master, is this mistress Satan?
Syr. Ant. It is the devil.

third person plural of verbs in '-s' is very common, cf. Abbott, 333–5; but here two verbs are involved, *is* and *puts*, and for the sake of the syntax, and here of euphony, it seems better to regard *ships* as an error.

36–8. Expedition . . . Delay] The names are chosen for the sake of the jest, cf. IV. i. 86ff. A *hoy* is a small coasting vessel.

38. *angels*] gold coins, worth between 6s. 8d. and 10s. according to the period, and having on one side the figure of St Michael overcoming the dragon; see note to 'evil angel', l. 19 above. Noble cites *Acts*, xii. 11 'that the Lord hath sent his Angel, and hath delivered me [i.e. Peter, from prison]'. Antipholus catches up the biblical echo in his call for providential deliverance (from witchcraft), l. 42, contrasting with his brother's mundane need of deliverance from arrest.

40–2.] Antipholus's tone has changed, as his sense of bewilderment and confusion has grown, from being willing to go 'at all adventures' (II. ii. 216), to a feeling that it is 'time that I were hence' (III. ii. 156), and so now to an appeal to the heavens for delivery. The feeling of growing oppression and

madness prepares the way for his wild behaviour later on, in the next scene.

42. S.D.] The Courtesan is presumably identified for the audience by her entrance from a door marked with the sign of her house, the 'Porpentine'; see III. i. 116–19, and Introduction, pp. xxxivff.

46–76.] Antipholus has all along been aware of Ephesus as a place of witchcraft and magic (see I. ii. 97ff.), but his attitude to this supernatural agency changes gradually through the play, as his pleasure in the gentle enchantments of Luciana, and the genial magic which, as he thinks, prompts everyone to greet him kindly, gives way to a growing sense of frustration, of wandering in illusions. He comes to think more in terms of sorcery, black magic, and finally, of evil, of the devil at work, as in his bitter attack on the Courtesan here; see IV. ii. 31–47 and n., and Introduction, p. xlvii.

46. *avoid*] be off; an echo of Christ's words to Satan at *Matthew*, iv. 10, 'Sathan avoid' (Geneva version; the Authorized Version has 'Get thee hence, Satan').

Syr. Dro. Nay, she is worse, she is the devil's dam;
 And here she comes in the habit of a light wench, and 50
 thereof comes that the wenches say "God damn
 me", that's as much as to say, "God make me a light
 wench". It is written, they appear to men like angels
 of light; light is an effect of fire, and fire will burn;
 ergo, light wenches will burn; come not near her. 55
Cour. Your man and you are marvellous merry, sir.
 Will you go with me? we'll mend our dinner here.
Syr. Dro. Master, if you do, expect spoon-meat, or be-
 speak a long spoon.
Syr. Ant. Why, Dromio? 60
Syr. Dro. Marry, he must have a long spoon that must eat
 with the devil.
Syr. Ant. Avoid then, fiend, what tell'st thou me of supping?
 Thou art, as you are all, a sorceress:
 I conjure thee to leave me and be gone. 65

52. as to] *Rowe;* to F. 57. me? . . . here.] *Var. 1778;* me, . . . here? *F.* 58.
you do,] *F2;* do *F;* you do *Rowe.* 63. then] *F;* thou *F4+*.

49. *devil's dam*] a catch-phrase, 'applied opprobiously to a woman' (*O.E.D.*, dam, sb.² 2b), and used several times by Shakespeare, as at *Shr.*, III. ii. 152; cf. Tilley, D 225.

51–2. *thereof . . . say*] cf. *Gent.*, III. i. 296ff., 'thereof comes the proverb . . . That's as much to say, "Can she so?" '; this close parallel in a contemporary passage of similar clowning fortifies the emendation here, though 'as much to say' (F) was a normal construction.

53–4. *It . . . light*] in *2 Corinthians*, xi. 14, 'Satan himself is transformed into an angel of light', a phrase which gave rise to a proverb, Tilley, D 231. Noble, p. 108, observes that the phrase 'It is written' itself echoes the Gospels, e.g. *Matthew*, iv. 4, 6, 7. The earlier play on 'angel', l. 38 above, is also recalled.

55. *light . . . burn*] i.e. infect with venereal disease; *O.E.D.* cites S. Fish, *Supplication* (1529; edited E. Arber, 1895), p. 7, 'These be they catche the pokkes of one woman, and bere theym to an other, that be brent with one woman, and bere it to an other'; cf. *Lr.*, III. ii. 84.

57. *mend*] supply what lacks, cf. III. i. 114. As N.C.S. notes, the Courtesan presumably points to her 'house' as she speaks.

58. *if you do*] *you* seems to have been accidentally dropped from F, but I see no reason to suspect, with Malone and N.C.S., that 'other words were passed over' by the compositor.

spoon-meat] liquid or soft food for eating with a spoon, here used to introduce Dromio's jest about the devil.

59–62. *long . . . devil*] a common proverb, cf. Tilley, S 771.

63. *Avoid*] See l. 46 and n.

then] usually emended to *thou* by analogy with 'Avaunt, thou', l. 76; *en* and *ou* could be confused in secretary hand.

64. *sorceress*] Cf. l. 11 above.

65. *conjure*] solemnly charge, the proper term for dismissing an evil spirit; cf. IV. iv. 55.

Cour. Give me the ring of mine you had at dinner,
   Or for my diamond the chain you promis'd,
   And I'll be gone, sir, and not trouble you.
Syr. Dro. Some devils ask but the parings of one's nail,
   a rush, a hair, a drop of blood, a pin, a nut, a cherry-   70
   stone; but she, more covetous, would have a chain.
   Master, be wise; and if you give it her, the devil will
   shake her chain and fright us with it.
Cour. I pray you, sir, my ring, or else the chain;
   I hope you do not mean to cheat me so?   75
Syr. Ant. Avaunt, thou witch. Come, Dromio, let us go.
Syr. Dro. Fly pride, says the peacock; mistress, that you know.
                    Exeunt [Antipholus and Dromio].
Cour. Now out of doubt Antipholus is mad,
   Else would he never so demean himself;

69–73.] *As F; verse Capell+,* Some . . . nail, / . . . pin, / . . . covetous, / (Some
devils / . . . rush, / . . . nut, / . . . covetous, / *Var. 1778;* Some . . . nail, / . . . pin, /
. . . cherry-stone; / . . . chain. / *Dyce*) . . . chain:— / . . . her, / . . . it.   77. S.D.
Exeunt . . . Dromio.] Exit. F.

66–7. *ring . . . chain*] Cf. III. i. 117–
19; the Courtesan has already dined
with Antipholus of Ephesus.

69–73.] These lines are usually
printed as verse, with a broken line at
'A nut, a cherry-stone', where editors
have suspected corruption or abridgement. It is true that the passage begins
with what might be two lines of verse,
but cf. the opening of Dromio's speech
at l. 49 above, which is printed as
verse in F. I suspect that Shakespeare
sometimes found it difficult as he was
writing to adjust from one rhythm to
another, and that a certain amount of
overlapping, as here, is the result.
Baldwin prefers to think that there
was 'a crowded insertion on the manuscript, part of which the printer
missed'.

72. *and if*] = if; see Abbott, 101,
103.

72–3. *the devil . . . it*] cf. *Revelation,* xx.
1–2, 'And I saw an Angel come down
from heaven, having the key of the
bottomless pit and a great chain in his
hand. And he laid hold on the dragon,

that old serpent which is the Devil and
Satan, and bound him a thousand
years' (Noble, p. 108).

77. *Fly . . . peacock*] The point of
Dromio's jest (the peacock is, of
course, an emblem of pride) is the
quibble on *pride* as meaning sexual
desire (*O.E.D.,* sb. 11); it is used in
this sense several times by Shakespeare, cf. *Sonn.* CXLIV. 7, 'And would
corrupt my saint [i.e. male friend] to
be a devil, / Wooing his purity with her
foul pride'. Pride, as the first of the
seven deadly sins, was often personified as a whore.

78. *Now . . . mad*] There has been
talk of madness previously (cf. II. i. 59,
II. ii. 11, III. ii. 53, etc.), but chiefly
between master and servant in jest, or
in private conversation; it is part of a
growing extension of private misunderstanding into public disorder
that the Courtesan should seriously
think Antipholus mad, and act on it
(cf. l. 92). See note to IV. i. 41–80, and
Introduction, p. xlvii.

79. *demean himself*] behave.

A ring he hath of mine worth forty ducats,   80
And for the same he promis'd me a chain;
Both one and other he denies me now.
The reason that I gather he is mad,
Besides this present instance of his rage,
Is a mad tale he told to-day at dinner   85
Of his own doors being shut against his entrance.
Belike his wife, acquainted with his fits,
On purpose shut the doors against his way—
My way is now to hie home to his house,
And tell his wife that, being lunatic,   90
He rush'd into my house and took perforce
My ring away. This course I fittest choose,
For forty ducats is too much to lose.   [*Exit.*]

SCENE IV

Enter ANTIPHOLUS *of Ephesus with the Officer.*

Eph. Ant. Fear me not, man, I will not break away.

93. S.D. *Exit.*] *F2; not in F.*

Scene IV
SCENE IV] *Capell, after Pope; not in F.*   S.D. *of Ephesus . . . the Officer*] *Ephes.
. . . a Iailor F.*   1. *Eph. Ant.*] *An. | F* (*Ant., Anti. to exit, l. 129*).

80. *ducats*] See IV. i. 30 and n.; Shakespeare returns here to what is, so to speak, the normal currency of the later part of the play, after making the coins in Adriana's purse English angels, for the sake of the quibble and its thematic importance, cf. l. 38 and n. above.

88. *way*] The immediate repetition of *way* in l. 89 (where it must be right) is odd; has it taken the place of a synonym such as *path* here?; cf. II. ii. 12, III. i. 54–6 and IV. i. 21.

89–92. *My way . . . choose*] The errors up to this point have all been those of honest misunderstanding; the Courtesan now bolsters up what she believes to be true (that Antipholus is mad) with a deliberate lie; see l. 78 and n.

89. *My way*] my best course of action, an obsolete usage, cf. *R3*, I. i. 78–80, 'I think it is our way . . . To be her men and wear her livery'.

91. *perforce*] by violence.

Scene IV
SCENE IV] Here disorder is reflected in violence, the beating of Dromio, the binding of Eph. Antipholus, the entry of Syr. Antipholus and Dromio with drawn swords driving the others off stage; the conflict of private worlds of experience leads to public disorder. After Dromio's last painful jesting in prose, the scene moves into blank verse which becomes the medium throughout most of this scene and the last act

I'll give thee ere I leave thee so much money
To warrant thee as I am 'rested for.
My wife is in a wayward mood to-day,
And will not lightly trust the messenger   5
That I should be attach'd in Ephesus;
I tell you 'twill sound harshly in her ears.

Enter DROMIO *of Ephesus with a rope's end.*

Here comes my man, I think he brings the money.
How now, sir? have you that I sent you for?
Eph. Dro. Here's that, I warrant you, will pay them all.   10
Eph. Ant. But where's the money?
Eph. Dro. Why, sir, I gave the money for the rope.
Eph. Ant. Five hundred ducats, villain, for a rope?
Eph. Dro. I'll serve you, sir, five hundred at the rate.
Eph. Ant. To what end did I bid thee hie thee home?   15
Eph. Dro. To a rope's end, sir, and to that end am I return'd.
Eph. Ant. And to that end, sir, I will welcome you.
                                                    [*Beats Dromio.*]
Offic. Good sir, be patient.
Eph. Dro. Nay, 'tis for me to be patient, I am in adversity.

5–6. messenger / ... Ephesus;] *This ed., after Capell;* Messenger, / ... *Ephesus, F;*
Messenger; / ... Ephesus, *F4+.*   7. S.D. *of Ephesus*] Eph. / F.   10. Eph. Dro.]
E. Dro. / F (*so down to l. 39*).   17. S.D. *Beats Dromio*] *Pope; not in F.*

for the culmination of the serious plot,
and its final resolution.

Entry. the Officer] evidently the
same as the 'Officer' of IV. i, though F
has 'Iailor' here.

2–3. *so ... as*] = as ... as; a common
usage, cf. Abbott, 275.

3. *warrant thee*] guarantee your
security, as at *Meas.*, IV. ii. 162 (*O.E.D.*
v. 8).

5–6. *messenger ... Ephesus;*] Editors
frequently place a stop after *messenger*,
but this is less satisfactory rhyth-
mically; the sequence of commas at
the ends of ll. 4, 5, and 6 in F offers no
clear guidance. Here 'trust' means
'rely upon the veracity of' (*O.E.D.*,
v. 4), cf. *Shr.*, IV. ii. 67; she will not
readily believe a messenger who
reports a thing so unlikely as his arrest.

6. *attach'd*] arrested.

10. *pay them all*] i.e. with a beating,
cf. IV. i. 15–21 above.

14. *serve ... rate*] i.e. supply five
hundred ropes for that amount.

16–17. *rope's end ... end*] quibbling
on *end* = purpose and (rope's) end =
a whipping, cf. IV. i. 16 and 98.

17, 41 S.D.] Disorder begins to
break out into violence, cf. IV. i. 41–80
and n.

18–19. *patient ... patient*] Antipholus
earlier showed his impatience in his
relation with Adriana, and now
bursts out in anger against his servant;
this disruption of relationships is part
of the play's theme; see Introduction,
p. xliv, and III. i. 85 and n.

19. *Nay ... adversity*] Cf. *Psalm* xciv.
13, "That thou mayest give him

Offic. Good now, hold thy tongue.   20
Eph. Dro. Nay, rather persuade him to hold his hands.
Eph. Ant. Thou whoreson, senseless villain.
Eph. Dro. I would I were senseless, sir, that I might not
feel your blows.
Eph. Ant. Thou art sensible in nothing but blows, and so   25
is an ass.
Eph. Dro. I am an ass indeed; you may prove it by my
long ears. I have served him from the hour of my
nativity to this instant, and have nothing at his hands
for my service but blows. When I am cold, he heats   30
me with beating; when I am warm he cools me with
beating; I am waked with it when I sleep, raised with
it when I sit, driven out of doors with it when I go
from home, welcomed home with it when I return,
nay, I bear it on my shoulders as a beggar wont her   35
brat; and I think when he hath lamed me, I shall beg
with it from door to door.

Enter ADRIANA, LUCIANA, *Courtesan, and a Schoolmaster,*
called PINCH.

35. wont] *F* (woont).   37. S.D. *Enter . . . Pinch.*] *As F; after l. 38, Dyce*+.

patience in time of adversity' (Prayer
Book version; cited by Noble, p. 108).
   20. *Good now*] a phrase of entreaty,
cf. *Ham.*, I. i. 70.
   25. *sensible . . . blows*] i.e. only blows
make you reasonable; but *sensible* also
means 'capable of feeling', cf. *Cor.*,
I. iii. 84, 'sensible as your finger'.
   26–8. *ass . . . ears*] reminiscent of the
similar dialogue between these two at
III. i. 15ff., and cf. II. ii. 199–201. The
sense of being transformed into an ass
is part of a thematic pattern relating
to loss and change in identity, cf. III. ii.
39–40 and n. There is a play on *ears*,
cf. next note.
   28. *ears*] quibbling on 'years', which
occurs as a form of *ears* in Devon,
Somerset, and Lancashire in the
19th century (Joseph Wright, *English
Dialect Dictionary*); 'ye(e)re' was a
possible spelling of 'ear', occurring, as

N.C.S. notes, at *2H4*, I. ii. 181 (Q).
The same quibble is involved in the
modern phrase 'for donkey's years' (=
a very long time); see *O.E.D.*, Supplement, s.v. *Donkey*, and Kökeritz, p.
103. Compare also the proverb, 'An
ass is known by his long ears', Tilley,
A 355.
   35. *wont*] not elsewhere used thus
absolutely by Shakespeare, but a
standard usage(*O.E.D.*, v. arch. 3b).
   36–7. *beg with it*] perhaps alluding to
the common punishment of beggars
and rogues by whipping; see *Shakespeare's England*, II. 489–91.
   37. S.D. Schoolmaster] presumably
the author's description of Pinch, who
is called 'conjurer' in the text (l. 45),
i.e. one who can deal with spirits, an
exorcist. He was thought of as a schoolmaster because only a learned man
would have the Latin with which to

Eph. Ant. Come, go along, my wife is coming yonder.

Eph. Dro. Mistress, *respice finem*, respect your end, or
     rather, to prophesy like the parrot, beware the rope's   40
     end.

Eph. Ant. Wilt thou still talk?   *Beats Dromio.*

Cour. How say you now? Is not your husband mad?

Adr. His incivility confirms no less.

     Good Doctor Pinch, you are a conjurer;   45
     Establish him in his true sense again,
     And I will please you what you will demand.

Luc. Alas, how fiery, and how sharp he looks.

Cour. Mark how he trembles in his ecstasy.

Pinch. Give me your hand, and let me feel your pulse.   50

40. to prophesy] *Dyce;* the prophesie *F;* prophesie *Rowe.*   42. S.D. *Dromio]*
Dro. | F.

address spirits in the language they
understood, cf. *Ham.*, I. i. 42, 'Thou
art a scholar; speak to it [i.e. the
Ghost], Horatio' (so N.C.S.). See also
2H6, IV. ii. 84ff., where Jack Cade's
rebels condemn the Clerk of Chatham,
a scholar and schoolteacher, as a 'conjurer' because he can read. Shakespeare develops the figure of a comic
pedant in *Shr.* and *LLL.* (Holofernes);
for the background to this type of
character, see K. M. Lea, *Italian
Popular Comedy*, II. 393ff.
     Pinch] so called because of his
'hungry, lean-fac'd' look, cf. v. i.
238ff.
     39–41. respice . . . *end*] alluding to
two jokes of the time; one was the substitution of *respice funem* (a rope, i.e.
hanging) for the common tag *respice
finem* (think on your end), cf. Nashe's
attack on Harvey in *Four Letters Confuted* (1592; McKerrow, I. 268), 'to bee
. . . bid *Respice funem*, looke backe to his
Fathers house' (Harvey's father was a
ropemaker, and see Tilley, E 125.
The other relates to the habit of teaching parrots to cry 'rope', and Shakespeare's immediate source was probably Lyly, cf. *Midas*, I. ii. 45, 'she wil
crie "walke knave, walke". Then I
will mutter, "a rope for Parrat, a

rope" ' (this occurs in a passage which
Shakespeare seems to echo earlier, see
III. ii. 99–143 and n.), and *Mother
Bombie*, III. iv. 54ff., where the parrot's
cry 'A Rope' is referred to in a context
relating to hanging. For further comment, and the probable source of the
joke about the 'rope's end', see T. W.
Baldwin, 'Respice Finem, Respice
Funem', *J. Q. Adams Memorial Studies*
(1948), pp. 141–55.
     44–5.] Adriana is ready not only to
believe her husband mad, but that he
is possessed by a fiend—so the belief
Antipholus of Syracuse has had, that
Ephesus is a place of sorcery and devil-
ish practice, becomes translated into
action. It is another sign of spreading
disorder; cf. IV. iii. 78 and n.
     44. *incivility*] not used elsewhere by
Shakespeare.
     45. *Doctor*] still at this time carrying
the sense of 'teacher' or 'learned man',
cf. *Ado*, v. i. 195.
     conjurer] See note on 'School-
master', l. 37 S.D. above.
     47. *please*] satisfy.
     48. *sharp*] angry, as at *2H6*, III. i. 156.
     49. *trembles*] a sign of possession by a
spirit, cf. *Tp.*, II. ii. 75, and ll. 52, 90,
105 below.
     ecstasy] frenzy, fit.

Eph. Ant. There is my hand, and let it feel your ear.
                                        [*He strikes Pinch.*]
Pinch. I charge thee, Satan, hous'd within this man,
        To yield possession to my holy prayers,
        And to thy state of darkness hie thee straight;
        I conjure thee by all the saints in heaven.   55
Eph. Ant. Peace, doting wizard, peace; I am not mad.
Adr. O that thou wert not, poor distressed soul.
Eph. Ant. You minion, you, are these your customers?
        Did this companion with the saffron face
        Revel and feast it at my house to-day,   60
        Whilst upon me the guilty doors were shut,
        And I denied to enter in my house?
Adr. O husband, God doth know you din'd at home,
        Where would you had remain'd until this time,
        Free from these slanders and this open shame.   65
Eph. Ant. Din'd at home? [*To Dromio.*] Thou villain, what
        sayest thou?
Eph. Dro. Sir, sooth to say, you did not dine at home.
Eph. Ant. Were not my doors lock'd up, and I shut out.
Eph. Dro. Perdy, your doors were lock'd, and you shut out.
Eph. Ant. And did she not herself revile me there?   70
Eph. Dro. Sans fable, she herself revil'd you there.

---

51. S.D. *He strikes Pinch.*] *As Dyce; not in* F.   66. Din'd] F; Din'd I *Theobald;*
I din'd *Capell.*   66. S.D. *To Dromio*] *This ed.; not in* F.   67. *Eph. Dro.*] *Dro.* /
F (*so to end of scene*).

52–5. *charge . . . conjure*] This passage
is nicely set against the dialogue of
Antipholus of Syracuse and the Courtesan in IV. iii; see especially ll. 46,
63–5. The word *conjure* = solemnly
charge) is the proper one for an exorcist to use.

58. *minion*] used contemptuously of
a mistress or loose woman; *O.E.D.*
cites Spenser, *Faerie Queene* (1590),
II. ii. 37, 'A mincing minion . . .
Who in her looseness took exceeding
joy'. Cf. II. i. 87 above, and l. 99
below.

customers] Antipholus speaks to his
wife as if she were a courtesan; the
irony is that while she was entertaining

his twin, he was himself with the
Courtesan.

59. *companion*] used as a term of contempt, as at *2H6*, IV. x. 30.

62. *denied*] not allowed; formerly a
common usage (*O.E.D.*, v. 9).

65. *slanders*] disgraces, or perhaps
disgraceful actions (*O.E.D.*, sb. 3c), as
the word is used several times elsewhere in the singular by Shakespeare,
cf. *Lucr.*, 1207, 'My blood shall wash
the slander of mine ill'.

66–74.] stichomythia, unrhymed,
but marked by repetition, giving a
formal note to the passage, as an
interrogation of a witness.

69. *Perdy*] assuredly (perdieu).

Eph. Ant. Did not her kitchen-maid rail, taunt and scorn me?
Eph. Dro. Certes she did, the kitchen-vestal scorn'd you.
Eph. Ant. And did not I in rage depart from thence?
Eph. Dro. In verity you did; my bones bears witness.   75
    That since have felt the vigour of his rage.
Adr. Is't good to soothe him in these contraries?
Pinch. It is no shame; the fellow finds his vein,
    And yielding to him, humours well his frenzy.
Eph. Ant. Thou hast suborn'd the goldsmith to arrest me.   80
Adr. Alas, I sent you money to redeem you
    By Dromio here, who came in haste for it.
Eph. Dro. Money by me? Heart and good will you might,
    But surely, master, not a rag of money.
Eph. Ant. Went'st not thou to her for a purse of ducats?   85
Adr. He came to me and I deliver'd it.
Luc. And I am witness with her that she did.

---

75. bears] *F* (beares); bear *F2*+.   85. ducats] *F* (Duckets).

72. *kitchen-maid*] As N.C.S. notes, this establishes the identity of Luce (see III. i. 47ff.), and Nell (see III. ii. 93ff.); cf. also Introduction, pp. xx, xxv.

73. *Certes*] certainly.
kitchen-vestal] See Syr. Dromio's description of her, III. ii. 94–100. This is an ironical allusion to virginity, and to 'her charge being, like that of the vestal virgins, to keep the fire burning' (Dr Johnson).

75. *bears*] Third person plural in *-s* is common in F; see Abbott, 333.

77. *soothe*] humour, cf. *R3*, I. iii. 298.

78–99.] Pinch at first thinks Dromio is merely humouring his master, but when it becomes clear that the remembered experience of Dromio clashes with that of Adriana, Pinch brands him as 'possess'd' like his master. The similar disagreement between what Adriana and Antipholus remember confirms them in their impatience (ll. 18–19 above, and IV. ii. 16), which now breaks out into public enmity.

78. *vein*] Cuningham compares II. ii. 20 above.

83. *Heart . . . will*] Cf. *MND.*, III. ii. 164, 'with all good will, with all my heart, In Hermia's love I yield you up my part'.

83–4. *Heart . . . money*] A rag of money seems to have been a cant phrase for a farthing (*O.E.D.* rag, sb.[1] 2c, where this is the earliest example cited). N.C.S. notes that the phrase 'heart and good will, but never a ragge of money' occurs in T. Nashe, *Four Letters Confuted* (1592; McKerrow, I. 301), and argues that 'unless both writers are quoting from some common source, we must suppose that Nashe was borrowing from Shakespeare', for elsewhere (McKerrow, I. 271–2) Nashe speaks of borrowing a sentence from a play. However, Baldwin cites Thomas Lodge, *Deaf Man's Dialogue* (1592), M1[v], commenting, as Nashe is in the passage cited, on a writer, 'oh it is a proper man, but never a rag of money'. In *Four Letters Confuted*, Nashe was attacking Gabriel Harvey, and it is odd that two of his jests against Harvey should turn up in this scene; see ll. 39–41 above and n.

Eph. Dro. God and the rope-maker bear me witness
    That I was sent for nothing but a rope.
Pinch. Mistress, both man and master is possess'd,   90
    I know it by their pale and deadly looks;
    They must be bound and laid in some dark room.
Eph. Ant. Say, wherefore didst thou lock me forth to-day,
    And why dost thou deny the bag of gold?
Adr. I did not, gentle husband, lock thee forth.   95
Eph. Dro. And gentle master, I receiv'd no gold;
    But I confess, sir, that we were lock'd out.
Adr. Dissembling villain, thou speak'st false in both.
Eph. Ant. Dissembling harlot, thou art false in all,
    And art confederate with a damned pack   100
    To make a loathsome abject scorn of me;
    But with these nails I'll pluck out these false eyes
    That would behold in me this shameful sport.
Adr. O bind him, bind him, let him not come near me.

Enter three or four and offer to bind him; he strives.

Pinch. More company; the fiend is strong within him.   105
Luc. Ay me, poor man, how pale and wan he looks.
Eph. Ant. What, will you murder me? Thou jailor, thou,

102. these false] *F;* those false *Rowe.*   104. S.D. *Enter . . . strives.] This ed.; after l. 103, F; after l. 105, Dyce.*   107. me? Thou . . . thou,] *Rowe;* me, thou . . . thou? *F.*

90. *is*] See l. 75 and n.
92. *bound . . . room*] a common treatment for the mad, cf. Sir Toby's confinement of Malvolio, *Tw. N.,* III. iv. 130, 'we'll have him in a dark room and bound'.
93, 95.*forth*] out, cf. I. ii. 37.
100. *pack*] conspiracy, or gang of rogues, cf. Malvolio's exit line, *Tw. N.,* v. i. 364, 'I'll be reveng'd on the whole pack of you.'
101–4.] The widening disorder grows more serious with this new outburst of violence in Antipholus's attack on his wife (cf. the beating of Dromio, l. 17 and n. above), and the fight on stage which follows.
104. S.D. strives] See l. 107 and n.

S.D.] after l. 103 in F, but often transferred, as by N.C.S. and Alexander, to follow l. 105; it may be anticipatory (the prompter or bookkeeper sometimes placed directions some lines in advance of a point of entry to serve as warning to him and the actors), but the permissive 'three or four' suggests an author's direction, and it looks as though they should come on as Adriana calls 'bind him', for Antipholus clearly moves as if to attack her. Pinch's cry, 'More company' may merely emphasize what a struggle Antipholus puts up.
107. *What . . . me*] Cf. Marlowe, *Edward II*, v. iii. 29, where the King speaks these same words, as he 'strives'

I am thy prisoner; wilt thou suffer them
To make a rescue?
Offic.   Masters, let him go;
He is my prisoner and you shall not have him.   110
Pinch. Go bind this man, for he is frantic too.
Adr. What wilt thou do, thou peevish officer?
Hast thou delight to see a wretched man
Do outrage and displeasure to himself?
Offic. He is my prisoner; if I let him go   115
The debt he owes will be requir'd of me.
Adr. I will discharge thee ere I go from thee;
Bear me forthwith unto his creditor,
And knowing how the debt grows, I will pay it.
Good master doctor, see him safe convey'd   120
Home to my house; O most unhappy day!
Eph. Ant. O most unhappy strumpet!
Eph. Dro. Master, I am here enter'd in bond for you.
Eph. Ant. Out on thee villain, wherefore dost thou mad me?
Eph. Dro. Will you be bound for nothing? Be mad, good 125
    master; cry "the devil".
Luc. God help, poor souls, how idly do they talk!
Adr. Go, bear him hence; sister, go you with me.
    Say now, whose suit is he arrested at?
        *Exeunt [Pinch and his assistants carrying off Antipholus and
                                        Dromio of Ephesus].*

108–10.] *As Pope; prose in* F.   127. help, poor] *Theobald;* help poor F.   idly]
Pope (idlely F).   128. go you] F; stay you *Pope.*   129. S.D. *Exeunt ... Ephesus.*]
Capell (subst.); Exeunt. Manet Offic. Adri. Luci. Courtizan | F; after l. 128, Malone.

against Matrevis and Gurney; see also
v. i. 170–3 and n., and Introduction,
p. xix.

108–10.] F prints as prose, and not
unreasonably, for it is the barest kind
of verse; cf. iv. iii. 69–73 and n.

109. *make a rescue*] remove by force
from legal custody, cf. *Cor.*, iii. i. 277
(*O.E.D.*, rescue, sb. 2).

111. *this man*] Dromio, cf. l. 125.

112. *peevish*] senseless, cf. iv. i. 94.

114. *displeasure*] injury, cf. v. i. 142
below.

117. *discharge*] pay.

120. *doctor*] See l. 45 above, and n.

124–6.] So F; again it is difficult to
distinguish verse from prose, cf. ll.
108–10 above.

126. *cry "the devil"*] The common expression of impatience, but Dromio is
still jesting on his supposed possession
by 'the fiend', l. 105.

127. *God help,*] a common interjection; F has no comma after *help*, but
'poor souls' clearly refers to Antipholus
and Dromio.

129. S.D.] For a comment on the
form of the stage-direction in F here,
see Introduction, p. xiv; cf. also v. i.
407, S.D. and n.

Offic. One Angelo, a goldsmith; do you know him?   130
Adr. I know the man; what is the sum he owes?
Offic. Two hundred ducats.
Adr.   Say, how grows it due?
Offic. Due for a chain your husband had of him.
Adr. He did bespeak a chain for me, but had it not.
Cour. When as your husband all in rage to-day   135
    Came to my house and took away my ring,
    The ring I saw upon his finger now,
    Straight after did I meet him with a chain.
Adr. It may be so, but I did never see it.
    Come, jailor, bring me where the goldsmith is;   140
    I long to know the truth hereof at large.

Enter ANTIPHOLUS *and* DROMIO *of Syracuse with rapiers drawn.*

Luc. God for thy mercy, they are loose again!
Adr. And come with naked swords; let's call more help
    To have them bound again.
Offic.   Away, they'll kill us!
    [*They*] *run all out, as fast as may be, frighted.*

134. for me] *F; omitted Hanmer.*   141. S.D. *Antipholus . . . drawn.*] *Dyce (subst.)*; *Antipholus Siracusia with his Rapier drawne, and Dromio Sirac. F.*   143–4. swords; let's . . . help / . . . again. Away . . . us!] *As Hanmer;* swords, / Let's . . . helpe . . . againe. / *Runne all out.* / Away . . . us. *F.*   144. S.D. *They run all out*] *Exeunt omnes F.*

135. *When as*] = when; a common usage.

141. S.D. *rapiers*] In F the S.D. names Antipholus only as entering 'with his rapier drawn', but see ll. 142–3. The dialogue is not consistent, for Dromio, l. 146, says Adriana runs from Antipholus, and at v. i. 34 she speaks only of Antipholus as having a sword. It is true that at v. i. 151 she says both attacked 'with drawn swords', but then she is inclined to exaggerate all that has happened, cf. v. i. 140–4 and n.

141–4.] This marks another stage in the growing disorder and violence, cf. ll. 101–4 and n., and Introduction, p. xlviii.

144. S.D. They . . . frighted] The verse is mislined here in F; 'Let's . . .

againe' is printed as the last line at the foot of column 1 on the page H6ᵛ, and squeezed below it is the S.D. 'Runne all out'; column 2 begins with the line '*Off.* Away, they'l kill vs', followed by another S.D., 'Exeunt omnes, as fast as may be, frighted'. Greg, *First Folio,* p. 201, says 'Exeunt omnes' was 'doubtless added (incorrectly) on the left [i.e. by the prompter], duplicating the author's original direction on the right', and compares v. i. 407 S.D. This is a possible explanation, and the splitting off of 'Runne all out' in F may have come about simply because the author's S.D. was divided into two lines in the margin, and the compositor set it up as it was written; but the division of this passage between two columns in F may itself account for its

Syr. Ant. I see these witches are afraid of swords.   145
Syr. Dro. She that would be your wife now ran from you.
Syr. Ant. Come to the Centaur, fetch our stuff from thence;
    I long that we were safe and sound aboard.
Syr. Dro. Faith, stay here this night, they will surely do
    us no harm; you saw they speak us fair, give us gold.   150
    Methinks they are such a gentle nation, that but for
    the mountain of mad flesh that claims marriage of
    me, I could find in my heart to stay here still and
    turn witch.
Syr. Ant. I will not stay to-night for all the town;   155
    Therefore away, to get our stuff aboard.   *Exeunt.*

145. *Syr. Ant.*] *S. Ant.* / *F.*   146. *Syr. Dro.*] *S. Dro.* / *F.*   150. saw ... speak ...
give] *F;* saw ... spake ... give *F2;* saw ... spake ... gave *Rowe 2;* see ... speak
... give *Capell.*   147, 155. *Syr. Ant.*] *Ant.* / *F.*   149. *Syr. Dro.*] *Dro.* / *F.*

peculiarities, see Introduction, p. xiii.
In any case, the argument of N.C.S.,
p. 73, that the original S.D. was
'Exeunt omnes' and the rest was added
later, is implausible guessing, designed
to bolster up a theory that a scribe
revised 'the stage-directions for theatrical purposes'; cf. Chambers, *W.S.*,
I. 306.

    145, 154. *witches ... witch*] applied to
both sexes, cf. III. ii. 155.

    146. *would . . . wife*] i.e. wished to
make out that she was your wife; see
Abbott, 329.

    147. *Centaur*] Cf. I. ii. 9 and II. ii. 2
above.

    147, 156. *stuff*] baggage.

    150. *saw*] often emended to 'see' (as
by N.C.S.), but such irregular
sequences of tenses as here are not
uncommon, and the sense is plain; cf.
Abbott, 370 and 347.

    155-6.] Here Antipholus again
promises to carry out his resolution to
leave Ephesus instantly, cf. III. ii. 183-
4; this helps to maintain tension, for
his proposal to go threatens to impede
a solution to the action.

K

ACT V

SCENE I

*Enter [Second] Merchant, and [*Angelo*] the Goldsmith.*

Angelo. I am sorry, sir, that I have hinder'd you,
    But I protest he had the chain of me,
    Though most dishonestly he doth deny it.
Sec. Mer. How is the man esteem'd here in the city?
Angelo. Of very reverend reputation, sir,   5
    Of credit infinite, highly belov'd,
    Second to none that lives here in the city;
    His word might bear my wealth at any time.
Sec. Mer. Speak softly; yonder, as I think, he walks.

Enter Antipholus *and* Dromio *[of Syracuse] again.*

ACT V
Scene i

ACT V SCENE I] *Pope; Actus Quintus. Scæna Prima. F.*   S.D. *Second*] *Dyce; not in F.   Angelo*] *not in F.*   1. *Angelo*] *Rowe; Gold. | F (and throughout, except for Goldsmith, l. 377).*   4. *Sec. Mer.*] *Mar. | F (so throughout scene).*   9. S.D. *of Syracuse*] *not in F.*

ACT V] So F, but the act-division may be the work of an editor; the S.D. at l. 9 points to a continuous action.

SCENE I] Like the last part of iv. iv, this returns (cf. i. i and ii) to blank verse to close the action, in which the prevailing atmosphere of confusion and violence threatens briefly to overshadow the earlier comedy; we are released back into this earlier mood at the very end, as the Dromios have a few lines in prose, and go off finally with a couplet recalling their tumbling, jesting verse.

Entry. the Goldsmith] Angelo is not named in F after iv. iv. 130, and figures in speech-headings and direc-

tions as Gold(smith).

1. *hinder'd you*] referring back to iv. i. 1 ff.

5. *reverend*] *reverent* F; see iii. ii. 88 and n.

8. *His . . . wealth*] i.e., as N.C.S. suggests, 'His word is worth my whole credit'—he might borrow so much on his word alone.

9. S.D.] Whoever wrote this direction was not thinking of the dialogue here as the beginning of Act V, but of a continuous action with no break. N.C.S. regards this S.D. as theatrical, but I think, with Greg, *First Folio*, p. 201, that it is the author's; see Introduction, p. xii.

88

Angelo. 'Tis so; and that self chain about his neck   10
    Which he forswore most monstrously to have.
    Good sir, draw near to me; I'll speak to him.
    Signior Antipholus, I wonder much
    That you would put me to this shame and trouble,
    And not without some scandal to yourself,   15
    With circumstance and oaths so to deny
    This chain, which now you wear so openly.
    Beside the charge, the shame, imprisonment,
    You have done wrong to this my honest friend,
    Who, but for staying on our controversy,   20
    Had hoisted sail and put to sea to-day.
    This chain you had of me, can you deny it?
Syr. Ant. I think I had; I never did deny it.
Angelo. Yes, that you did, sir, and forswore it too.
Syr. Ant. Who heard me to deny it or forswear it?   25
Sec. Mer. These ears of mine thou know'st did hear thee.
    Fie on thee, wretch, 'tis pity that thou liv'st
    To walk where any honest men resort.
Syr. Ant. Thou art a villain to impeach me thus;
    I'll prove mine honour and mine honesty   30
    Against thee presently, if thou dar'st stand.
Sec. Mer. I dare, and do defy thee for a villain.

They draw. Enter ADRIANA, LUCIANA, *Courtesan and others.*

12. to me] *F;* with me *Hudson, after Collier.*   23, 25, 29. Syr. Ant.] *Ant.* | *F.*
26. thee.] *As F;* thee, sir *Capell;* thee swear *conj. Grant White;* thee swear it *Cuningham.*

10. *self*] same; see Abbott, 20.

12. *to me*] commonly emended to *with me*, which certainly makes more obvious sense; but I take it that Angelo beckons to the Merchant to stay by him as he moves to speak to Antipholus, and there is no need to emend.

16. *circumstance*] detailed argument.

18. *charge*] expense, or perhaps inconvenience, echoing 'trouble', l. 14.

imprisonment] It is not explained how Angelo comes to be walking here freely with the Merchant, who had him arrested on his last appearance (IV. i. 69–71); not that this troubles the

spectator. For other minor inconsistencies, cf. I. i. 124, 128, V. i. 400 and notes.

26. *These . . . thee*] often emended, as short of a syllable and accent, but effective as it stands, and there are other examples in Shakespeare, see Abbott, 505–10.

31. *presently*] immediately.

32. S.D. They draw] i.e. Antipholus and the Second Merchant, who twice refers to drawing his sword on Antipholus, at ll. 43 and 263. There is nothing to suggest that Angelo also has a weapon out.

Adr. Hold, hurt him not for God's sake, he is mad;
    Some get within him, take his sword away;
    Bind Dromio too, and bear them to my house.   35
Syr. Dro. Run master, run, for God's sake take a house;
    This is some priory; in, or we are spoil'd.
             Exeunt [Antipholus and Dromio] to the priory

Enter [EMILIA, *the*] *Lady Abbess.*

Abbess. Be quiet, people; wherefore throng you hither?
Adr. To fetch my poor distracted husband hence;
    Let us come in, that we may bind him fast   40
    And bear him home for his recovery.
Angelo. I knew he was not in his perfect wits.
Sec. Mer. I am sorry now that I did draw on him.
Abbess. How long hath this possession held the man?
Adr. This week he hath been heavy, sour, sad,   45
    And much, much different from the man he was;
    But till this afternoon his passion
    Ne'er brake into extremity of rage.
Abbess. Hath he not lost much wealth by wrack of sea?
    Buried some dear friend? Hath not else his eye   50

---

33. God's] *F3;* God *F.*   37. S.D. *Antipholus and Dromio] not in F.*   *Emilia, the*]
not in F.   38. quiet, people] *Theobald;* quiet people *F.*   46. much, much]
F2; much *F.*

32–7.] This is the final stage in a crescendo of violence marked by the beating of Dromio, the fight, and binding of Antipholus of Ephesus, followed by the entry of Antipholus and Dromio of Syracuse with drawn swords, in IV. iv; normal order and normal relationships are thoroughly disrupted, and a sense of magic has become a sense of evil (see IV. iii. 46–76 and n.). It is at this point that the Priory is first mentioned, with its hint of a providential solution of difficulties. For the importance of this in the play's action, see Introduction, p. xlviii.

34. *within him*] inside his guard, at close quarters; the correct term (*O.E.D.*, prep. 8b.).

36. *take*] i.e. enter for refuge (*O.E.D.*, v. 25), cf. *Troil.*, v. iv. 18.

37. *spoil'd*] destroyed, ruined.

S.D. to the priory] perhaps one of the doors on the stage, marked with an appropriate sign, cf. IV. iii. 42 S.D. and n., and Introduction, p. xxxiv. See too l. 156 below, where Adriana says the Abbess 'shuts the gates on us'.

44. *possession*] Cf. IV. iv. 52–3.

45. *sad*] grave.

46. *much, much*] Cuningham compares *Mer. V.,* III. ii. 61; it was probably a slip of the compositor to drop one *much* from F.

47. *passion*] affliction, disorder, cf. *Mac.,* IV. iii. 114; the word has three syllables here, cf. III. i. 106 above.

48. *rage*] madness, cf. IV. iii. 84.

49. *wrack*] the form invariably used by Shakespeare.

Stray'd his affection in unlawful love,
A sin prevailing much in youthful men,
Who give their eyes the liberty of gazing?
Which of these sorrows is he subject to?

Adr. To none of these, except it be the last,   55
Namely, some love that drew him oft from home.

Abbess. You should for that have reprehended him.

Adr. Why, so I did.

Abbess.   Ay, but not rough enough.

Adr. As roughly as my modesty would let me.

Abbess. Haply in private.

Adr.   And in assemblies too.   60

Abbess. Ay, but not enough.

Adr. It was the copy of our conference;
In bed he slept not for my urging it,
At board he fed not for my urging it;
Alone, it was the subject of my theme;   65
In company I often glanc'd at it;
Still did I tell him it was vile and bad.

Abbess. And thereof came it that the man was mad.
The venom clamours of a jealous woman
Poisons more deadly than a mad dog's tooth.   70
It seems his sleeps were hinder'd by thy railing,
And thereof comes it that his head is light.
Thou say'st his meat was sauc'd with thy upbraidings;

66. glanc'd at it] *Pope;* glanced it *F.*   67. vile] *F* (vilde), *Rowe.*   69. venom]
F (venome)*; venom'd *Pope.*   70. Poisons] *F;* Poison *Pope.*

51. *Stray'd*] not used transitively
elsewhere by Shakespeare (cf. *O.E.D.*,
v^2 4 c).

61.] A short line, cf. I. i. 61 and n.
The repartee here is not regular in
pattern and leaves over this half-line.

62. *copy*] theme, treated with full-
ness (*copia verborum*). For further discussion of the technical senses of the
word as used here, see T. W. Baldwin,
Shakspere's Small Latine, II. 184–5, and
Hilda Hulme in *Neophilologus*, XXIV
(1958), 73–4.

66. *glanc'd at*] I think *at* probably
dropped out here in a similar way to
much, l. 46. Most edd. now keep

glanced (F), and *O.E.D.* records this as
the earliest and only example of a
figurative use. It is tempting to rely on
the form in F as indicating an inflected
–ed, but F is not regular, cf. I. i. 130,
laboured for *labour'd*; l. 215 below, *disturbed* for *disturb'd*.

67–8.] Adriana falls into the Abbess's trap, and the rhyme here marks
its closure.

67. *vile*] *vilde* (F) was a common
form of the word.

69. *venom*] formerly common as an
adjective, cf. *R2*, II. i. 19.

69–70. *clamours ... Poisons*] See IV. iv.
75 and n.

Unquiet meals make ill digestions;
Thereof the raging fire of fever bred,   75
And what's a fever but a fit of madness?
Thou sayest his sports were hinder'd by thy brawls;
Sweet recreation barr'd, what doth ensue
But moody and dull melancholy,
Kinsman to grim and comfortless despair,   80
And at her heels a huge infectious troop
Of pale distemperatures and foes to life?
In food, in sport and life-preserving rest
To be disturb'd, would mad or man or beast;
The consequence is then, thy jealous fits   85
Hath scar'd thy husband from the use of wits.

Luc. She never reprehended him but mildly,
When he demean'd himself rough, rude and wildly;
Why bear you these rebukes and answer not?

Adr. She did betray me to mine own reproof.   90
Good people, enter and lay hold on him.

Abbess. No, not a creature enters in my house.

Adr. Then let your servants bring my husband forth.

Abbess. Neither. He took this place for sanctuary,
And it shall privilege him from your hands   95
Till I have brought him to his wits again,
Or lose my labour in assaying it.

Adr. I will attend my husband, be his nurse,

79. moody and] *F;* moody, moping and *Hanmer;* moody, heavy and *Cuningham.*
80. Kinsman] *F;* A'kin *Hanmer.*   81. her] *F;* their *Malone, conj. Heath;* his
Collier 2, conj. S. Walker.   86. Hath] *F;* Have *F2.*

79. *But . . . melancholy*] Cf. l. 26 and
n.; emendation seems to me to weaken
the line, and Abbott, 484, cites many
parallels.

80. *Kinsman*] used generically;
emendation of 'her', l. 81, is unnecessary; Ritson compares *Mer. V.,* III. ii.
164–6.

82. *distemperatures*] ailments.

85–6. *fits | Hath*] Cf. ll. 69–70 above.

88. *demean'd himself*] a verb used
only in this play and in *2* and *3H6* by
Shakespeare.

94. *took*] Cf. 'take', l. 36 and n.

sanctuary] The right of taking refuge

from the law in a church or sacred
place was not abolished in criminal
cases until 1625, and in civil cases
until the end of the 17th century; see
O.E.D., sb.[1] 5.

98–9.] Noble, p. 109, suggests that
Adriana may be alluding to the
phrase in the marriage service, Book
of Common Prayer, 'to have and to
hold . . . in sickness and in health'.

98–101.] Adriana's desire to have
her husband all to herself recalls her
fastening on Antipholus of Syracuse,
II. ii. 173–80; and reflects her jealous
and over-possessive love, a love dis-

Diet his sickness, for it is my office,

And will have no attorney but myself,   100

And therefore let me have him home with me.

Abbess. Be patient, for I will not let him stir

Till I have us'd the approved means I have,

With wholesome syrups, drugs and holy prayers,

To make of him a formal man again.   105

It is a branch and parcel of mine oath,

A charitable duty of my order;

Therefore depart, and leave him here with me.

Adr. I will not hence and leave my husband here:

And ill it doth beseem your holiness   110

To separate the husband and the wife.

Abbess. Be quiet and depart, thou shalt not have him. [*Exit.*]

Luc. Complain unto the duke of this indignity.

Adr. Come, go, I will fall prostrate at his feet,

And never rise until my tears and prayers   115

Have won his grace to come in person hither,

And take perforce my husband from the abbess.

Sec. Mer. By this I think the dial points at five;

Anon I'm sure the Duke himself in person

Comes this way to the melancholy vale,   120

The place of death and sorry execution

Behind the ditches of the abbey here.

---

112. *Exit.*] *Theobald; not in* F.   121. death] *F3; depth* F.

ordered; for further comment on this
aspect of the play, see J. R. Brown,
Shakespeare and his Comedies, pp. 54–
7.

100. *attorney*] substitute to act for
me.

102. *patient*] See IV. ii. 16 and n.

103. *approved*] tried.

105. *formal*] properly formed, regular, hence normal, sane; cf. *Tw. N.*, II.
v. 128, 'this is evident to any formal
capacity'.

106. *parcel*] part, item.

117. *perforce*] Cf. IV. iii. 91.

118. *five*] Cf. I. ii. 26 and IV. i. 10;
the action has pointed towards five
o'clock, supper-time (III. ii. 173) as a
point of resolution, when Antipholus

of Syracuse, the Merchants and
Angelo arrange to meet to settle the
affair of the chain; it now turns out,
appropriately, to be the time fixed for
Egeon's execution too.

120–2. *vale . . . here*] T. W. Baldwin,
in his *William Shakspere Adapts a
Hanging* (Princeton, 1931), sees here
an allusion to the execution of a
seminary priest, William Hartley, on
5 October 1588, in Finsbury Fields,
behind the ditches of Holywell Priory,
close by the Theatre and Curtain,
where he believes the play was
originally acted. For discussion see
Introduction, p. xvii.

121. *sorry*] causing sorrow, cf. *Mac.*,
II. ii. 20.

Angelo. Upon what cause?

Sec. Mer. To see a reverend Syracusian merchant,
Who put unluckily into this bay,   125
Against the laws and statutes of this town,
Beheaded publicly for his offence.

Angelo. See where they come; we will behold his death.

Luc. Kneel to the Duke before he pass the abbey.

Enter [SOLINUS] *the Duke of Ephesus, and* [EGEON] *the Merchant
of Syracuse barehead, with the Headsman and other Officers.*

Duke. Yet once again proclaim it publicly,   130
If any friend will pay the sum for him,
He shall not die, so much we tender him.

Adr. Justice, most sacred duke, against the abbess.

Duke. She is a virtuous and a reverend lady,
It cannot be that she hath done thee wrong.   135

Adr. May it please your grace, Antipholus my husband,
Who I made lord of me and all I had
At your important letters, this ill day
A most outrageous fit of madness took him;
That desp'rately he hurried through the street,   140
With him his bondman, all as mad as he,

129. S.D. *Solinus*] not in F.   *Egeon*] not in F.   137. Who] *F;* Whom *F2+.*
138. letters, . . . day] *Pope, after F2;* Letters . . . day, *F.*

123.] Cf. l. 61 and n.
124. *reverend*] See III. ii. 88 and n.
129. S.D. the Merchant] Egeon is
not named, and there is already one
merchant on stage; see l. 195 S.H. and
n. below. Egeon comes on 'bound', as
indicated in l. 294 below.
130–94.] On the conflicting claims
for justice here, and the working out of
the resolution of the action, see Introduction, p. xlviii.
132. *tender*] have regard for; or perhaps take pity on, cf. *1H6,* IV. vii. 10.
137. *Who*] for *whom,* as commonly,
cf. *Mac.,* III. i. 122, 'Who I myself
struck down' (Abbott, 274).
138. *important*] pressing, urgent, cf.
Ado, II. i. 74. Steevens thought Shakespeare might have had in mind here

the sovereign's right of marrying his
wards to anyone of equal rank (see
Shakespeare's England, I. 386–7), as later
in *All's W.,* II. iii. 50ff., the King offers
Helena her choice among the bache-
lors who, he says, 'stand at my
bestowing'.
140–4.] Adriana accepted the Courtesan's lie that Antipholus broke into
her house and stole her ring (see IV.
iii. 89–92 and n.), but now she extends
it in her anger to make him and
Dromio responsible for general outrage and widespread robbery; what
she imagines here contributes to the
sense of confusion and disorder in
Ephesus.
140. *desp'rately*] with reckless violence.

Doing displeasure to the citizens
By rushing in their houses; bearing thence
Rings, jewels, any thing his rage did like.
Once did I get him bound, and sent him home,   145
Whilst to take order for the wrongs I went,
That here and there his fury had committed;
Anon, I wot not by what strong escape,
He broke from those that had the guard of him,
And with his mad attendant and himself,   150
Each one with ireful passion, with drawn swords
Met us again, and madly bent on us,
Chas'd us away; till raising of more aid
We came again to bind them. Then they fled
Into this abbey, whither we pursu'd them,   155
And here the abbess shuts the gates on us,
And will not suffer us to fetch him out,
Nor send him forth that we may bear him hence.
Therefore, most gracious duke, with thy command
Let him be brought forth, and borne hence for help. 160
Duke. Long since thy husband serv'd me in my wars,
And I to thee engag'd a prince's word,
When thou didst make him master of thy bed,
To do him all the grace and good I could.
Go some of you, knock at the abbey gate,   165
And bid the lady abbess come to me.
I will determine this before I stir.

Enter a Messenger.

Mess. O mistress, mistress, shift and save yourself;
My master and his man are both broke loose,

150. with] *F;* here *Capell.*   155. whither] *F* (whether).   168. *Mess.*] *F2; not in F.*

142. *displeasure*] offence, harm, cf. IV. iv. 114.
144. *rage*] Cf. l. 48 above.
146. *take order for*] make arrangements for settling.
153. *raising of*] *of* was commonly used after a participle; see Abbott, 178.
156. *shuts the gates*] Cf. l. 37 S.D. and n.

160. *help*] cure, relief, cf. *Sonn.* CLIII. 11, 'I, sick withal, the help of bath desir'd . . . But found no cure'.
168. S.H. Mess.] The speech-heading is omitted from F, as at IV. iii. 1; see Introduction, p. xiv, n. 2.
169–77.] The syntax is confused, but allows for the shift of attention from present danger to what has hap-

Beaten the maids a-row, and bound the doctor,   170
Whose beard they have sing'd off with brands of fire,
And ever as it blaz'd, they threw on him
Great pails of puddled mire to quench the hair;
My master preaches patience to him, and the while
His man with scissors nicks him like a fool;   175
And sure (unless you send some present help)
Between them they will kill the conjurer.

Adr. Peace, fool, thy master and his man are here,
And that is false thou dost report to us.

Mess. Mistress, upon my life I tell you true,   180
I have not breath'd almost since I did see it.
He cries for you, and vows if he can take you
To scorch your face and to disfigure you.   *Cry within.*

175. scissors] *F* (Cizers).   183. scorch] *F;* scotch *Hanmer.*

pened (*are . . . broke . . . beaten . . . have sing'd*), leading back to a focus on the present (*nicks*) and future (*will kill*).

170–3.] H. F. Brooks points out the echo here of *Edward II*, a play in which Marlowe followed historical sources in making Matrevis and Gurney wash the King's face in 'puddle water' and shave away his beard; later Edward says he has stood 'in mire and puddle' (v. i. 58); see also iv. iv. 107 and n.

170. *a-row*] one after another; not used elsewhere by Shakespeare (cf. Abbott, 24).

173. *puddled*] stirred up and foul.

174.] Apparent alexandrines are common in Shakespeare, but a slurring or elision of light syllables is probably intended (cf. Abbott, 494–8).

patience] It is a nice touch that the constantly impatient Antipholus of Ephesus (cf. iv. iv. 18–19 and n.) should now preach patience to Pinch.

175. *scissors*] With the spelling *Cizers* (F) possibly Shakespeare's, cf. *The Two Noble Kinsmen*, i. ii. 59, 'Cizard' (= scissored).

nicks . . . fool] alluding to the traditional habit of the professional fool of shaving his head, or wearing his hair cut like a monk's, cf. R. H. Goldsmith, *Wise Fools in Shakespeare* (Liverpool,

1958), pp. 1–2; Malone appositely cited S.R., *The Choice of Change* (1585), K1v, 'They [the monks] are shaven and notcht on the head, lyke fooles'. It is not clear whether Dromio simply cuts out patches of Pinch's hair haphazardly, or gives him a special sort of haircut.

177. *conjurer*] See iv. iv. 37, S.D. and note.

181. *not . . . almost*] We would now say 'hardly', or 'almost not' (Abbott, 29).

183. *scorch*] cut or gash; often needlessly emended to *scotch*, like *scorch'd* (*scotch'd*) at *Mac.*, iii. ii. 13. Here *scorch* seems to follow from 'brands of fire', l. 171, and N.C.S. imagines a striking tableau at l. 189 of Antipholus and Dromio entering with burning brands. There is no warranty for this, but there is less still for emendation, especially since *scotch* is not used in Shakespeare's early works, as Cuningham noted. In Warner, Menaechmus, feigning madness, cries to his wife '*Apollo* commaunds me that I should rende out hir eyes with a burning lampe' (Bullough, p. 37), where the Latin has 'you [Apollo] bid me not to spare my fists at all on her face' ('pugnis me votas in

Hark, hark, I hear him, mistress—fly, be gone.
Duke. Come, stand by me, fear nothing; guard with halberds.
Adr. Ay me, it is my husband; witness you   186
    That he is borne about invisible;
    Even now we hous'd him in the abbey here,
    And now he's there, past thought of human reason.

Enter ANTIPHOLUS *and* DROMIO *of Ephesus.*

Eph. Ant. Justice, most gracious Duke, O, grant me justice,
    Even for the service that long since I did thee   191
    When I bestrid thee in the wars, and took
    Deep scars to save thy life; even for the blood
    That then I lost for thee, now grant me justice.
Egeon. Unless the fear of death doth make me dote,   195
    I see my son Antipholus and Dromio.
Eph. Ant. Justice, sweet prince, against that woman there—
    She whom thou gav'st to me to be my wife;
    That hath abused and dishonour'd me,
    Even in the strength and height of injury.   200

189. S.D. *Dromio of Ephesus*] E. *Dromio of Ephesus | F.*   195. *Egeon.*] *Johnson;*
Mar. Fat. | F.   195–6.] *As Rowe 2; prose in F.*   199. dishonour'd] *Rowe;* dis-
honored *F.*

huius ore quicquam parcere', l. 848).
    185. *halberds*] Some of the 'other
officers' of l. 129 S.D. draw near and
set up their weapons, a combination of
spear and battle-axe, for defence.
    187–9.] The final link in the chain
of evidence which has now convinced
Adriana that a supernatural agency
controls her husband; the association
of Ephesus with witchcraft, which
began in rumour, in what Antipholus
of Syracuse had heard about the city
(I. ii. 97), has become a frightful
reality not only for him, but for
Adriana too. See Introduction, p.
xlvii.
    188. *hous'd*] pursued into a house.
    189. S.D.] Chambers, *W.S.,* I. 306,
and Greg, *First Folio,* p. 201, attribute
the duplication here in F, 'E. Dromio
of Ephesus', to a prompter, who, they
think, added the last two words. I
think it is just as likely to be the com-

positor's casual expansion of MS.
'Enter E(phes.) Antipholus and E.
Dromio'; see Introduction, p. xiv.
    190. *Justice*] See note to l. 130.
    192. *bestrid*] the form always used by
Shakespeare, who never has *bestrode.*
    195. S.H. Egeon] F has '*Mar. Fat.*',
following the entry at l. 129, which
lists Egeon as '*the Merchant of Siracuse*',
and so distinguishes in speech-heading
between him and the Merchant who is
on stage. Later, from l. 283 onwards,
the heading for Egeon becomes '*Fa.*'
(*Fath., Father.*); the name Egeon does
not appear in headings or directions,
although it occurs in the text, cf. ll.
337, 341, 344.
    195–6.] These lines are printed as
prose in F, possibly because there was
no space to print *dote* in l. 195.
    199. *dishonour'd*] F may be correct, if
the word can be slurred into *dis-
hon'red* in pronunciation (H.F.B.).

Beyond imagination is the wrong
That she this day hath shameless thrown on me.
Duke. Discover how, and thou shalt find me just.
Eph. Ant. This day, great duke, she shut the doors upon me
     While she with harlots feasted in my house.   205
Duke. A grievous fault: say, woman, didst thou so?
Adr. No, my good lord. Myself, he, and my sister
     To-day did dine together; so befall my soul
     As this is false he burdens me withal.
Luc. Ne'er may I look on day, nor sleep on night,   210
     But she tells to your highness simple truth.
Angelo. [*Aside*] O perjur'd woman! They are both forsworn,
     In this the madman justly chargeth them.
Eph. Ant. My liege, I am advised what I say,
     Neither disturb'd with the effect of wine,   215
     Nor heady-rash, provok'd with raging ire,
     Albeit my wrongs might make one wiser mad.
     This woman lock'd me out this day from dinner;
     That goldsmith there, were he not pack'd with her,
     Could witness it; for he was with me then,   220
     Who parted with me to go fetch a chain,

212. S.D. *Aside*] *This ed.; not in* F.   215. disturb'd] *Rowe;* disturbed F.

205. *harlots*] originally meaning
'rogue', 'low fellow', this word was
later applied to men, and more commonly women, 'of loose life', as *O.E.D.*
puts it. N.C.S. observes that Shakespeare generally 'uses it in relation to
fornication', as at *Wint.*, II. iii. 4, 'She
th' adultress; for the harlot king / Is
quite beyond mine arm', and no doubt
this is the sense intended here; cf. II. ii.
136 and IV. iv. 99 above, and IV. iv. 58,
where Antipholus addressed Adriana
as a prostitute.

208.] apparently an alexandrine,
but no doubt *together* was softened into
toge'er, cf. IV. i. 60 (Abbott, 466).

208-9. *so . . . As*] For the construction here, cf. *R3*, II. i. 11, 16, and
Abbott 133.

210. *on night*] = at night, cf. Abbott,
181.

212. *Aside*] Angelo speaks out only at
l. 255, where he addresses the Duke.

214. *I am advised*] I am well aware of.
cf. *Shr.*, I. i. 181.

219-30.] Antipholus was arrested at
Angelo's instigation (IV. i. 80) on what
seemed to him a false claim of payment for a chain never delivered.
Later Antipholus assumes that Angelo
was working in collusion with Adriana
who had 'suborn'd' him (IV. iv. 80).
So, in his imagination, Angelo becomes a main agent in the conspiracy
(cf. l. 237) he believes his wife has
engineered against him. His violent
comments on Angelo here follow
naturally from his initial supposition. N.C.S. found this attack odd
in relation to Angelo's remarks in
ll. 212-13, but if these two lines are
taken as an aside, the difficulty
vanishes.

219. *pack'd with*] in league with; cf.
IV. iv. 100 and n.

221. *parted with*] departed with.

Promising to bring it to the Porpentine,
Where Balthasar and I did dine together.
Our dinner done, and he not coming thither,
I went to seek him. In the street I met him,   225
And in his company that gentleman.
There did this perjur'd goldsmith swear me down
That I this day of him receiv'd the chain,
Which, God he knows, I saw not. For the which
He did arrest me with an officer;   230
I did obey, and sent my peasant home
For certain ducats; he with none return'd.
Then fairly I bespoke the officer
To go in person with me to my house.
By th'way we met   235
My wife, her sister, and a rabble more
Of vile confederates; along with them
They brought one Pinch, a hungry lean-fac'd villain;
A mere anatomy, a mountebank,
A thread-bare juggler and a fortune-teller,   240
A needy-hollow-ey'd-sharp-looking-wretch;

235-6.] *As Malone; one line in F.*   237. vile] F (vilde); *Rowe.*   241. needy-
hollow-ey'd-sharp-looking-wretch] F; needy, hollow-ey'd, sharp-looking wretch
Theobald+, after Pope.

223. *Balthasar*] This is the only
reference to him outside III. i, the one
scene in which he appears. N.C.S.
regards him as a 'ghost' character, a
relic of an older version of the play,
but see Introduction, p. xxviii.

226. *that gentleman*] Angelo was
accompanied by the Merchant, cf.
IV. i.

231. *peasant*] Cf. II. i. 81 and n.

233. *bespoke*] requested.

235. *By . . . met*] A short line, cf. l. 61
above; there is no need to see evidence
of cutting with N.C.S., or of omission
with Cuningham. In F it is printed as
one line with l. 236.

237. *vile*] *vilde* in F; cf. l. 67 and n.

238-42. *Pinch . . . dead man*] Allison
Gaw, 'John Sincklo as one of Shake-
speare's Actors', *Anglia*, neue Folge,
XXXVI (1926), 289-303, drew atten-

tion to a number of parts for a thin,
serious faced actor in Shakespeare's
earlier plays, Starveling in *MND.*, an
Officer in *2H4*, the Apothecary in
Rom., and identified this actor plausibly as John Sincklo, who is named in
a direction in the Quarto of *2H4*, and
in other texts. He argues that the
description here fits this actor. See
also Greg, *First Folio*, pp. 115-16. The
epithets 'lean-fac'd' and 'hollow-ey'd'
are used to describe a rogue, who does
not appear, in *Arden of Feversham*
(1592), II. ii. 51-2, but this is probably
a coincidence; 'hollow-eyed' was certainly a common epithet. See Introduction, p. xix.

239. *anatomy*] skeleton.

240. *juggler*] sorcerer, cf. IV. iv. 56
and I. ii. 98-9 above.

241.] The punctuation here may

A living dead man. This pernicious slave
Forsooth took on him as a conjurer,
And gazing in mine eyes, feeling my pulse,
And with no-face (as 'twere) out-facing me,   245
Cries out, I was possess'd. Then all together
They fell upon me, bound me, bore me thence,
And in a dark and dankish vault at home
There left me and my man, both bound together,
Till gnawing with my teeth my bonds in sunder,   250
I gain'd my freedom; and immediately
Ran hither to your grace, whom I beseech
To give me ample satisfaction
For these deep shames and great indignities.
Angelo. My lord, in truth, thus far I witness with him,   255
    That he din'd not at home, but was lock'd out.
Duke. But had he such a chain of thee, or no?
Angelo. He had, my lord, and when he ran in here
    These people saw the chain about his neck.
Sec. Mer. Besides, I will be sworn these ears of mine   260
    Heard you confess you had the chain of him,
    After you first forswore it on the mart,
    And thereupon I drew my sword on you;
    And then you fled into this abbey here,
    From whence I think you are come by miracle.   265
Eph. Ant. I never came within these abbey walls,
    Nor ever didst thou draw thy sword on me;
    I never saw the chain, so help me heaven;
    And this is false you burden me withal.
Duke. Why, what an intricate impeach is this?   270
    I think you all have drunk of Circe's cup:
    If here you hous'd him, here he would have been;

---

246. all together] *Rowe* (altogether *F*).   252. hither] *F* (hether).

represent Shakespeare's deliberate compression of the lines into one breathless word.

243. *conjurer*] exorcist, cf. iv. iv. 37, S.D. and n.

247–8. *bound . . . vault*] See iv. iv. 92 and n.

263. *drew my sword*] See l. 32 above, where he accepted the challenge of

Antipholus of Syracuse, and they both drew swords.

270. *impeach*] charge; also used at *3H6*, i. iv. 60.

271. *drunk . . . cup*] The allusion is to the *Odyssey*, Book 10, cf. iii. ii. 163 and n. This line is the culmination of the images of transformation.

272. *hous'd*] Cf. l. 188 above.

If he were mad, he would not plead so coldly.
You say he din'd at home, the goldsmith here
Denies that saying. Sirrah, what say you?   275
Eph. Dro. Sir, he din'd with her there, at the Porpentine.
Cour. He did, and from my finger snatch'd that ring.
Eph. Ant. 'Tis true, my liege, this ring I had of her.
Duke. Saw'st thou him enter at the abbey here?
Cour. As sure, my liege, as I do see your grace.   280
Duke. Why, this is strange: go, call the abbess hither.
I think you are all mated, or stark mad.
                                        Exit one to the Abbess.
Egeon. Most mighty duke, vouchsafe me speak a word;
Haply I see a friend will save my life,
And pay the sum that may deliver me.   285
Duke. Speak freely, Syracusian, what thou wilt.
Egeon. Is not your name, sir, call'd Antipholus?
And is not that your bondman Dromio?
Eph. Dro. Within this hour I was his bondman, sir,
But he, I thank him, gnaw'd in two my cords;   290
Now I am Dromio, and his man, unbound.
Egeon. I am sure you both of you remember me.
Eph. Dro. Ourselves we do remember, sir, by you.
For lately we were bound as you are now.
You are not Pinch's patient, are you sir?   295
Egeon. Why look you strange on me? you know me well.
Eph. Ant. I never saw you in my life till now.
Egeon. O! grief hath chang'd me since you saw me last,
And careful hours with time's deformed hand
Have written strange defeatures in my face;   300
But tell me yet, dost thou not know my voice?

283. *Egeon.*] *Fa.* | *F* (*Fa., Fat., Fath., or Father to end of scene*).   293, 303. *Eph. Dro.*]
Dro. | *F.*   299. deformed] *F;* deforming *Capell.*

274. *You*] Adriana; cf. l. 208.
282. *mated*] bewildered, stupefied.
For comment on the Duke's function
here, see Introduction, p. xlviii.
299. *careful*] full of care, as at *R3*,
I. iii. 83.
deformed] usually glossed as 'deform-
ing' (so Onions), by analogy with
other passages where passive participles are loosely used in an active

sense, as at *Oth.*, I. iii. 289, 'If virtue no
delighted beauty lack' (cited Cuningham; for other examples, see Abbott,
374); but Shakespeare may rather
have been thinking of the withered
hand of Father Time, as commonly
personified and depicted, cf. II. ii. 68-9
above and n.
300. *defeatures*] disfigurement; literally 'ruins', cf. II. i. 98 and n.

Eph. Ant. Neither.

Egeon. Dromio, nor thou?

Eph. Dro.   No, trust me sir, nor I.

Egeon. I am sure thou dost?

Eph. Dro. Ay sir, but I am sure I do not, and whatsoever   305
a man denies, you are bound to believe him.

Egeon. Not know my voice? O time's extremity,
Hast thou so crack'd and splitted my poor tongue
In seven short years, that here my only son
Knows not my feeble key of untun'd cares?   310
Though now this grained face of mine be hid
In sap-consuming winter's drizzled snow,
And all the conduits of my blood froze up,
Yet hath my night of life some memory;
My wasting lamps some fading glimmer left;   315
My dull deaf ears a little use to hear—
All these old witnesses, I cannot err,
Tell me thou art my son Antipholus.

Eph. Ant. I never saw my father in my life.

Egeon. But seven years since, in Syracusa, boy,   320
Thou know'st we parted, but perhaps, my son,
Thou sham'st to acknowledge me in misery.

Eph. Ant. The duke, and all that know me in the city,
Can witness with me that it is not so.

302, 319, 323. *Eph. Ant.*] *Ant.* / *F.*   305. Ay sir] *F* (I sir), *Capell.*   305–6.] *As
F; verse Capell*, Ay sir, / ...whatsoever / ...him.   307. extremity] *F* (e tremity),
F2.   317–18. witnesses, ...err, / Tell me] *As Pope;* witnesses, ...erre. / Tell
me, *F.*   320. Syracusa, boy,] *F* (*Siracusa* boy), *Capell;* Syracusa bay, *Rowe.*

303. *Dromio . . . I*] It may be accidental that this makes a verse; short
questions and answers often stand outside the verse pattern, cf. ll. 123, 366,
371.

306. *bound*] alluding to Egeon's
bonds, cf. l. 294.

307. *extremity*] extreme severity.

308. *splitted*] Cf. I. i. 103 and n.

310. *feeble . . . cares*] 'the weak and
discordant tone of my voice, that is
changed by grief' (Douce).

311. *grained*] furrowed, lined like the
grain of wood, cf. *Cor.*, IV. iv. 108,
'My grained ash an hundred times

hath broke . . .' (so Onions, Cuningham); Baldwin suggests dyed in
grain, burnt by exposure, a possible
sense.

313. *froze*] for *frozen;* see *arose,* l. 388
and n.

315. *lamps*] eyes; Cuningham is one
of a number of editors who emend to
'lamp' (presumably = spirit).

317.] The broken syntax well ex-
presses Egeon's incredulity; N.C.S.,
however, finds the construction awkward, and suggests emendation.

320. *seven years*] See I. i. 132 and l.
400 and n. below.

I ne'er saw Syracusa in my life.   325
Duke. I tell thee Syracusian, twenty years
    Have I been patron to Antipholus,
    During which time he ne'er saw Syracusa.
    I see thy age and dangers make thee dote.

Enter [EMILIA] *the Abbess with* ANTIPHOLUS *and* DROMIO
of Syracuse.

Abbess. Most mighty duke, behold a man much wrong'd. 330
                    All gather to see them.
Adr. I see two husbands, or mine eyes deceive me.
Duke. One of these men is *genius* to the other;
    And so of these, which is the natural man,
    And which the spirit? Who deciphers them?
Syr. Dro. I, sir, am Dromio, command him away.   335
Eph. Dro. I, sir, am Dromio, pray let me stay.
Syr. Ant. Egeon art thou not? or else his ghost.
Syr. Dro. O, my old master, who hath bound him here?
Abbess. Whoever bound him, I will loose his bonds,
    And gain a husband by his liberty.   340
    Speak old Egeon, if thou be'st the man
    That hadst a wife once call'd Emilia,
    That bore thee at a burden two fair sons?
    O, if thou be'st the same Egeon, speak—
    And speak unto the same Emilia.   345
Duke. Why, here begins his morning story right:

329. S.D. *Emilia*] *not in* F.   *and Dromio of Syracuse.*] *Siracusa, and Dromio Sir.* |
F.   339. loose] F (lose).   346–51.] *As* F; *transposed to follow l. 361 by*
Capell+.

330. S.D.] This direction suggests   life, governing his fortunes, cf. *Troil.*,
that the group around Egeon and the   IV. iv. 49. Thomson, *Shakespeare and the*
Duke have been absorbed in their   *Classics*, p. 51, cites a fine description
argument, and do not notice the entry   of the *genius* from Spenser's *Faerie*
of the Abbess until she speaks; it marks   *Queene*, II. xii. 47.
an effective dramatic moment as all   343. *bore . . . sons*] Cf. I. i. 50.
turn to look at the new arrivals on the   346–51.] Capell has been followed
scene; the twins are brought together   by most edd. (including Cuningham
here for the first time in the play.   and Alexander) in transposing these
  332. genius] attendant spirit (the   lines of the Duke to follow Emilia's
Greek *daemon*), which was supposed in   next speech, i.e. after the present l. 361.
ancient times to be allotted to a man at   He argued that 'her urging of her
birth, and to accompany him through   wrack at sea' (l. 349) is not supported

L

These two Antipholus', these two so like,
And these two Dromios, one in semblance,
Besides her urging of her wrack at sea.
These are the parents to these children,   350
Which accidentally are met together.
Egeon. If I dream not, thou art Emilia;
If thou art she, tell me, where is that son
That floated with thee on the fatal raft?
Abbess. By men of Epidamnum, he and I   355
And the twin Dromio, all were taken up;
But by and by, rude fishermen of Corinth
By force took Dromio and my son from them,
And me they left with those of Epidamnum.
What then became of them I cannot tell;   360
I, to this fortune that you see me in.
Duke. Antipholus, thou cam'st from Corinth first.
Syr. Ant. No, sir, not I, I came from Syracuse.
Duke. Stay, stand apart, I know not which is which.
Eph. Ant. I came from Corinth, my most gracious lord.   365
Eph. Dro. And I with him.

347. Antipholus'] *F* (Antipholus).   355, 359. Epidamnum] *Pope;* Epidamium
F.

by anything in Emilia's first speech. But, as N.C.S. notes, she says nothing of the wreck in her second speech either. N.C.S. goes on to postulate a cut, pointing out that Emilia's second speech 'appears to continue the account of the 'wrack' which should have been begun in her first'. This is pressing the matter of the wreck hard; I find it difficult to believe that an audience, knowing from Act I all about the shipwreck, would be troubled by the slight inconsistency here. The point surely is that Shakespeare reminds us of Egeon's story without allowing Emilia to repeat what is well known. If any difficulty is felt, the simplest solution would be to emend 'her urging' (l. 349) to 'his urging', as Collier suggested.

347. *Antipholus'*] The plural '–es' of nouns ending in '–s', '–se', and the

like, is frequently not printed or pronounced in Shakespeare, cf. Abbott, 471.

348, 350. *semblance, children*] trisyllabic; Abbott, 477, gives many examples of lines in which 'R and liquids in disyllables are . . . pronounced as though an extra vowel were introduced between them and the preceding consonant'; so these lines should be read as full pentameters. He cites Spenser's usage, cf. *Faerie Queene,* I. viii. 28 'handeling', and 34, 'enterance'.

355–61.] Cf. I. i. 110–11; Egeon had erred in thinking that his wife and son were 'taken up By fishermen of Corinth'. Emilia does not explain how she came from Epidamnum to Ephesus. See Introduction, p. xxxi.

366, 371, 383.] short lines; cf. l. 61 and n.

Eph. Ant. Brought to this town by that most famous warrior,
Duke Menaphon, your most renowned uncle.
Adr. Which of you two did dine with me to-day?
Syr. Ant. I, gentle mistress.
Adr.   And are you not my husband?
Eph. Ant. No, I say nay to that.   371
Syr. Ant. And so do I, yet did she call me so;
And this fair gentlewoman, her sister here,
Did call me brother. [*To Luciana.*] What I told you then,
I hope I shall have leisure to make good,   375
If this be not a dream I see and hear.
Angelo. That is the chain, sir, which you had of me.
Syr. Ant. I think it be, sir, I deny it not.
Eph. Ant. And you, sir, for this chain arrested me.
Angelo. I think I did, sir, I deny it not.   380
Adr. I sent you money, sir, to be your bail
By Dromio, but I think he brought it not.
Eph. Dro. No, none by me.
Syr. Ant. This purse of ducats I receiv'd from you,
And Dromio my man did bring them me.   385
I see we still did meet each other's man,
And I was ta'en for him, and he for me,
And thereupon these errors are arose.
Eph. Ant. These ducats pawn I for my father here.
Duke. It shall not need, thy father hath his life.   390
Cour. Sir, I must have that diamond from you.
Eph. Ant. There, take it, and much thanks for my good
cheer.

374. S.D. *To Luciana*] *Clark and Glover; not in F.*

368. *Menaphon*] not mentioned elsewhere; the name was possibly borrowed from Marlowe's *Tamburlaine* (printed 1590), or Greene's *Menaphon* (1589). See Introduction, p. xxxiv.

376. *dream . . . hear*] Compare *Gent.*, v. iv. 26, 'How like a dream is this I see and hear' (N.C.S.), *MND.*, iv. i. 190–1, and ii. ii. 181 above and n. Antipholus's earlier thoughts of sorcery and witchcraft soften into fantasy, but he cannot at once accept the new reality offered to him.

384, 389. *ducats*] See iv. i. 30 and n.
386. *still*] continually.
388. *arose*] Abbott, 343, explains this use of preterite for past participle (cf. *froze*, l. 313 above), as arising through a tendency to drop the *–en* inflection from past participles; where the curtailed form (*arisen–arise; taken–take*) might be confused with the infinitive, the preterite was used. See *Shakespeare's England*, ii. 551–2.

391. *diamond*] her ring, spoken of at iv. iii. 66–7.

Abbess. Renowned duke, vouchsafe to take the pains
    To go with us into the abbey here,
    And hear at large discoursed all our fortunes;   395
    And all that are assembled in this place,
    That by this sympathised one day's error
    Have suffer'd wrong, go, keep us company,
    And we shall make full satisfaction.
    Thirty-three years have I but gone in travail   400
    Of you, my sons, and till this present hour
    My heavy burden ne'er delivered.
    The duke, my husband, and my children both,
    And you, the calendars of their nativity,
    Go to a gossips' feast, and joy with me,   405
    After so long grief, such felicity.

398. wrong, go] *Rowe;* wrong. Goe *F.*   400. Thirty-three] *F;* Twenty-five *Theobald;* Twenty-three *Capell.*   402. burden ne'er] *Dyce;* burthen are *F;* burthens are *F2;* burden not *Capell.*   405. joy] *Rann;* go *F.*   406. felicity] *Hanmer;* Natiuitie *F;* festivity *Dyce, after Johnson.*

397. *sympathised*] shared in by all equally; an odd use of the word, extending the sense in which it is used at *LLL.,* III. i. 45, and in other passages in Shakespeare's early work, of 'matched', 'harmoniously contrived'.

400. *Thirty-three*] Theobald added the 'eighteen years' of I. i. 125 to the 'seven years' of l. 320 above and emended here to 'Twenty-five', as the number of years which had elapsed since the shipwreck. But the inconsistency is Shakespeare's, who did not trouble about minor discrepancies that no audience would notice; compare the confusion in *AYL.* (I. i. 105; II. i. 2) as to how long the Duke has been banished, and cf. I. i. 128 and n. above. At I. i. 132 Egeon says he has been searching for 'five summers', a statement which seems to conflict with l. 320.

402. *burden ne'er*] The sense requires *ne'er,* and the compositor may simply have misread a badly written *burthen nere* in MS.; perhaps the words were run together and he misdivided them. N.C.S. thinks F's *burthen are* can only

be explained as a mishearing, not a misreading; but see Introduction, p. xv.

404. *calendars*] i.e. the Dromios; see I. ii. 41 and n.

405. *gossips' feast*] a feast of sponsors at a christening, a baptismal feast; each of the main characters is to be, as it were, named, to discover, or rediscover, his or her real identity. See Introduction, pp. xlv, xlix.

joy] a generally accepted emendation; perhaps the attraction of 'Go' earlier in the line is sufficient to account for F's error.

406. *felicity*] F's 'Nativitie' (like *go* in the previous line) is probably to be explained as an error due to the attraction of the last word of l. 404, as Dr Johnson noted (it is, however, strongly defended by Sisson, *New Readings,* I. 97–8); the compositor's attention seems to have been lax in this passage. Any substitute is a guess, and I prefer *felicity* as better than the usually preferred *festivity* only because it does not simply echo the word 'feast', ll. 405 and 407.

Duke. With all my heart, I'll gossip at this feast.
            Exeunt; the two Dromios and two Brothers [Antipholus]
                                        remain behind.
Syr. Dro. Master, shall I fetch your stuff from shipboard?
Eph. Ant. Dromio, what stuff of mine hast thou embark'd?
Syr. Dro. Your goods that lay at host, sir, in the Centaur. 410
Syr. Ant. He speaks to me; I am your master, Dromio.
            Come, go with us, we'll look to that anon;
            Embrace thy brother there, rejoice with him.
                            Exeunt [the two Antipholuses together.]
Syr. Dro. There is a fat friend at your master's house,
            That kitchen'd me for you to-day at dinner;   415
            She now shall be my sister, not my wife.
Eph. Dro. Methinks you are my glass, and not my brother:
            I see by you I am a sweet-fac'd youth;
            Will you walk in to see their gossiping?
Syr. Dro. Not I, sir, you are my elder.   420
Eph. Dro. That's a question, how shall we try it?
Syr. Dro. We'll draw cuts for the senior; till then, lead thou
            first.
Eph. Dro. Nay then, thus:
            We came into the world like brother and brother,   425
            And now let's go hand in hand, not one before another.
                                        Exeunt.

FINIS

---

407. S.D. *Exeunt; the . . . two*] *Exeunt omnes. Manet the two | F.*   *Antipholus remain
behind. Not in F.*   413. *Exeunt . . . together.*] *Exit. F.*   420–4.] *As F; verse Pope,*
question: | . . . senior: | . . . thus—.   422. senior] F (*Signior*); *Rowe 2.*

407. S.D.] The form of this direction
in F is a fairly common Shakespearian
one; see Introduction, p. xiii and
IV. iv. 129, S.D. and n.

408, 409. *stuff*] baggage, cf. IV. iv.
147.

410. *at host . . . Centaur*] Cf. I. ii. 9;
host means 'inn', and is related to
'hostel', being a different word from
host = landlord.

413. S.D. *Exeunt . . . together*] F
merely has *Exit*, but the two Antipholuses are surely meant to go off

here in harmony, as the two Dromios
do at the end. See Introduction, p.
xlix.

415. *kitchen'd*] entertained in the
kitchen; cf. III. ii. 92–4.

418. *sweet-fac'd*] good-looking.

422. *draw cuts*] draw lots, in the form
of straws of unequal length.

424–6.] so F; Cuningham may be
right in reading these as two lines of
doggerel, but Dromio's 'thus' seems to
set off what he is about to say, to mark
off his couplet.

APPENDIX I

SOURCES

There is no need to reprint all the play's sources; Warner's translation of Plautus's *Menaechmi*, extracts in translation from *Amphitruo*, the passages from John Gower's *Confessio Amantis* which deal with the story of Apollonius (the source of the enveloping action of Egeon and Emilia), and George Gascoigne's *Supposes* are all reprinted in Geoffrey Bullough's *Narrative and Dramatic Sources of Shakespeare*, Volume I (1957). However, I have decided to include here summaries of the action of Plautus's two plays, drawing attention, in the passages in square brackets, to the most significant connections between the Latin texts, Warner's translation of *Menaechmi*, and *The Comedy of Errors*. These will illustrate the argument of the section in the Introduction on sources, and also provide a handy reference-chart to Shakespeare's main borrowings. I am printing also extracts from the Bible in a version known to Shakespeare; the full importance of Acts and Ephesians as sources for Shakespeare does not seem to have been noticed, not even by Bullough, and the relevant passages are gathered together here.

1. *Menaechmi*
(*Prologue*) A Prologue [omitted in Warner's translation; it may have suggested the figure of Egeon] relates that an old Syracusan merchant had twin sons; when these were seven years old, he took one with him to Tarentum, where the boy strayed from his father, and was taken up by a merchant of Epidamnum, who carried him off to his home. The father died of grief at Tarentum, and when news of this reached Syracuse, where the other twin had remained with his mother, the grandfather changed the name of the remaining twin to that of the lost one, and called him Menaechmus. The merchant of Epidamnum adopted the boy he found, gave him a wife, and died, leaving him rich. The action opens in Epidamnum as Menaechmus of Syracuse, now a man, arrives in search of his brother.
(Act I) Peniculus, a parasite, enters on his way, as is his habit, to Menaechmus of Epidamnum, in expectation of food. Menaechmus comes from his house complaining about his wife's constant prying into his activities, and proposes to dine with a courtesan

[Warner: 'a sweet friend of mine'; see III. i. 109–11]. He has a cloak of his wife's, which he intends to present to the courtesan, and invites Peniculus to join them at dinner. They call on the courtesan, Erotium, present the cloak, and bid her get ready a fine dinner, while Menaechmus takes Peniculus off with him to do some business in the city. Erotium calls her cook Cylindrus, and sends him off to buy food.

(Act II) Menaechmus Sosicles of Syracuse enters with his servant Messenio, relieved to be on land; they have been searching for his brother for six years [Warner: 'six yeares now have roamde about thus, *Istria, Hispania, Massylia, Ilyria*, all the upper sea, all high *Greece*'; see I. i. 132–4. The Latin text has 'Graeciamque exoticam']. Messenio tells his master that Epidamnum is a town of rakes, swindlers and harlots [Warner: 'a place . . . exceeding in all ryot and lasciviousnesse; and . . . as full of Ribaulds, Parasites, Drunkards, Catchpoles, Conycatchers, and Sycophants, as it can hold: then for Curtizans, why here's the currantest stamp of them in the world'; see I. ii. 97–102]. Cylindrus returns as they are talking, and addresses Menaechmus, to his surprise, speaks of the dinner he is to prepare, and goes indoors, to tell his mistress. Erotium enters to greet Menaechmus affectionately, who thinks she must be mad or drunk to address a stranger so effusively [see II. ii. 147–67]. He protests he does not know her, but she knows his name and something of his family history, so that he accepts the situation, goes in to dinner, and agrees to take the cloak she says he gave her to be dyed and trimmed. Before entering her house, he sends off Messenio with his purse to find an inn [see I. ii. 8–10; II. ii. 1–2].

(Act III) Peniculus comes on complaining that Menaechmus of Epidamnum has given him the slip at the law-courts; but as he laments his loss of a dinner, Menaechmus Sosicles comes from Erotium's door, carrying the cloak. Menaechmus is amazed when Peniculus accuses him of cheating him out of a dinner, grows angry, and Peniculus reacts by going off to tell the wife that her husband, as he supposes, has been with a courtesan. Erotium's maid then comes out to commission Menaechmus to take a bracelet to be refurbished at a jewellers' [Warner: 'take this chaine with you, and put it to mending at the Goldsmythes'; see III. i. 114–19; Shakespeare added the character Angelo, a goldsmith, in his play]. Menaechmus rejoices in his good fortune, plans to sell the cloak and bracelet, and leave the town as quickly as he can [cf. III. ii. 149–51].

(Act IV) The wife now appears, with Peniculus, and bitterly complains of her husband's supposed behaviour in going to the courtesan. They draw aside as Menaechmus of Epidamnum comes on, also complaining of having been kept all this time by a client at the forum, and consoling himself with the thought of visiting Erotium. His wife and parasite, overhearing him men-tion the courtesan, accost him, and sarcastically ask him to fetch the cloak back from the dyers, then accuse him of giving it to the courtesan, and eating her dinner. Menaechmus is overwhelmed by all this, lamely excuses himself by saying he merely lent it to her, and is shut out of his own doors until he returns it. He believes he will find welcome instead at Erotium's door [cf. III. i. 116–21]. So he knocks there, and when Erotium comes asks her to return the cloak. She in turn grows angry, protesting that she gave him the cloak and a bracelet, and slams her door in his face. So he goes off to seek counsel of his friends. Peniculus, meanwhile, rejected by wife and husband, goes off annoyed to the city.

(Act V) Menaechmus Sosicles returns, having failed to find Messenio, to be accosted by his brother's wife, who sees him carrying the cloak, and takes him for her husband. She rails at him, and when he reproaches her and questions her sanity, she sends a servant for her father, and, when he comes, complains to him. The old man is inclined to think she must be at fault, and addresses Menaechmus Sosicles as if he would make peace; but when Menaechmus swears he knows neither of them, and never set foot in the house, they decide he must be insane [see IV. iii and iv, where the motif of madness in Shakespeare's play becomes prominent]. He decides to pretend to be mad, in the hope of getting rid of them, and in his feigning abuses them [he cries, 'Apollo from his oracle bids me burn her eyes out with blazing brands' (Warner 'a burning lampe'); cf. V. i. 171]. The old man proposes to fetch servants to tie up Menaechmus and carry him home [cf. IV. iv. 104ff., 129 S.D.]; so Menaechmus decides to scare them off by threatening them with injury [cf. IV. iv. 141–5], and, succeeding in this, he rushes off to his ship [cf. IV. iv. 147–56].

The old man returns with a doctor, to encounter Menaechmus of Epidamnum, complaining of his misfortunes. The doctor tries to question him about his supposed madness, and when Menaechmus curses him in anger, he really believes his patient is mad [cf. IV. iv. 45ff.], and demands four of the father's men to carry him to his house. As the Doctor and old man go off, Messenio returns, just in time to help his supposed master to escape from the four servants who come to take him to the Doctor's house [cf. IV. iv]. As a reward Messenio begs his freedom, which Menaechmus of Epidamnum, protesting he is not Messenio's master, grants, and Messenio goes to fetch the money he has had in charge. Menaechmus, perplexed, goes to try once more Erotium's mercy. At this point Messenio returns, with Menaechmus Sosicles, who denies being rescued or giving him his freedom, but is stopped in his anger by the entry of Menaechmus of Epidamnum from Erotium's house. The twins now meet for the first time, and their recognition brings a solution to all perplexities; Messenio is given his freedom indeed, and the play ends with Menaechmus of Epidamnum proposing to auction all his property, including his wife, and return to his own country.

2. *Amphitruo*

(Prologue) As the play opens, Amphitryon, general of the Theban armies, is returning from a battle in which he has won a notable victory. Jupiter, who has taken a fancy to his wife Alcmena, comes down to earth with Mercury, and, adopting the appearance of Amphitryon and his servant Sosia, they enter Amphitryon's house. Jupiter prolongs the night while he lies with Alcmena, and Mercury keeps watch outside.

(Act I) The real Sosia, Amphitryon's slave, comes on, sent ahead by his master to announce his safe arrival in Thebes to Alcmena. But the timorous slave is accosted by his double, Mercury-Sosia, who beats him for saying he is Sosia, and claiming that he has just arrived from Port Persicus [a port in the Euboean Sea, but the Latin phrase 'portu Persico' (ll. 403, 412, 823) may have prompted Shakespeare to make his Second Merchant propose a journey to Persia, iv. i. 4]. Gradually, by showing that he knows all the details of the battle, and of Sosia's behaviour there, he almost persuades Sosia that he is transformed [l. 456, 'ubi immutatus sum?', cf. ii. ii. 195]. Finally, Sosia, denied entrance to his own house [cf. iii. i] returns to the harbour to seek out his master there. Jupiter enters from the house to part affectionately from Alcmena, and leave with Mercury.

(Act II) The real Amphitryon and Sosia arrive home. Alcmena is naturally surprised to see her husband so soon after Jupiter-Amphitryon left her, and out of their misunderstanding, a quarrel is generated. Amphitryon thinks she has been seduced, and that he will be able to settle the question of her disloyalty to him by appealing to Alcmena's own relative, Naucrates, who dined with him on his ship the previous evening, at a time when Alcmena says she was eating with him.

(Act III) While Amphitryon is away, Jupiter-Amphitryon returns to confuse matters by apologizing to Alcmena, and getting rid of Sosia, so that he can divert himself with Alcmena again. Mercury-Sosia is instructed to keep the real Amphitryon out of the house by any device.

(Act IV) Amphitryon returns home weary, having failed to find Naucrates, and is kept out of his house by Mercury-Sosia (cf. iii. i). There is a gap in the manuscript here, but evidently further quarrels arise between Aphitryon and Alcmena, and between him and his servant Sosia. Finally Jupiter comes out of the house, to abuse and be abused by Amphitryon, who is finally discomfited when his friend the pilot Blepharo refuses to take his part. In his anguish Amphitryon threatens revenge, and shouts that he will murder everyone in the house [cf. iv. iv].

(Act V) A flash of lightning strikes Amphitryon, who recovers to learn that his wife has borne twin sons in miraculous fashion; and finally Jupiter appears to explain that one (Hercules) is his child, the other Amphitryon's.

3. *The Bible*

It has long been recognized that Shakespeare was thinking of Acts xix and St Paul's Epistle to the Ephesians when he changed the setting of his play from the Epidamnum of *Menaechmi* to Ephesus, and that he recalled the biblical association of this city with witchcraft and 'curious arts'. He also seems to have had in mind St Paul's exhortations to wives and husbands and to servants and masters to maintain a proper harmony in their relationships. The full extent of his debt to the Bible, however, does not seem to have been noticed, and as the versions he knew are no longer readily accessible, the relevant passages are printed here.

It seems almost certain that Shakespeare was familiar with the Bishops' Bible, first published in 1568, and the Geneva version, issued first in 1560, as well as the Book of Common Prayer. Richmond Noble has shown, in his *Shakespeare's Biblical Knowledge* (1935), that what looks like a straightforward quotation from one version, such as 'Satan avoid' (iv. iii. 46; Matthew iv. 10, Geneva version), may be Shakespeare's inversion of 'Avoid Satan', which appears in early issues of the Bishops' Bible and in the prayer-book, where the passage is included among those to be read during Lent. We cannot be certain which version Shakespeare used for a play; he seems to have had both at recall. The passages below are cited from a Geneva Bible of 1560 which has been collated with a Bishops' Bible of 1586, and significant differences in this version are inserted in round brackets. Abbreviations in the text are expanded.

References to *The Comedy of Errors* are given in square brackets before each excerpt from the Bible; these are intended merely as a guide, for Shakespeare's debt to the Bible in this play is more evident in the themes and atmosphere than in verbal borrowings.

Acts xix

[I. i. 132–4, 111] 1. And it came to pass, while Apollos was at Corinthus, that Paul when he passed through the upper coastes, came to Ephesus, and founde certain disciples.

2. And this was done (continued) by the space of two yeres, so that all they which dwelt in Asia, heard the word of the Lord Jesus ...

[I. ii. 97–103; II. ii. 188–92; II. i. 62; IV. iii. 10–11; IV. iv. 45–6, 52–7]
13. Then certeine of the vagabonde Jewes, exorcistes, toke in

hand (tooke upon them) to name over them which had evill
spirits, the name of the Lord Jesus . . .
16. And the man in whome the evil spirit was, ran on them, and
overcame them . . .
17. . . . and the name of the Lord Jesus was magnified.
19. Many also of them which used curious artes (craftes), broght
their bokes, and burned them before all men . . .
[The Priory of Act V corresponds to the temple of Diana. In the
Biblical account, Demetrius protests against the preaching of
Paul, and confusion results]
27. . . . the temple of the great goddesse Diana shulde be nothing
estemed, and . . . her magnificence, which all Asia and the
worlde worshippeth, shulde be destroyed.
28. Now when they heard it, they were ful of wrath, and cryed
out, saying Great is Diana of the Ephesians.
29. And the whole citie was ful of confusion.

Ephesians iv
[IV. iii. 12–14]
22. That is, that ye cast off (lay downe), concerning the conversation in time past, the olde man, which is corrupt through the
deceiveable lustes (accordyng to the lustes of errour)
23. To be renued in the spirite of your mind;
24. And to put on that newe man which after God is created
(shapen) in righteousnes and true holines.

Ephesians v
[II. i. 7–25; II. ii. 110–46]
22. Wives, submit your selves unto your husbands, as unto the
Lord.
23. For the housband is the wives head, even as Christ is the head
of the Church, and the same is the saviour of his bodie.
24. Therefore as the church is in subjection to (is subject unto)
Christ, even so let the wives be to their housbands in everie thing.
25. Housbands, love your wives, even as Christ loved the
church . . .
28. So ought men to love their wives, as their owne bodies: he
that loveth his wife, loveth him self.
33. . . . let everie one love his wife even as him self, and let the
wife se that she feare (reverence) her housband.

Ephesians vi
[Master and servant also quarrel in the play, cf. especially II. ii.
22–5, IV. iv. 42–4]
5. Servants, be obedient unto them that are your masters.
9. And ye masters, do the same things unto them, putting away
threatning.
[See especially III. ii. 140–7, and IV. iii. 41ff.]

11. Put on the whole armour of God that ye may be able to stand against the assaults of the devill.

12. For we wrestle not against flesh and blood, but against principalities (rulers), against powers, and against the worldlie governours, the princes of the darkenes of this worlde, against spiritual wickednesse, which are in the hie (heavenly) places.

13. For this cause take unto you the whole armour of God, that ye may be able to resist in the evil daye, and having finished all things, stand fast.

14. Stand therefore, and your loines girde about with verity (the trueth), and having on the brest plate of righteousnes . . .

16. Above all, take the shield of faith, wherewith ye may quench all the fyrie dartes of the wicked.

17. And take the helmett of salvation, and the sworde of the Spirit, which is the worde of God.

APPENDIX II

THE GRAY'S INN PERFORMANCE OF 1594

Below is an extract from *Gesta Grayorum: or, the History of the High and Mighty Prince Henry, Prince of Purpoole . . . Who Reigned and Died, A.D. 1594.* This account of the Christmas revels at Gray's Inn, beginning 20 December 1594, and extending well into the new year 1595, was first printed in 1688. Late on the night of 28 December, a 'Comedy of Errors', 'like to Plautus his *Menechmus*', was presented by common, i.e. professional, players, and the references to it leave little doubt that it was Shakespeare's play. Before the play was performed the evening was marred by some disorders which drove away the ambassador of the Inner Temple, and the mock-inquiry held the following night into these disorders clearly refers to, and includes, the play among them. There are references to 'Errors', to 'a Play of Errors and Confusions', to 'vain Representations and shows', 'vain Illusions', as well as to 'Sorceries and Inchantments' and 'Witchcraft', all of which are terms which seem to apply directly to the play, with its atmosphere of witchcraft, and use of a vocabulary related to it—cf. 'sorcerers' (I. ii. 99 etc.), 'witches' (I. ii. 100 etc.), 'enchanting' (III. ii. 160), 'illusions' (IV. iii. 43). An interesting point to note is that a stage was built, presumably in the great hall, and scaffolds (? tiered-seating) set up 'to the top of the House'.

The date raises a difficulty, for the accounts of the Treasurer of the Chamber show that payments were made to Shakespeare's

company, the Lord Chamberlain's Men, for performances at the
Court, which was at Greenwich, on the evenings of 26 and 28
December 1594. The same accounts also show a payment to the
Lord Admiral's Men for a play on 28 December, and possibly the
entry relating to the Chamberlain's Men for this day has been mis-
dated, and really belongs to 27 December.[1] There seems to be no
other way out of the difficulty.

The passages cited below are reprinted, by permission of the
Council of the Malone Society, from the edition of *Gesta Grayorum
1688* prepared by W. W. Greg (Malone Society Reprints, 1914),
pp. 20–4.

The next grand Night was intended to be upon *Innocents-Day* at
Night [28 December]; at which time there was a great Presence of
Lords, Ladies, and worshipful Personages, that did expect some
notable Performance at that time; which, indeed, had been
effected, if the multitude of Beholders had not been so exceeding
great, that thereby there was no convenient room for those that
were Actors; by reason whereof, very good Inventions and Con-
ceipts could not have opportunity to be applauded, which otherwise would have been great Contentation to the Beholders. Against
which time, our Friend, the *Inner Temple*, determined to send their
Ambassador to our Prince . . . The Ambassador came very
gallantly appointed, and attended by a great number of brave
Gentlemen, which arrived at our Court about Nine of the Clock
at Night. . .

When the Ambassador was placed, as aforesaid, and that there
was something to be performed for the Delight of the Beholders,
there arose such a disordered Tumult and Crowd upon the Stage,
that there was no Opportunity to effect that which was intended
. . . The Lord Ambassador . . . thereupon would not stay longer at
that time . . . After their Departure the Throngs and Tumults did
somewhat cease, although so much of them continued, as was able
to disorder and confound any good Inventions whatsoever. In
regard whereof, as also for that the Sports intended were especially
for the gracing of the *Templarians*, it was thought good not to offer
any thing of Account, saving Dancing and Revelling with Gentle-
women; and after such Sports, a Comedy of Errors (like to *Plautus*
his *Menechmus*) was played by the Players. So that Night was begun,
and continued to the end, in nothing but Confusion and Errors;
whereupon, it was ever afterwards called, *The Night of Errors*.

This mischanceful Accident . . . gave occasion to the Lawyers of
the Prince's Council, the next Night, after Revels, to read a Commission of *Oyer* and *Terminer*, directed to certain Noble-men and
Lords of His Highness's Council, and others, that they should

1. See W. W. Greg, *Gesta Grayorum 1688*, pp. v–vi; Chambers, *W.S.*, II.
319–20.

enquire, or cause Enquiry to be made of some great Disorders and Abuses lately done and committed within His Highness's Dominions of *Purpoole*, especially by Sorceries and Inchantments; and namely, of a great Witchcraft used the Night before, whereby there were great Disorders and Misdemeanours, by Hurly-burlies, Crowds, Errors, Confusions, vain Representations and Shews, to the utter Discredit of our State and Policy.

The next Night upon this Occasion, we preferred Judgments thick and threefold, which were read publickly by the Clerk of the Crown, being all against a Sorcerer or Conjurer that was supposed to be the Cause of that confused Inconvenience. Therein was contained, How he had caused the Stage to be built, and Scaffolds to be reared to the top of the House, to increase Expectation. . . Also that he caused Throngs and Tumults, Crowds and Outrages, to disturb our whole Proceedings. And Lastly, that he had foisted a Company of base and common Fellows, to make up our Disorders with a Play of Errors and Confusions; and that that Night had gained to us Discredit, and it self a Nickname of Errors . . . The Prisoner appealed to the Prince his Excellency for Justice . . . The Prince gave leave to the Master of the Requests that he should read the Petition; wherein was a Disclosure of all the Knavery and Juggling of the Attorney and Sollicitor, which had brought all this Law-stuff on purpose to blind the Eyes of his Excellency, and all the honourable Court there, going about to make them think, that those things which they all saw and perceived sensibly to be in very deed done, and actually performed, were nothing else but vain Illusions, Fancies, Dreams and Enchantments, and to be wrought and compassed by the Means of a poor harmless Wretch, that never heard of such great Matters in all his Life . . . the Prince and States-men (being pinched on both sides, by both the Parties) were not a little offended . . , and thereupon the Prisoner was freed and pardoned, the Attorney, Sollicitor, Master of the Requests, and those that were acquainted with the Draught of the Petition, were all of them commanded to the Tower . . . And this was the end of our Law-sports, concerning the Night of Errors.